D1486916

WORD

Mykel Mitchell

For Everybody
Who Thought
Christianity
Was for Suckas

WORD

 NEW AMERICAN LIBRARY

PUBLIC LIBRARY
EAST ORANGE, NEW JERSEY

248.4
M682

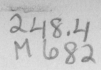

NEW AMERICAN LIBRARY
Published by New American Library, a division of
Penguin Group (USA) Inc., 375 Hudson Street,
New York, New York 10014, USA
Penguin Group (Canada), 10 Alcorn Avenue, Toronto,
Ontario M4V 3B2, Canada (a division of Pearson Penguin Canada Inc.)
Penguin Books Ltd., 80 Strand, London WC2R 0RL, England
Penguin Ireland, 25 St. Stephen's Green, Dublin 2,
Ireland (a division of Penguin Books Ltd.)
Penguin Group (Australia), 250 Camberwell Road, Camberwell, Victoria 3124,
Australia (a division of Pearson Australia Group Pty. Ltd.)
Penguin Books India Pvt. Ltd., 11 Community Centre, Panchsheel Park,
New Delhi - 110 017, India
Penguin Group (NZ), cnr Airborne and Rosedale Roads, Albany,
Auckland 1310, New Zealand (a division of Pearson New Zealand Ltd.)
Penguin Books (South Africa) (Pty.) Ltd., 24 Sturdee Avenue,
Rosebank, Johannesburg 2196, South Africa

Penguin Books Ltd., Registered Offices: 80 Strand, London WC2R 0RL, England

First published by New American Library, a division of Penguin Group (USA) Inc.

First Printing, February 2005
10 9 8 7 6 5 4 3 2 1

Copyright © Mykel Mitchell, 2005
All rights reserved

Scripture taken from the HOLY BIBLE, NEW INTERNATIONAL VERSION®, Copyright 1973, 1978, 1984 International Bible Society. Used by permission of Zondervan Publishing House. All rights reserved.

The "NIV" and "New International Version" trademarks are registered in the United States Patent and Trademark Office by International Bible Society. Use of either trademark requires the permission of the International Bible Society.

NEW AMERICAN LIBRARY and logo are trademarks of Penguin Group (USA) Inc.

Library of Congress cataloging-in-publication data is available upon request.

Set in Galliard

Printed in the United States of America

Without limiting the rights under copyright reserved above, no part of this publication may be reproduced, stored in or introduced into a retrieval system, or transmitted, in any form, or by any means (electronic, mechanical, photocopying, recording, or otherwise), without the prior written permission of both the copyright owner and the above publisher of this book.

The scanning, uploading, and distribution of this book via the Internet or via any other means without the permission of the publisher is illegal and punishable by law. Please purchase only authorized electronic editions, and do not participate in or encourage electronic piracy of copyrighted materials. Your support of the author's rights is appreciated.

12.95
2/15/05
DS

6 12 357 595 DA

In Loving Memory of
Baby Mitchell
&
Isaiah Alexander Williams

Acknowledgments

Let me just say from jump . . . I know I'm going to forget some-body, so cut me some slack. . . . Moving on.

To my wife, Sheeri: You are the manifestation of God's grace in my life. I could not have come this far in life or completed this book without you . . . you my nuckah.

To my children, Chase, Max and Blake: I purpose to live my life in such a way that you'll never be ashamed to call me your Papi. I love you.

To Bobbi: Your determined optimism convinced me early on that I could do anything I set my mind to. Thank you.

To Bill: Your courageous effort to rebuild our relationship inspires and humbles me. I look forward to many more years together.

To Stan: Your leadership and protection in my youth literally made the difference between life and death. I appreciate your many sacrifices.

To Markist and Matthew: I'm grateful for your love and support in my life.

To Vera: Your generosity and hospitality are unmatched. Thank you for your unmerited support.

To Marian, Gregory and Natalie: Your unconditional love for me has been evident from the start. Thank you for embracing me.

To my folks, Troyvoi, Ingrid, Derrick Wade, Kevin, Angela G., Jacin, Brad and Angie, Travon, Fred and Daven: You have been there from day one. For the loyalty and love I have for you, there are no words.

To Antoine: We go back like sweat socks and flip-flops. Can you believe how far God has brought us?

To Sean Gascie: What predates history??? Us!

To Charles Brooks: You have taught me more about being a man than any other person in my life. Thank you for taking a personal interest in me. I love you. On to the Benz dealership!

To Jody Moore: You are one of the few men whom I not only like but admire. I am proud to call you my pastor and even prouder still to call you my friend.

To Bishop Kenneth C. Ulmer, Pastor Donald Bell, Travon Potts and Dr. Kerry Brooks: It is because of your passion for the Word and your ability to rightly divide it that I am the man of faith I am today. Thank you for your diligence and transparency.

To Marc Gerald: Thanks for sharing the vision and helping to put legs to it. I appreciate your professionalism and friendship.

To Denise Silvestro: Thanks for the beautiful struggle. This book is a much better read because of your skill and effort. Let's do more. Call Marc.

Shout-outs: My Grandmas, Greg Mack, Mao LaBeet, Damon and Joi Hawkins, Donald and "Miss Beverly" Scott, the Stephens family, Diane "the Biz" Bisgeier, Dr. Kerry and Ruthie Brooks, the Spencer family, the Herbert family, the White family, AMQ brothers, Praise Tabernacle Bible Church family, Faithful Central Bible Church family, Grace Bible Church family, James Andrews and family, James Lopez and family, Tarvenia and Kijana and family, the Davis family, the Tatum family and the Webb family.

God bless you all.

Contents

Foreword

Sheeri Mitchell

As I watched the young man ascend the steps to the pulpit, it occurred to me how odd he must look to the members of the congregation. He with his shaved head, diamond stud earrings, proudly wearing a Raiders jersey, baggy jeans, and white Nikes with the gray swoosh (to match the silver in his jersey—of course), not to mention the fact that he is black and thirty-five years old. And the congregation? Well, nearly half of them are at least fifty years old and, except for one Indonesian family and one black family (that of the young man), they are all white. Every one of them is receptive to what he has to say, silently encouraging him with broad smiles and nods of approval. *If I sold tickets, no one would believe me,* I think to myself. This is odd on so many levels. Not just the fact that Mykel Mitchell is about to deliver a sermon at Grace Bible Church in Riverside, California, but that Mykel Mitchell is about to deliver a sermon anywhere.

Mykel Mitchell, who, only just over a decade ago, hustled for a living, carried a gun at times, slept with every woman in sight, and who would just as soon beat a man for stealing from him without as much thought as he would give to brushing his teeth. This Mykel

Mitchell was now standing up before Grace Bible Church to teach them about Jesus Christ. Wow. If I didn't know him so well, I would think that he must be a fraud. But as his wife of eight years, I can tell you, he's the real deal. He's really saved. He's really flied out, all the time. He's no less black and he has no less flava than he did back in the day when (as he puts it) he was "doin' dirt." He is a devoted, faithful husband, a doting father to his three children, a patient son-in-law, and a loyal son and brother. He is an entrepreneur, a publisher, an author, a consultant, and a visionary. In short, he is remarkable.

What makes him so unique is that he flies in the face of all preconceived notions of what Christianity is and isn't. Corny he is not. A punk—never was. Conservative—only in his theology, but hardly in his dress or manner. A gentleman—always. He has far too much respect for the God he serves to behave as though J.C. (Jesus Christ—if you not knowin') never died for him. But don't piss him off, though. You wouldn't like him when he's angry. He is wise beyond his thirty-five years and possesses an attitude so positive that it's practically contagious. He has love for all God's people, showing respect as readily to the homeless as he does to jet-setters. Like the God he serves, he is no respecter of persons.

About the only thing that has survived from Mykel's past, apart from his wicked sense of humor and his tattoo, is his love of hip-hop. An original "head" from the eighties, he not only produced "Greg Mack's Afternoon Drive Show" on Los Angeles's first (yes, before Hot 97 and Power 106) all-rap radio station, KDAY, he ate, slept, and breathed hip-hop in all its forms. And he remains loyal to the culture. He can bump Jay-Z and 50 Cent just as easily as he can bump Dawkins & Dawkins or Pastor Michael Lowry. To many people he seems like a walking contradiction. And he is. But he moves as effortlessly through the doors of NYC's Violator Management as he does through those of Inglewood, California's Faithful Central Bible Church. His is a complex world, but not at all complicated. He prays, works out, works it out, makes money, and always gives

God his share. Although he is saved and "walking," I'll guiltily confess he don't look it—at least not at first glance. And I kid you not, if he rolled up on me on a dark street, I'd cross over and clutch my purse . . . y'know, if I didn't know him. Yet he manages never to lose his originality or compromise his faith. He is far from sinless, but in the words of his bishop, Kenneth C. Ulmer, he does "sin less," or at least differently.

Because of his "presentation" many of the old guard—the conservative Christians, both black and white—openly frown upon him and his kind. But he doesn't sweat the fact that Sistah So-and-so thinks "he looks a mess in those big ol' pants," or that Mr. Jones disapproves of his pierced ears and tatted arm. He continues on, living his life to please only one person—J.C.

Besides, most people who misjudge him quickly change their minds and (if they're honest) admit their error, once he opens his mouth. I have chuckled to myself many a time as conservative whites try not to drop their jaws when they set eyes upon him and then again when they listen to him speak. The outside doesn't match the inside—or so they think. He is a deep brotha, able to engage a street nig or a Bible scholar. He can flow with CS Lewis as easily as Stan Lee. The son of a tenured university professor (and former street hustler), he himself boasts nothing higher than a high school diploma and some college. He is in the world, but not of it (at least not anymore). He can hold his own on the corner or in the boardroom. He is equally comfortable with 'hoodrats or Hamptonites, and usually they with him. He is not easily impressed, nor is he concerned about impressing anyone. He is who he is. If you can roll wit' it, good for you; if not, your loss. With an amazing confidence (not in himself), he manages to remain humble and easygoing, fully aware of Who's got his back. Mykel Mitchell is a man unique to this age. He is a man who successfully navigates within and between two cultures and represents the perfect marriage of them both. If Christianity and hip-hop birthed a son, he'd be it. To hear his story in his own words, just turn the page.

Preface

I was watching ESPN's *Sports Center* one day when the news broke about Ricky Williams's retirement. The newscast explained that the main reason Ricky had decided to check out was that he was just tired of football and needed "to find himself." Now the first thought I had was, *How could that fool be tired of stackin' all that loot? Man! He must be crazy.* But then I found myself remembering how I felt about thirteen years ago. I was making a good living, working for a mega rock star and his family. My ends were nowhere close to Ricky's, but you could say they were meeting. I lived in the marina (a good address to have by most people's standards) and I drove a late-model BMW. I wasn't lacking for female company; and I had plenty of friends—or so I thought. To the average observer, ya boy was doing a'ight. But those closest to me would have told you that I was buggin' out. I was forever complaining to my boys that I was tired of all the BS—the different women, the different clubs, the smokin', the gettin' faded . . . the whole regular routine. I was sick of it.

A typical week in my life at the time went like this: Monday: go to work for the rock star at one of his big estates, either in Beverly

Hills or Brentwood. Get off that night, call up a female, smoke a blunt, get laid. Tuesday through Thursday: wake up and do it all over again. The only difference Friday through Sunday was that me and my boys smoked more blunts and had more time for sex. Insert some shopping and a few parties here or there, and that was my week, my month, my year, my life! *Pathetic* didn't even begin to describe it.

I told my roommate and best friend at the time that I thought I was going crazy. I confided in him that I needed a change and that I needed my life to matter. I wanted a good woman, someone I could trust and build with. But I didn't even know where to start looking! My moms had always been on me about the way I treated women. I remember telling her on the phone one night about how tired I was of the type of woman I had been kickin' it with and that I wanted a good girl. She laughed at me and demanded to know why in the world did I think God would give me one of His daughters when I would just treat them like s%*t? The question was a rhetorical one. And of course I knew the answer. She went on (like she often did) to tell me that I should read the *In Touch* magazines she had been sending me for the better part of a year and that I should go to church.

My initial response was my usual "Whatever, Ma. . . ." But a few days later I found myself digging through a pile of *Source* magazines looking for an *In Touch*. Before I realized it, I had read it cover to cover. And that pretty much did it. I don't remember the exact subject, nor any Scriptures in particular. I just know that something clicked. Suddenly a lot of bits and pieces of information I had always known about God, my life, and my purpose just came together. I understood that if I wanted a better life, I had to become a better man.

That realization kicked off a whole new season of my life when I separated myself from the rest of the world for the next six months. Don't get me wrong—I still went to work (a brotha still had to eat). But I pretty much cut out everything else. My life had been too fast and too crazy. I needed a quiet place where I could be solo with my thoughts, so I could figure some things out. I needed—don't laugh—to find myself. I basically stopped hangin' out with the crew. I stopped "dating." I fasted from women. On occasion, when I got desperate, I'd attempt to make a booty call. But I seldom finished dialing before I hung up. I was enjoying the peace my new life had brought me. And I wasn't that ready to give it up, even for really good sex. For the most part, I just sat in the house, read my Bible and the Christian study materials my moms kept sending, and smoked a blunt every once in a while between working out and watching TV. I know Bibles and blunts don't mix, but back then they were working for me. I had given up sex and drinkin'. The occasional blunt was all that stood between me and cabin fever. I still had the urge to "hit it" every now and again. But even the thought made me feel bad. Maybe *bad* is not the correct word. *Conflicted* is what I really mean. The old ways just didn't feel as good or right as they used to.

What I didn't know was that God was cleaning me up. He was preparing me for the answer to my prayers, and most important, He was preparing me for a relationship with Him. I had thought that I needed to find myself. That was partly true. What it took me a while to understand was that as a created being, the root of my identity and purpose was to be found only in my Creator. I wasn't so much searching for myself as I was searching for myself in relation to my Savior.

During that six-month fast from the world and from women, God began preparing me for all of my heart's desires. He had every intention of prospering my life on all fronts. But in His wisdom He took the time to make me ready—so that I wouldn't get out there, act like a fool, and screw it all up.

Thirteen years later I stand on the other side of many answered prayers and a truckload of undeserved blessings, all made sweeter by the hard times God personally led me through. When I looked into the face of my firstborn child just moments after his birth, I knew instantaneously that his life would be nothing like mine. I vowed to teach him every good thing that I knew—especially about Jesus—so that he wouldn't have to be stupid like I had been for so long. But then it occurred to me: What about all those young cats who are just like me? Those young men on the verge of adulthood, ready to do big things but operating in ignorance, with no one to show them the way? What about them? I feel for the young upstarts with no pops in the home, either emotionally or physically, who are making it the best they know how. Dudes who have to piece together a model of manhood from magazines, history, and MTV—those are the ones who have my heart.

To those young men I say: I don't have much to offer in the way of wisdom, but what I do have is yours. There are certainly more seasoned men, like Bill Cosby or Nelson Mandela, who have much more life experience than I do. And God knows there are many more men with better education—especially on matters of theology—like Reverend TD Jakes. But I believe that God has invested in me a message for you. I've written this book for anyone who has ever wanted some real answers about real, everyday topics, like sex, money, homosexuality, women, and marriage—and who might be curious about how God fits into all those areas. I've written this book for anybody who has ever been sick and tired of how things are, and who wants tools to improve their situation. I hope you can find something you can use in the pages of this book. I hope that you can find the hope to continue on your own path, doing the right things, believing that you will be rewarded for a life well lived, knowing that you are not alone in your journey. I pray that something you read on these pages will touch your inner spirit and ignite in you a fire that can never be put out. And if you don't find any of those things, maybe you'll get a laugh out of what an idiot I used to be.

Mykel Mitchell

Introduction

For a Good Time, Push "Play"

I will never forget the first time I heard hip-hop music. The year was 1977. I was eleven years old, hangin' out in the basement at my cousin Oliver's house in San Francisco. Oliver, me, and his brothers were just kickin' it, reading comic books and crackin' on each other, when I noticed a cassette tape lying on the table. I didn't think much of it because I always brought tapes to Oliver's house. They were full of stuff I had taped off the radio (KDIA). Back in the day, I didn't bother to edit anything. My tapes had songs, commercials, background noise from home, my voice singing along with the music, police sirens from the street—everything. When I visited Oliver, I'd listen to my tapes while we were chillin'. I thought this was just another one of my tapes, but I was wrong. "Listen to this!" Oliver said, pushing it toward me. "I bet you ain't never heard nothin' like this before." So I popped the tape into a nearby cassette player. I pushed the "play" button, and what I heard next changed my life.

Someone had just recorded the goings-on at what sounded like a typical house party. But what made it special was the man on the tape. It was DJ Hollywood, mixin', scratchin', rhymin', and (what I would later learn was called) rappin'. I pushed "play" and the party came to life. As an eleven-year-old, I would never be allowed to attend a party like that unless my parents were present, and even then I wouldn't have been in with the grown-ups; I probably would have been in some room with all the kids whose parents were at the party, watching TV or playin' kids' games or something. But this tape transported me to the middle of all the action. I felt as though I was there with everybody having a good time.

I had listened to music before. I listened to music all the time, especially at home, where my mother and my stepfather played everything from James Brown to the Dramatics. One of my stepfather's favorites was a group called the Last Poets. I remember their album cover. It was a black-and-white photograph of them, a group of black men, posed on a basketball court. Now that I think about it, they were probably the forerunners of rap music. My stepdad played that album all the time. And the songs were just guys reciting poetry over what we then called "soul music." I remember liking that album a lot as a kid and never really thinking about why.

I had been exposed to a great deal of music in my life, but Oliver was right: I had never heard anything like this new music before. When I listened to any of my parents' records, I could dance and even sing some—that is, until the music faded into the snap, crackle, and pop inherent in vinyl recordings. But on this party tape, the music didn't end! It kept going. The tape had movement. It was hot on so many levels! Not just the fact that the music was continuous, but that DJ Hollywood was the focus. In between songs he would rap, talk, and engage the partygoers. He was controlling all the action at the party. He would say stuff like, "Up my back and around my neck, who got the girls in check," "Come on now," "Shake it." He was directing the party! And the people loved it. When he said something funny, they laughed. When he said something they liked, they yelled back, "All right!" or "Sho' 'nuff!" or "Okay!" When he cracked on somebody, they said "Oooh!" And it was all happening to the beat of the music, which never ended. It was kind of like being in church, except the deejay was the preacher and the partyers were the congregation. He was calling and they were responding. It was a trip. And it was fun! That's what I remember the most. It was fun on tape. It was an instant good time . . . and all you had to do was push "play." And that was so important to me, especially at that time in my life.

My moms had remarried eight years prior, and I was living with her, my stepfather, and my younger brothers in Oakland, California. At the time I didn't know that he was my stepfather; I thought that he was my real father, because he was the only father I had ever known and no one, including him, had told me any different. I even carried his last name. I would find out at a later date that my biological father was a man named William "Bill" Mitchell, who lived in Sacramento and was a professor at California State University, Sacramento. I would learn a lot about Bill's relationship with Bobbi (my mom) and all that led up to her marrying my stepfather, Stan. I would eventually even meet Bill face-to-face. But in the meantime I lived with Bobbi, my brothers, and Stan.

To say that life with Stan was sometimes unhappy would be a gross understatement. Life with Stan at times was active, living misery. My brothers—who are his and Bobbi's biological sons—and I lived for the times when he was away from home, because his presence brought with it an oppressed, heavy atmosphere. A marine drill sergeant by occupation, after he was honorably discharged Stan became a jailer at Oakland City Jail, a position for which he won many honors. He was and continues to be (to the best of my knowledge; we're no longer on speaking terms—my choice, not his) a hard man. He was a tough dad to have for any child, let alone for a precocious, gregarious, reasonably confident ten-year-old such as myself. He ran our home as though it were a combination boot camp/jailhouse. We got up, ate, studied, played, and went to bed according to his rigid schedule. And there was no room for deviation or creativity. The only time we got a break was when he was gone and my mother was in charge. So we were happy about whatever would call him away from home. It seemed as though when Stan wasn't around, we could just breathe—period!

For me, joy was in short supply in those days, so when I found it—or as close to it as I had experienced—on tape, I had to have it. I wanted what those people on the tape had. I envied them as much as I wanted to be like them. I wanted to be at that party. I wanted to feel like they did. I tried everything I knew to get my cousin to let me take that tape home, but that wasn't gonna happen. Oliver told me that it wasn't his tape. Some friend of their family had brought it over, and Oliver was not about to let me take it. I was disappointed. I was mad. Pissed off. I had found that something and I couldn't take it home. But the fire had been lit. I made up my mind that every time I went to Oliver's house I was going to listen to that tape over and over again until I had it memorized. Since my family visited Oliver's family about every two weeks, all I had to do was wait. Two weeks until I was back at the party.

So when I returned in two weeks and Oliver had lost the tape, I could have smacked him upside the head. And I think I probably would have, except that he was bigger than I was back then. He didn't realize what he had done. I could tell he wasn't feelin' it like I was. I got over it eventually, but it was hard. . . .

I didn't know it at the time, but my next encounter with hip-hop would be just weeks away in another very familiar place.

It happened at a bus stop in Oakland, California, on High Street. I was just standing there waiting for the bus when this kid broke out rappin'. It wasn't deep. And I can't really say that he was flowin'. But he was rhyming on beat and I recognized it right away. And this time, the how of what was being said wasn't as important as the what. He was talking to me! It took me a minute to realize that he wasn't rappin' something he had heard, but that he was making it up as he went along. He was an "older" guy, maybe twelfth grade or so to my fifth. And he looked cool enough. He was rappin' about his books, about people on the street, about the bus stop, about cars going by—everything! And in his rap he was telling me that I could do it, too! He was saying that he could do it; I could do it; everybody could do it. Everybody could rap just like DJ Hollywood was doing on that mix tape! I was hyped!

As I sat there listening to him, watching him, and absorbing his ways and style, I guess I realized that he was right. I mean, it's not like he was singing or something like that. He was talking in rhyme to a beat. I could do that. Even though I did sing in church on Sundays (which I hated doing—both singing in church and going to church, which I was forced to do with my grandmother), I didn't really consider myself a singer. Not like Michael Jackson or Al Green. But I could rap. I had never done it, but I knew if ol' boy at the bus stop could bust one out, then so could I. And then I had it! That young man didn't know it at the time, but he was proverbially teaching me to fish. Now I didn't need Oliver's lost party tape. I could make the party wherever I went! I could rap!

My plunge into hip-hop had to have been predestined. It was layered into my life: first the Last Poets, then the mix party tape, then the guy at the bus stop. The only thing left was the final layer. And that layer was put in place in September of 1979, when a little record by an unknown group called the Sugar Hill Gang exploded through my radio speakers. "Rapper's Delight" galvanized my love of hip-hop and pushed me over the edge—as it did so many others—into my journey as a "hip-hop head." That song started a revolution and literally changed the course of my life. I practically ate that record. I remember going to Eastmont Mall in Oakland and buying the big vinyl twelve-inch single. I even remember the album cover, a baby-blue joint with a multicolored, sprawling cornucopia on it. It was the second record I had ever bought with my own money (the first had been Funkadelic's *One Nation Under a Groove*—of course). I say I ate that record because I played it nonstop, day and night. I memorized every line, every verse, every beat, every nuance. I can still recite the rhymes by heart . . . as can most of my contemporaries, including my wife. But the best thing about the Sugar Hill Gang was that they made rap legit. I wasn't listening to a homemade mix party tape or some kid on the corner. "Rapper's Delight" was a real, physical record that I could touch and play! (I ain't got nothin' against CDs, but nothing feels as good as vinyl.) It was a product I could buy in a store, which made it official.

I didn't know it then, but I was one of many young people who caught the bug and drove their parents crazy with the bass-line instrumental from Chic's "Good Times." My mother, my stepfather, my aunts, and every adult I knew straight-up hated "Rapper's Delight." I would go as far to say that they despised it. They said it was low-class, ghetto. Forgetting that their parents and grandparents had said the exact same thing about doo-wop, the blues, jazz, and rock 'n' roll, they called rap "garbage" and "nigga mess." They said it was just a fad that would never last. They said it would never go any farther than the ghetto, and that no one who had anything to do with it would ever become successful. I am so glad that I did not listen to them. Rap was the best thing to come into my life at that point, and I knew my parents and their generation had just missed the boat. I was convinced that rap was destined to rule the world. And you know what? I was right.

If my experience with rap music had been one of the best, most critical parts of my life, then my first experience with Christianity proved to be just the opposite. No, scratch that. Not my experience with Christianity—my experience with Christians and Christian culture, as it were. On this side of the cross, it is obvious to me that my early experiences in church had nothing to do with Jesus Christ, and that the people I encountered were either ignorant of the message of the Gospel and the power in it or were apathetic toward them both. I have since come to understand more fully that true believers, those men and women who have taken God's Word to heart, live extraordinary lives filled with love, purpose, hope, gratitude, and an unquenchable need to serve others. I have come to understand that the teachings of Jesus Christ, if embraced, have the power to transform lives. His message is so radical that most of the men in His day just could not wrap their tiny minds around it, so they rejected it and decided to kill Him. It's no different today. Most people have formed opinions about Jesus Christ's identity and teaching based on someone else's misinformed opinion, poor behavior, or hypocritical attitude, and have never bothered to investigate on their own what God's Word has to say about Him. This shared ignorance has resulted in a lot of myths for both the Christian and the non-Christian alike. This same shared ignorance characterized my first experience with organized religion and colored my view of Christians, church, and Jesus Christ Himself.

My grandmother, the late Willie White, used to drag me to church every Sunday back in the early seventies when I lived with her in Pittsburgh, Pennsylvania. We lived in the projects, the now-defunct Saint Claire Village, and the church we attended was about a block away from our home in the basement of a nearby building in the same housing project. I don't remember how my grandmother found out that I could sing, but once she did, she forced me to sing praise and worship songs in this basement church in front of the forty-or-so-member congregation, made up mostly of her peers—other grandmothers in their fifties and sixties. I hated it. I hated singing there. I hated going there. I just hated it. The place was always packed, no ventilation, hot, folks sweatin' . . . and there I was at six years old singing old Negro spirituals in front of a bunch of old people.

I remember that the pastor was a man much younger than my grandmother, possibly in his early thirties. He was outgoing and very animated—especially when he preached. Church was a very confusing place for me at that age. All I remember is people shouting back and forth to the preacher and staying for a long time. No one ever bothered to explain to me the point of going, the significance of the different parts of the service, let alone what I was supposed to get out of it. The confusion added to the heaviness of the place. And man, was it boring! I got my snooze on whenever I could, whenever my grandmother wasn't jabbing me awake.

I couldn't articulate it as a child, but I know now that what I felt was oppression. It was the kind of heaviness that made you want to escape. It was that kind of oppression that makes alcoholics and drug abusers out of sane men and women. It was all over Saint Claire Village—and especially in the basement church. There was no joy, little hope (on this side of death), and absolutely no victory in the lives of these people. And who could blame them? They lived in the projects in Pittsburgh. They were the bottom rung of American society. But what made no sense to me was why they would get together only to become even sadder. So at age six, I decided church and everything affiliated with it meant boredom, oppression, and defeat. And just when my opinion couldn't sink any lower, something happened that would forever change my perception of so-called "men of the cloth."

Sunday in and Sunday out, I'm facing the chore of attending and singing in the basement church, when I get the news that we're moving. Not my biological family, but my church family. As it turns out, the congregation had been saving and giving toward the effort of purchasing a church home. And apparently this one Sunday the pastor shared the news that we were now owners of a nearby property, an actual house where we could have regular services and room for Bible study and other ministries. The people were excited— the only excitement I ever remember witnessing.

The next weekend my grandmother dragged me with her to a wreck of a house on a corner lot near my elementary school. To say this house was a fixer-upper would be an understatement. It was to' back: waist-high weeds overrunning the yard, paint falling off in chunks, chain-link fence bent back and over—it was a mess! For an entire two days, we (my grandmother and me), along with the other forty or so members, pulled weeds, moved rocks, and tilled soil. The few male church members who were there painted the exterior and trimmed hedges. I didn't know this at the time, but my grandmother later told me that some people even took off work in order to help prepare our new church home. This fact makes what happened next even more heinous.

The following week the members all returned to the site so that we could start work on the inside of the house. But it was locked. My grandmother and I stood there with several other people, confused but confident that the pastor would arrive soon with the key. He never did. As a matter of fact, no one ever saw him again. To add insult to injury, it was later discovered that he had never even approached the owner of the property! The house had never been purchased, gone through escrow, or anything. And most important, no money had ever changed hands. And he was gone. You do the math.

My grandmother and her friends were devastated and angry, to say the least. This young man had deceived and used them. I know now that what that man had done was an act of spiritual rape. Many of those people never recovered, including my grandmother. (I think this event ultimately led to her rejecting Christ totally and joining the Jehovah's Witnesses—a cult, by conservative Christian standards.) This pastor's act was the worst kind of treachery because it had been done in the name of Jesus. Most people expect to get hustled every now and then. That's just part of life. People expect politicians and businessmen to get over on them. And now people expect it from preachers, too. They especially expect it from preachers. The difference is that when politicians and businesspeople do it, only your faith in people is affected. But when pastors do it, your faith in God is affected. And the most important thing about any of us is what we believe about God.

At the time that this happened, it wasn't really that deep to me. I was just happy because it meant I didn't have to go back to the basement and sing anymore. But even though I didn't know it at the time, it affected me much more deeply. This had been my first experience with religion, and it had been jacked up. And it colored my view forever. In the back of my mind, even as an adult, I doubted the integrity of most pastors I came in contact with—particularly the more popular ones—and especially the ones with their own television shows. I think I suspected that they were all in it just for the money. Even now I place little value on religion, per se. It seldom leads to anything good, as far as I can tell. But if anything positive came from this experience it was the lesson that religion and people fail you, but God never does. It would take a long while for me to understand the difference between being religious and having a personal, intimate love relationship with the one true living God. But once I finally got it, I would never look at the world the same way again.

1

Jesus: God, Prophet, Madman, or Jackleg?

Let me set it straight from jump: This book is not an attempt to convince anybody to convert to Christianity. I could never do that. I don't possess those skills. Only God Himself can speak to you. Only the Holy Spirit can convict your heart. I'm just puttin' it down so that whatever choice you make, it will be a more informed one. This is not even an attempt to make you believe in Jesus' diety. That is my belief. This book simply explains why I believe. If you agree, good for you. If you don't, more power to you.

Here's what I know. Out of all the major religions the world over—Judaism, Islam, Hinduism, Buddhism, Taoism, Confucianism—no one ever came to earth and declared himself God. And for those of you not knowin', Jesus did not claim to be the son of Allah. He did not call himself a prophet or even a "good man." He declared himself to be one with God, the Father, Jehovah, the God of Abraham, Isaac, and Jacob, El Shaddai, Jehovah Jireh/Tsidkenu/Shammah/Shalom—you get the picture (John 17:11). He proclaimed himself to be "the Way," "the Truth," and "the Life" (John 14:6—capitalization mine). He did not offer to show us *a* way, tell us *some* truth, or point us in the *direction of* life. He declared that "before Abraham was born, I am," a statement that really pissed off the religious leaders of the day (John 8:58). "I Am" is the same name Jehovah gave to Moses, when during ol' boy's burning-bush encounter, Moses asked God's name. Make no mistake: Jesus claims equal status with God the Father. And for good measure, in case fools didn't get it, he explained that "No one comes to the Father except through Me" (John 14:6).

If you don't believe me, good. Go read it for yourself. The entire account can be found in the gospel of John. And even if you do believe me, go read it for yourself anyway. There's a gang of Christians out there that are just as ignorant as non-Christians. Fools be claimin' Jesus as Lord and Savior, but live foul and don't know jack about the Word of God. That's why it's so easy to lead us astray. If I meet one more former Baptist who is now a member of "the Nation," I'm gon' flip out. I'm sick of fools spouting out to me some rehearsed rhetoric that they heard in mosque, on the street corner, or from the pulpit. My nigga, did you read it for yourself? Did you interact with the text one on one? And please, Christians, don't come at me asking me to *study* the Koran. I'll leave that to Muslims. A true Christian needs to adopt the principles of the Canadian Mounties. When being trained to identify counterfeit bills, they don't examine the details of the counterfeit. They commit the real deal to memory so that they can then spot the fakes. Study God's Word so that you can't be punked by imitators! 'Cause there are a gang of cults and false religions out there.

Would-be-informed brothas, don't come at me with the lie that Christianity is the white man's religion. Just to set the record straight, Jesus was a Jew from Africa. And although most of the Jews in his day rejected him, the very first Christians were Jews. The first church consisted of people of many races, ethnicities, and cultures (Acts 2). Have some Europeans and white Americans misused and misrepresented Christianity in order to justify atrocities, such as the Crusades in medieval times and slavery in the antebel-

lum South? Yes, of course! No one denies that. But their misuse
does not negate the power of God's Word incarnate in the person
of Jesus Christ. Be mad at white people if you must. Work through
your issues with racism and discrimination. But know this: Jesus
Christ is neither white nor American. He transcends them both. As
a matter of fact, he transcends all cultures. He's just "AM." That's
"bad grammar, but good theology, y'all," as Bishop Kenneth Ulmer of Faithful Central Bible Church in Inglewood, California,
often says. And on top of that, please don't think He don't know
what a brotha is going through when you get pulled over by the
po-pos for DWB (drivin' while black). You sittin' on the curb, with
your pride in your hands (which are handcuffed behind your back,
by the way), sportin' your Prada, next to your V-1-2-6-0-0, while
ol' boy checks your glove box for "tobacco and firearms" because
you—ahem, let me make sure I get it right—"fit the description."
Yeah, yeah, to all that I say that J.C. has been there, done that, and
come back with the T-shirt and the hat. Again, if you don't believe
me, I encourage you to read it for yourself. Pick a gospel: Matthew,
Mark, Luke, and John all chronicle the account. See what He went
through at the hands of the Pharisees (the religious leaders of the
day), the Romans, and His fellow Jews. Mock trials in the middle of
the night, a kangaroo court, back shredded with a cat-o'-nine-tails,
whupped up from head to toe, beat down, spat upon, cursed out—
and if that wasn't enough, then nailed to a tree in His draws in
front of His mama and His boys (the ones who didn't bone out)
and crucified for no real crime. Oh, yeah, J.C. knows a little bit
about civil rights violations. He knows about loneliness, abandonment, being lied on, gettin' beat down, and literally being left for
dead, too. So don't come at me with that "white man's religion"
crap—that just makes me wanna give you the boot. But—so that
we're clear—I wouldn't do that, because to do so would not glorify
the God I serve. I'm just sayin' that's how pissed I get at that
widely accepted lie. But alas, I digress.

Moving on, like I said, Jesus makes some pretty bold claims in the four gospels and in the book of Acts, and every last one of them lines up with the prophecies spoken about Him in the Old Testament. And no matter what anyone tells you, no matter how much "proof" you amass, no matter who witnesses to you, no matter how many sermons you hear, no matter how many theologians bombard you with apologetics, the truth is this: Belief in Jesus Christ as the Messiah, the Son of God, the alpha and omega is, at the end of the day, a choice. You hear the gospel, the good news, and make a decision.

Understand that even no decision is a decision. Jesus is pretty clear about this. You are either for Him or against Him. You either gather with Him or scatter. You in or you out. You down or you ain't. There is no in-between. There is no riding the fence; there is no "well, let me think about it and get back to you." Jesus presents Himself in such a fashion as to force the choice. He claimed to be God. Not a prophet. Not a good man. God. And that's it. Either He was: a) telling the truth, b) a nut with a serious messiah complex, or c) a jackleg, like that preacher who got my grandmama. Whatever you choose to believe is on you. But the choice is *yours*, and so are the consequences of it. Don't say you believe because "Mama an' dem" told you to. Don't reject Him either because Haikim, that brotha down the way, been spittin' some mad knowledge at you. Read the Word, the Holy Bible. Better yet, start by just reading the book of John. Pray and ask God to help you understand it. Then decide for yourself. Just understand that whatever your ultimate choice is, even if it's by default, you will live with the consequences of that choice for *eternity*. Again—don't believe me? Look it up.

Okay, so the first thing people usually say to me is this: "But I'm a good person. I don't steal or rob or cheat on my spouse. I'm an upstanding member of the community . . . blah, blah, blah." Translation: "God wouldn't possibly condemn me to hell, because I'm one of the good guys." Alternate translation: "I'm cool, so I don't need a savior." I usually address these types of statements with an analogy that I heard a long time ago. The human condition is like being a guy who has a long-standing debt over three generations at his local grocery store. His family has been so poor for so far back that the store owners for three generations have just allowed them to do business "on credit." The debt has grown so large that no one in the current generation can ever pay it off. Then one day the guy gets a job and starts paying cash up front for all his groceries. The owner is geeked, accepts the money, and allows the man to continue to do business. The only problem is that the man still has an unpaid debt. Who is going to cover that? Clearly since the man just started working, he can't make up for all those generations of debt. To attempt to do so would break his family. So he just continues to pay cash, knowing that one day someone will have to settle his account. In essence, this is what it means to be human. You may have *become* a good person (which I maintain is an oxymoron), but you weren't always one and you can't always be one every minute of every day. At some point you slip. You have slipped. You do slip.

If you even think about it in terms of karma, what goes around really does come around. Think it don't? Well, get this. One day you will die, and you will have to settle your account. You will stand before God and have to answer for every wrong thing you have ever done in your entire life. Think about that. Every lie, every time you talked about somebody behind their back, (when as a shorty) every time you disobeyed your moms, every girl you ever sexed (who wasn't your wife), every scam you ever pulled (even if you got caught and did time, you still got to answer for all that, yo), gettin' yo' hustle on, chasin' that paper at all costs, that shorty you left yo' moms to raise, that nigga you shot . . . all dat. In the end—and we all have one—you will have to answer for *all* your dirt. And here's what it comes down to: God will exact payment.

Now here's where your choice today comes in. You can pay for all your dirt with your soul—that's right, here comes the fire-and-brimstone part—by going to hell (a place not created for human beings, by the way), or you can consider the debt paid in full by Jesus' death on the cross. It seems like a simple choice to me. But again, that's just me. And the cool part about that "debt paid" stuff is that it cancels out that karma thing once and for all while you're still living. What goes around stops coming around once you get saved, because you are no longer under law, but under grace. Now that's some deep stuff, right there.

That's not to say that you won't reap what you sow, that you won't harvest what you have planted. Some consequences of sin cannot be erased. You been sexin' it up outside of marriage; then you contracted AIDS. That's simply a consequence. Yes, God could cure you. But your getting the bug is simply a consequence of sexin'. You can't be mad at nobody but you on that one. You stole a car with your boy and now you're behind bars. Choice followed by consequence. The fact that you were sexin' a billion times before and never got the bug, that you have stolen a gang of cars and never got caught, is just evidence of God's mercy. You should have recognized it and stopped when you had the chance. Now, unless God reveals to some scientist how to cure the bug or moves the heart of some judge to pardon you, you just stuck. If you are in Christ, you don't have to live under God's wrath, but you do have to deal with the results of your behavior. What you don't have to do is live in fear of every wrong deed catching up to you, because you no longer live under God's wrath. You are forgiven. Your slate has been wiped clean. Your account is settled. Jesus picked up your tab. You feelin' me? So again, the choice is yours. There's a gang of other benefits of following Jesus, like peace (even though you may feel like you goin' through hell), true love (as opposed to—forgive me, ladies—pu——y), living up to your worth as a human being, operating in your purpose, and living free from fear, poverty, or emptiness. But like I said, I ain't tryin' to convert you; I'm just tryin' to break it down so that you can understand where I'm coming from with the rest of this book. I just want to make it clear to you, so that whatever you choose, your choice is an informed one.

I made my choice to embrace Christ only after finally admitting to myself that the best the world was capable of offering could never satisfy me. For a long time I stayed away from the "Jesus thing," as I used to call it, because the church met me with judgment, condemnation, and condescension. Religion disappointed me. But eventually, even after that drama at my grandma's church, I gave Jesus one more try because my life sucked.

Truthfully, my "return" was really a first attempt. When I had been a part of my grandma's church, it had been against my will. I had no say in the decision to "come to Christ," in part because I was a minor. My opinion as to which congregation we belonged didn't matter. She wasn't listening. Mama, as we used to call her, was straight old-school. Just to clarify the matter, I don't harbor any resentment against her. If anything, I support her decision to bring me up in the Lord. The fact that she got duped by a phony is really too bad, but it does not invalidate her desire for me to know the Lord. That was right and good. She was my acting guardian at that time. To her, taking me to church and introducing me to Jesus Christ was as essential as teaching me to read, which she also did. I agree with her decision to "train [me] up . . . in the way [I] should go" (Proverbs 22:6, King James Version). I agree so much that I'm doing the exact same thing with my children. It's no more an option for the Mitchell children to attend church than it is for them to learn to speak English.

Although the way we rock the church thing is real different from the way Mama did it, the basics are the same. My children's relationship with the Lord is the most important one they will ever have, so Sheeri and I do our best to cultivate an environment that reflects His Lordship in our lives. We instruct them whenever possible. We live out our faith in front of them. They are free to ask questions about what they don't understand. We do our best to explain God's mysteries as clearly as we can in a manner they can grasp. That's no joke either. You try explaining the concept of free will versus predestination to a six-year-old who's really listening. As parents we would be really triflin' if we never took the time to help our children cultivate a relationship with the most important Person who has ever existed and will ever exist. I don't get parents who don't pass on their beliefs to their children. How could you not? I've actually heard people say, "I'll let them decide what they believe when they're older." As though that relieves the parent of the responsibility to teach their children right from wrong. If you are convinced that something is right and good, you've *got* to share it with your children, or you set them up for failure. They may never embrace your values. They may even hate you for "forcing" your values on them. But, hey, suck it up. Parenthood is not a popularity contest. You are not put here to be your children's friend. You gotta set the standard and expect your kids to meet it. Otherwise you're just a punk. That's what Mama did for me. She set the standard.

I regret that I never made the effort to thank her while she was alive for making me go to church. I never thanked her for her prayers for me. But I am grateful to God that she lived to see me personally embrace Jesus Christ. Even though He no longer had her heart, she believed she had done right by me and told me as much. She had contributed to my becoming a good man. Her attitude was, if I couldn't be a Jehovah's Witness, being a Christian was the next best thing.

So like I said, my "return" was really a first attempt. I had reached a plateau. I had made as much money as I was gon' make—doin' what I was doin', if you feel me. I had all the gear, all the trinkets, all the bells and whistles, all the women I wanted, all the fine dining, and all the cash to make me happy. Except I wasn't. I had done all the stuff people tell you to do that supposedly makes you happy. I had done it all, or at least I had done enough to know what "all" would look like if I persisted. I could see where it was leading; I wasn't impressed.

So at the point when I began to thirst for something more than the expensive toys, the fly gear, and the expensive girlfriends, God began to do a work in me. I can't explain it, but one day I looked up and I saw it all for what it was: death. I looked at the fools I was smokin' with, dying . . . slowly dying. Some of them still are. I looked at the women I was running. Educated though some of them were, they were just stupid . . . no woman who knew her real worth would let a man treat her the way I treated some of the women I dated. I looked at some of my colleagues—more death. Folks selling their souls in exchange for paper. And the ones with legal jobs were no better. Still exchanging their lives for a regular biweekly paycheck. It became so clear. It was all so useless. All of it. I was sick to my stomach and had had enough.

So I just sat back. I pulled out. I kept doing my thing, but all the frivolity stopped. No more clubs, no more ho'in', no more scammin', no more shopping sprees. For about six months I just stopped. And I started going to church. It was a pathetic experience, so I won't share where, but I got some Truth out of it; enough to know I needed to be going somewhere else. The problem was, I was still met with the looks. You know the looks. In some white people, it's when their eyes become dime slits and their pupils slide to the side to get a better view of you as you stroll by. For them, it's that look that allows them to see all they can without actually having to turn around and call attention to themselves. From some older black folks the "look" is much more pronounced. It's that one where, when someone first catches sight of you, he looks you up and down from head to toe and back again before rolling his eyes, pursing his lips, and turning his back to you. Those were the looks I got. And in my carnal state, they pissed me off. And you know what? In my more spiritually mature state, they still piss me off. Because now I know enough about Jesus to know that when He walked the earth, He never looked at anyone like that. And seated at God the Father's right hand, He still doesn't. He never viewed me the way the "saints" did and, if the truth be known, the way the saints still do in some parts. I know now that He looks at a man's heart, not his clothes. And that He would never turn anyone away from His house of worship because they didn't *look* holy. That would totally defeat His purpose for having come!

I'm thankful that at that point in my life, my heart had purposed to do right. Had I been any less determined a man, those looks might have been enough to send me back to my old lifestyle. But thank God that He had instilled in me the determination to persist. And He rewarded me big-time by deepening my relationship with Him, by leading me directly to the woman who would become my wife, my best friend, and the mother of my children (I knew she was the one by our third date), and to a church home where I was fed, groomed, and discipled by real, authentic black men, themselves lovers of Christ, who embodied everything positive in men, and who embraced me just as I was, baggy jeans, tatts, pierced ears, and all. They were the first men ever to show me what Jesus means in Matthew 11:28, where He entreats, "Come to me, *all* you who are weary and burdened, and I will give you rest" (emphasis mine). I already knew I was weary. And *burdened* didn't even begin to describe the weight I was operating under. But the real Christian men I met made me understand that *all* applied to me, too. The love they showed a brotha was just like the love I got from other heads, except much more so because it was rooted in the very source of love (1 John 4:7, 16). So I came to Christ and never looked back.

My boys also schooled a brotha. They helped me to understand that I didn't have to stop listenin' to hip-hop in order to be an authentic Christian. This was news to me. A lot of people, especially many Christians, believe that hip-hop and the Gospel of Jesus Christ have nothing in common. Nothing could be farther from the truth. I have actually heard people call hip-hop the music of the devil. They maintain that Christians should have nothing to do with it. Plain and simple, that's just not true. Let me explain.

Hip-hop as it exists today has become its own culture. It has its own values, its own language, its own style of dress, and most notably its own music. But hip-hop, like the Gospel of Jesus Christ, is all-inclusive. It easily exists side by side with other cultures and for the most part is an "equal opportunity employer," for lack of a better phrase. Even though its origins are in black American culture (or African-American culture, if you prefer—honestly I get confused sometimes), its universal appeal speaks volumes. I remember when I hosted an online hip-hop show from Hollywood, California, we would get listeners/viewers from as far away as Israel and Japan. Hip-hop and hip-hop heads really don't discriminate against anybody except posers or Johnny-come-latelies. All heads want to know is, Are you down from the beginning? Do you remember and/or give props to the original playas, like the Treacherous 3, Melle Mel, Slick Rick, and Red Alert? And I tell you, it doesn't matter if a cat is from Harlem or Warsaw. If he's authentic, if his love for hip-hop is real, if he is down, and especially if he (or she—lest the ladies think they get no love) has got skills, (s)he will be welcomed. It's really no more complicated than that.

Jesus is the exact same way. The biblical accounts of His dealings show Him forever in the company of whoever wanted to be down. He didn't care if His followers were male or female. It might be difficult for Western women or men of this day and age to appreciate how radical that fact is. In our culture men and women operate side by side. Women lead almost as often as men. We haven't gotten the equal-pay thing right yet, but the rights Western women enjoy today are certainly closer to God's plan than those of the women in Jesus' day. The culture He operated in had a view of women similar to that of modern-day conservative Muslim nations. Women had very specific duties and roles, which were designed to keep them apart from men. They did not enjoy the same basic rights men did. In every sense they were second-class citizens. In many cases they were considered just barely a step above slaves and livestock. They had no political voice, no authority, and no relevance in society beyond their ability to marry as virgins and to bear male heirs. No one bothered to educate them. Jesus ignored this practice. It was common for women not only to follow Him, but to sit at His feet, a position traditionally reserved for students. Jesus taught women alongside men. He allowed them to ask questions and to engage Him. He didn't merely tolerate them; He welcomed them. He valued them. You might call Him the first feminist.

Another group that Jesus valued was children. If women were given no regard back in the day, children were virtually ignored. Jesus even had to check His own disciples. On one particular occasion recorded in the tenth chapter of Mark's gospel, word was out that Jesus was in town. Folks were bringing their little ones to be blessed. Probably thinking they were doing Jesus a favor, the disciples rebuked the people. Verse 14 in the NIV reads "When Jesus saw this, he was indignant. He said to them, 'Let the little children come to me, and do not hinder them, for the kingdom of God belongs to such as these.' " Verses 15 and 16 continue: " 'I tell you the truth, anyone who will not receive the kingdom of God like a little child will never enter it.' And he took the children in his arms, put his hands on them and blessed them." I have to say, this is one of my favorite accounts. Jesus loves children! But what messes me up is that not only does He halt the practice of shoving them aside; He charges us to be like them! Throughout the gospels He's always doing that. He takes what society then and now says is important and what's unimportant and swaps them out. Children were of no consequence in biblical times. But Jesus says they are the perfect models of the human spirit. I won't go into all the virtues of children. That topic all by itself is a sermon fit for someone with a much more scholarly background. But I can tell you this: Jesus didn't trip about what most of society tripped about. He still don't.

He didn't trip about the sick. He sought them out. He embraced lepers. Today that would be the equivalent of hugging somebody who you know has AIDS. I know AIDS is communicable only through the exchange of bodily fluids, but when was the last time you kissed somebody on the cheek who had stage IV lesions on their forehead? Yeah. That's what I mean. Leprosy, on the other hand, is contagious upon contact. But again, Jesus wasn't trippin'. He hung with tax collectors (ancient versions of loan sharks and bank robbers), prostitutes, and the multitudes of unclean people—those who weren't fit to commune with God or His people. He taught the ignorant. His chosen twelve were not scholars. They were longshoremen; they fished for a living. And you can tell by a lot of the questions they asked Jesus, they were not the sharpest knives in the drawer. I worked the docks one summer with them cats. I can tell you from firsthand experience, we didn't always smell so good. And that's with deodorant. I'd bet good money the apostles were not a fresh-smelling bunch. But Jesus didn't care. He ate with them, traveled with them, slept side by side with them. Why? Because He loved them. He had purposed for them, before they were ever born, that they would carry His message of good news to the world. And He took the time to train and equip them for the task. And he did it all in three years! Talk about the accelerated course. The point is, He handpicked them. He could have chosen kings, priests, philosophers, scholars, but He didn't. He deliberately chose common men, because He is not a respecter of persons. He knew their hearts and He knew that whatever He had purposed for them, He was more than adequate to enable them to achieve it. The results speak for themselves. Twelve ragamuffins started out with a message. Two thousand years later . . . well, you get the point.

I love an underdog. Give me the kid on the street who don't know what's goin' on, but he's got a dream. Show me the 'round-the-way girl who is determined to start her own business, not the debutante. I prefer David to Goliath any day. That's really why I love hip-hop. It's the underdog that rules the world. It started out with some dudes who had nothing but a beat and some rhymes. Now it's an empire. When hip-hop started, it was all about the music, all about the flow. But as its fans have matured and taken on different roles, like parent, spouse, business owner, they have brought the concerns that those roles foster to the forefront, and hip-hop has expanded to address those concerns. And what's cool is that hip-hop's fans bring their sensibilities to those roles. So, for instance, when my kids ask for a story before bedtime, it isn't beyond me and my wife to recite Slick Rick's "Children's Story" in unison from memory (a task made more enjoyable by the fact that the song contains no profanity). And believe you me, the irony of it all isn't lost on us. (If you don't understand, get your hands on a copy.)

As my personal roles have grown to include spouse, parent, literary agent, entertainment/marketing consultant, publisher, and now writer, my concerns for my business, my home, my children, my marriage have all surfaced. And what I have needed and sought for so long is Someone who can relate to me in all these areas without judgment, condemnation, or worse, condescension. I need a reliable source to go to for truth, not hearsay, wives' tales, popular opinion, or myth. I need an immovable, unchanging standard by which to align my life, my values, even my thoughts. Most of the stuff I'm doing now I have never done before in my life. And I don't mind tellin' you, I don't know what I'm doing most of the time. I have never been a husband, a father, an owner of multiple businesses. I have never had to deal with balancing family and ministry. I have never had to think about how to effectively raise children of privilege or how to verbally correct my daughter in a way that doesn't bring her to tears. I need real, applicable answers to my very real, hard questions about my life as it is right now, as well as how it will be. How do I handle a disobedient child? How do I structure my business? What does it take to make my marriage a screaming success? My need for answers to these questions makes me no different from any man in any other generation. And like so many men before me, I turn to Christ for insight, confidence, and provision. The only difference is that the way I rock mine is distinctly, undeniably hip-hop, a fact for which I refuse to apologize. And from what I gather from the Gospel, it is a fact for which no apology is expected (at least not from God Almighty).

2 | The Right Question

I think part of the reason I appreciate most rap artists is because I identify with them so much. There are the most obvious ways: Most of them are black, and so am I. Many of them are, or are close to, my age. Most of them grew up in the so-called " 'hood," as did I. Many of them hustled for a living—like me. But the thing I appreciate most is their determination to be someplace better. It's as though at some point each one had to look around and think, *There's gotta be something better than this!* That's not an original thought when you live in poverty or are surrounded by people who want to see you fail. What is rare is, having had the thought, you then find the cojones to do something about it. Most hip-hop artists, especially rap artists, are this way.

Clearly their desire for a better life and their willingness to chase it down make them (and, for that matter, me) no different from anyone who has ever pursued the American dream. What sets them apart, however, from many achievers is race and (closely related) starting point. Most of the dudes in the rap game start with a huge deficit. They hail from Jamaica in Queens, Harlem, Compton, East Oakland, Long Beach (not the good part either), and places like that. Did I mention that they are black? It may seem like I'm harping on that point, but let's be real—we are talking about the United States here, where being black became en vogue only recently. Don't sleep—our civil rights are barely fifty years old. We've all heard the stats: Brothers are more likely to get shot, go to jail, live in poverty, get shot, get arrested, get shot, go anywhere else but college, get shot, father babies out of wedlock as teens, get shot, die of colon cancer, experience rejection from a major lending institution—all at a much more alarming rate than their white counterparts in almost any age group. That's crazy!

When you look at rap artists and hip-hop artists, many of them are walking statistics: One or two baby's mamas, little or no college education, arrest records (hell, rumor has it, rap began in East Coast prisons in the seventies before it hit the streets of New York and made its way west. So did saggin', for that matter—except I think saggin' had a much earlier start date, but who knows or cares? The two pretty much go hand in hand anyway), and, let's not forget—no legacy.

Most rap artists are like so many blacks in the United States—scratch babies. I wish I could take credit for the term, but I heard it in a sermon given by Bishop Eddie Long of Newbirth Missionary Baptist Church in Atlanta. He proclaimed that most of us black folks are scratch babies. Everything we get in each generation we had to build from scratch, digging it up ourselves, seldom amassing enough of anything beyond debt to pass on to the next generation, damning them to start from—you guessed it—scratch.

Most rap artists fit this profile, but few of them forget that they have an obligation to their children and their children's children. Say what you want about Master P, but Lil' Romeo and any kids he may have got the bomb hookup. Pops has made sure that his son has a recording career, some airtime, some investments, and so forth. Lil' man ain't gon' be hurtin' unless something goes really, really wrong.

You may be thinking that that's what fathers should do. They should provide for their families and for future generations. I agree. The Word says that "A good man leaves an inheritance for his children's children" (Proverbs 13:22). God is truly generational. But you have to appreciate just how forward-thinking that is for a generation of men who grew up mostly without fathers to teach them by example, surrounded by a culture (by this I mean African-American) that spends millions annually on consumer goods. Almost every rap artist I can think of represents first-generation wealth. That's both sad and great at the same time. Many of them are the first people in their family to own homes—most of them buying homes for their mothers, who raised them alone. Until the advent of their careers, many of them never traveled outside of their 'hoods, let alone abroad! Most of them are determined to branch out into other avenues: owning/running their own music labels, film companies, clothing lines, beverage companies, sports franchises . . . you name it. It's as though they are trying to make up for all the years that the harvest was devoured by the locusts of ignorance, poverty, racism, and just plain stupidity.

They remind me of the tribes of Manasseh and Ephraim in the Old Testament. In the book of Joshua, chapter 14, when the promised land is being divided up among the twelve tribes of Israel, the two tribes who are Joseph's descendants tell Joshua that their allotment is not enough. At first glance it might seem an ungrateful statement. But as my pastor, Reverend Jody Moore, so eloquently pointed out one Sunday, they asked because they knew who they were. Joseph's sons had been personally blessed by Jacob/Israel, as recorded in Genesis, chapter 48. Knowing who they were and what they were entitled to, they demanded of Joshua their due.

Today's hip-hop-preneurs are like that. They know their history. They know they are descendants of kings and queens. They know they have survived the worst America has to offer. They know that the only difference between them and America's old money is opportunity. Where they've found none, they have created it. Where a door has remained closed to the patient knocking of their forefathers, the leaders of this generation have torn it off its hinges. In an interview I saw on PBS, Russell Simmons stated that part of the reason he created Phat Farm was because no white designers would hire him. The men of my generation have simply said to the world at large, "It's not enough." They are smart men, or at the very least have excellent advisers to whom they are smart enough to listen. They are men (and women, lest the sistahs feel slighted) of vision and should be commended for their achievements.

Nobody could have seen hip-hop's explosion worldwide— nobody except God. I am convinced that He has used it as a means to elevate an otherwise oppressed and disenfranchised people. Please don't think that I discount traditional means of advancement, like education. That's not what I'm sayin', so don't send me any hate mail. I simply see how God can and does use the "foolish things to confound the wise." I have no stats at all, but I would be interested in knowing how many young black millionaires have come into being either directly or indirectly as a result of hip-hop's growing influence. Just a thought.

Anyway, like I was sayin', cats in the game are smart. They ain't givin' up nothing! No publishing, no royalties, no rights. Gone are the days when managers could jack unsuspecting ghetto kids out of their cash. If you want to do anything legit within or involving the hip-hop community, you gon' have to deal with some black folks somewhere. 'Cause brothers done got hip to how this game is played, and you ain't gettin' *nathan* for free. Keep it up, y'all . . . elbow your way into your rightful place at the grown-ups' table. I'm right behind you. But the point I'm trying to make is that every successful rap artist began his journey in that moment after he examined his circumstances and decided not to settle. After he asked the right question: "Is this all there is?" And decided the answer was no.

That's pretty much my story, too. My mom and stepdad were working-class folks. They owned their own home. They were raising three boys (my two brothers and me) plus any given number of cousins here and there. Both had "good" jobs—i.e., regular paychecks. We were far from wealthy. We were like everybody else we knew—just okay. I observed early on, however, that mom and stepdad were miserable. They didn't really enjoy their work. They just did it because it was required. They hated Mondays and looked forward a little too much to the weekends. They seemed to me to be tolerating the majority of their lives. I looked around at all of my neighbors, relatives, friends . . . they seemed miserable, too. We kids were happy—in the way that kids are before they know anything about bills and responsibilities and selling their souls for a paycheck. We were happy, but the world we inhabited was a lot less so. If I had to choose a color to paint my childhood environment, it would be a dull shade of gray. It would look like film from cigarette smoke residue or something like that.

I knew as a young kid that whatever the grown-ups were sellin', I wasn't buyin'. I remember sitting outside one day with my best friend at the time, Sean Gascie, and some other dudes from our block. We were all about seventeen years old, or close to it. Our conversation drifted around to career choices. In other words, what we would be when we grew up. Somebody threw out butcher. Someone else said firefighter or policeman. When it was my turn I said, "I'm gon' make movies." There was a long pause before the group broke into laughter.

"Nigga, please!" was mostly what I remember hearing. I laughed, too. But I wasn't joking. I just knew I was destined for something better.

How I knew, I couldn't tell you. I mean, none of my folks drove luxury cars. Our 'hood was okay. We had some gangstas, and there were fights, domestic disputes, occasional gunfire, but it wasn't a battleground. We didn't travel. We didn't dine at fine restaurants. We just worked (myself included—I acquired my first paper route at age ten), went to school, and got our party on whenever and wherever we could. There was nothing spectacular about my life. I didn't know anybody who had it any better, and I had no natural reason to believe that I could or deserved to be anything other than what I saw around me. Nobody encouraged me. If anything, everything in my immediate environment discouraged me. For instance, I had a serious interest in sports. I threw shot put and discus and played football. But since neither my mom nor my stepdad ever came to any of my games, I figured sports weren't important, so I didn't take them seriously. I was a smart kid—when I felt like showing it. But I was on the under with mine. Mediocrity was the order of the day, so I didn't let anybody know just how bookish I was except family. But they weren't necessarily a supportive bunch either. One time some "cousins" (I had a grip of them) actually preempted my leisure reading to solicit my help in purse snatching in a nearby neighborhood. I won't lie—I helped. But they were really annoyed that after we got back, I picked up my book where I left off. They mocked me with comments like "bookworm" and "Einstein." They told me I acted like I was goin' to college or "some sh——." At the time it seemed funny. I don't think I fully appreciated just how jacked-up their attitudes were until I began writing this book. I thank God that none of the negativity in my life mattered too much. I just knew that I was destined for something far better than what I was being shown.

Anyway, most of the folks I knew reasonably well were mediocre and miserable. Those who weren't miserable were numb, just going through the motions. I wish I could tell you that I knew some Christians who just had it goin' on, but I didn't. In my neck of the woods, it was difficult to tell the saints from the ain'ts unless you got up early enough on Sunday to see who was leaving for church—provided there was no major football game on television. Other than that, there really was no discernable difference. If there had been, I might have gravitated toward Christ sooner. But as it stood, everybody was busted.

But the folks who were ballin'—the dudes with the gear, the

women, the Beamers and Benzes, chains, etc.—they were all pushin' product. And you know what else? They seemed pretty enthusiastic about life to me. They were having a good time (closer inspection from the inside out would prove my initial assessment full of error—but at the time I knew only what I saw); their joyful, carefree fronts were enough to convince me that I needed to be down. I won't give any specific details, as some of the folks I hooked up with are still in the game, but let's just say I got in with a real productive crew and became upwardly mobile.

As I stated earlier, my new financially prosperous life got stale, too. I was just reluctant to let go of the loot. But eventually I got real tired of constantly watching my back, havin' no real friends, being unable to connect with anybody about the demons that haunted my every waking moment. In some careers you can express reservations and misgivings to your peers or to your superiors. And in some cases doing so can even effect positive change, or at least get you some free counseling. But I wasn't working for FedEx. And in my profession, expressing anything could get a nigga "broke off."

When I got weary and worried enough, I left. And that was truly the Holy Spirit. Back in the day I used to call it my "spidey sense." I know some fools who call it instinct. But I know now it was none other than the third person of the Trinity, Himself. God the Holy Spirit was warning me that it was time to go. My grace was running out. I'm so glad I listened. Again, no details possible, but let's just say that things started shaping up in my organization in such a way that made me real uncomfortable. I had a feeling—no proof, mind you, just a feeling—that I was marked and I had little time left. So without discussing my plans with anyone—not even my moms, really—one night I packed up in the wee hours of the morning and headed south. I never looked back.

I knew enough to know when I got to LA that I didn't want to start that mess all over again, so I stayed clear of the underground. (The closest I came was getting my hands on a fat sack now and then. I had lost my taste for "wild" living, but not my taste for the good life, nor the smoke.)

Broke, no degree—I had completed only two years of college—no prospects, I was really ass-out, flappin' in the breeze. Calling on the experience I had as a behavioral specialist, which is just a fancy term for a job coach for the mentally challenged, I managed by the grace of God to get a job at a large southern California company that appreciated my skills with the developmentally disabled and who paid me accordingly. So just like that I went from ballin' to teaching developmentally disabled men and women how to do things like mop floors and clean toilets at Taco Bell and Barnes & Noble.

Most developmentally disabled people learn best by example. So there I was moppin' floors and cleaning toilets—all in the name of a paycheck. It was a worthwhile gig. I'll admit, the first time one of my clients, who had the mental capacity of a six-year-old, learned how to catch the bus on her own to and from work, I experienced the pride of a parent.

It was a job, but I really grew to care about my clients as people. I see now that God used that job to soften my hardened heart. I mean, to see a grown man break down and cry because he can't remember how to tie his shoe is something that would affect the most hardened of criminals. It wasn't long before I became invested. I really wanted to help all these people succeed. It helped that most of them were determined to do so at any cost. They knew most people found them repulsive. They wouldn't let that stop them. They drew inspiration from anywhere they could. When one potential employer interviewed one of my clients, she did what most people who aren't used to dealing with the handicapped do: She spoke really slowly and really loudly. After the interview, my client said to me that he didn't know they let retarded people manage restaurants. Do you get it? He thought that his interviewer was developmentally disabled like him, and he was inspired. Who was I to tell him any different?

Most of my clients had the goods. They just needed direction. I guess I had more in common with them than even I realized. Maybe that was why I understood them so well.

Fuzzy feelings aside, my new job paid well, but not nearly as well as my old job—know what I mean? Truthfully the decline in pay was not a bad trade-off for a good night's sleep—no waking up with a start at the slightest noise, no sharing a bed with a rottie and a bullmastiff (two breeds whose farts know no mercy), no gun under my pillow. (Well, okay, I still had the gun—old habits die hard—but I didn't need it anymore. And that was a good feeling.) I settled in okay to my new square life. But it was unsatisfying, too. I couldn't really put my finger on it, but I figured it must have had something to do with the pay (or lack thereof). So, old tapes still playing, off to get another job I went.

It turns out that my skills as a job coach and my connections within that company landed me a job working for an international rock star and his family. Which, when you think about it, makes complete sense. Working with and for the very rich can be barely discernible from working with retarded people. Actually, retarded people are much easier because they know they're retarded. My gig had the title of behavioral specialist—one of this guy's kids was kind of a "problem child"—but my title turned out to be a glorified term for "personal assistant." I've heard nightmares about what celebrities' personal assistants go through. Most of it is true. But my guy was really cool. He, too, had come from humble beginnings. He had worked menial jobs in his youth while pursuing his dream of international stardom. He appreciated my style—that and the fact that I didn't know who the hell he was when I first met him. He had and still has so many groupies that I think it must have been refreshing to be treated like a man instead of a demigod. He was so impressed with the fact that I wasn't impressed with his celebrity or his wealth that he hired me on the spot.

So I'm thinkin', *Cool—more cash. Things should be looking up.* And they were for a while. Until dissatisfaction crept back in—dirty bastard. Okay, so now I was really confused. I had thought that my lack of inner peace had been because I was doing dirt (which was partially true)—so I had walked. Then I thought it was because I wasn't getting paid enough. So I made a move. Between the two jobs I had more than enough loot. True, it still wasn't what I was bringing in back in the day, but by most folks' standards, it was a pretty good living—even after taxes, which, by the way, I resented the hell out of. I was single. No kids. No drama. Really, I had more than enough to do some things with. So naturally I spent it. I got another Beamer. I lived on the west side. I had nods from the honeys. I dressed well. I was a respected professional. I had respectable road dawgs. I didn't have a care in the world. So why the hell wasn't I happy? This was really starting to bug me. I had all the ingredients, but the recipe wasn't working. It was starting to piss me off.

God bless my boys, but a lot of them cats was some shallow-ass niggas. We would be smokin' and I'd try to get "deep" and ask a question like, "Y'all ever feel like something is missing?" I got responses like "Yeah—where the women at?" or "You know it, dawg—you got some chips?" Needless to say, I didn't try often. Rarely would I ask females what they were looking for. So again, in the midst of all this "fun" I was miserable and alone. I decided to just keep doing what I was doing. Maybe satisfaction would come along at some point. I just had to try harder. So I had more sex. I drank more alcohol. I smoked more bud. I went clubbin' with the homies more—ad nauseam, literally. But only on the weekends, of course. I had to chase my paper during the week. I didn't realize it then, but I had lapsed into the same lifestyle that my mom and stepdad had had. I was living for the weekend so I could get my party on.

Interestingly enough, I hadn't ever voiced my dissatisfaction to my moms. I guess I figured that she couldn't help me—so why bother? As far as I could tell, she was searching, too. But my mom and I have always been really close. She, much like my wife, rolls like a dude sometimes. She and I used to talk about everything. We still pretty much do. Usually if we didn't talk about something, it was because it didn't occur to me to tell her about it. The only secret I ever purposely kept from her was what I used to do for a living back up north. I knew she wouldn't approve, and I knew it would have stressed her out. Most important, I knew she would have confided in someone eventually, and that would have been it for me. So I just didn't tell her. I was so closemouthed about it, I'm almost certain that she still has no idea. As a matter of fact, I will have to break my silence before this book gets published.

Anyway, my mom is so cool, my brothers and I don't even call her "Mom." Although her birth name is Norma, everybody calls her Bobbi. Her fiesty disposition and red hair as a child earned her the nickname Bobcat. Over the years it kinda morphed into Bobbi. So that's who she is to everybody who's close to her. My brothers and I even call her Bob when we address her face-to-face. She refuses all titles and monikers. To cousins, children, nieces, nephews, brothers, sisters, and grandchildren alike, she's just Bobbi. And you know what? It's a good fit.

So Bobbi and I were talking on the phone one day. I was bragging about my latest sexual conquest (that's how tight we are), when she just cut me off. She said something to the effect of loving me with all her heart, but not liking or respecting me at all. I really can't remember my response now, but I think at the time I just laughed it off. But in truth, it really stung.

When I was growing up with her, my mom had lost her temper with me countless times. I used to get butt-whippin's on the regular as a boy. I deserved every one. When I got too old and too big to spank, she would cuss me out. I was all kinds of "m-f-ahs" and "bastards" and "niggas" back in the day. My younger brothers still joke that for a long time they thought my name was That-niggamykel. I didn't mind it so much, really. I often deliberately provoked her because I found her tirades really funny. There was never any lasting damage.

Yeah, Moms and I had some real rough patches when she and

my stepdad were divorcing. She was in danger of losing the house, and I was in the midst of my less-than-legal career. It was a stressful time. It got bad enough for me to leave home a couple of times (read: thrown out), but never so bad that I couldn't come back. I was paying almost all of our bills, but she was still trying to school me. I wasn't havin' it. She exploded daily. We laugh about it now. What infuriated her most was how I always remained so calm, even jovial during our arguments. Sometimes I just broke out laughing when she was puttin' it on me. I really didn't do it to bug her. It's just that she was really funny to me. She's so little—maybe five-two on a good day, in half-inch heels. She has a really high-pitched, squeaky voice, which goes up at least an octave when she's pissed. Those two facts combined made it feel like I was being rolled up on by a mad elf or a dangerous gnome or something. I couldn't help but laugh.

All that's to say, even at our worst, I never doubted my mom's love for me or that she liked me. Whenever I got in trouble she always made it clear that it was my behavior that she didn't like, not me. I have done some pretty to'-up stuff, too. But Bobbi always assured me that I was nothing less than wonderful to her. So when, in this particular conversation, she said she didn't like or respect me, she blindsided me. I pretended that I didn't care, but I was messed up. I had never lived in a world without Bobbi's approval. It sucked. And although I had never really given much consideration to her respect for me, I didn't like losing it.

I would like to be able to say here that I resolved then and there to become a better man. Nope! I think my initial response was something like, "F—— her! How she gon' judge me?" Yeah, real eloquent and cerebral. But, hey, I was not saved yet, and my flesh was not feeling the truth. But I love my moms, and I just couldn't stay angry at her that long. Still, I sho' as hell wasn't gon' call her first. She apparently felt the same way, because we went from talking three or four times a week to zero. I don't even remember now how long that lasted. But it was effective.

In the meantime, I had to deal with the fact that I had become a jackass. I had turned into the kind of guy even my own mother couldn't stand. I could see if I had become a serial killer or a crackhead, like Leonardo DiCaprio's character in the movie *The Basketball Diaries*. There's a scene where his mom won't let him in her apartment because he's fiendin' for some rock. It's a wild scene. Now that I'm a parent I can't imagine how painful it would be to have to take such a hard line with my kid. But I'd do it in a heartbeat if that's what it took to save any of their lives. I'm hard-core, and so is my wife. Our motto at home is "No punks!" We love our children, which is why we put the smack down on the regular. 'Cause ain't nobody walkin' out of the Mitchell home not knowin'. Once they are out on their own, that's between them and the Lord. Naturally my wife and I will always have our say. In the meantime, though, whatever it takes . . . you feelin' me? Whatever it takes. 'Cause we just that committed.

In her own way, that's what Bobbi was doing to me when she cut me off. I couldn't see it then. But I felt it.

At first, all I wanted to do was prove her wrong. But the closer I looked at my life, the more I realized she was right: I was a bastard. No, I wasn't doin' anything illegal—unless you count the chronic. I wasn't lying, cheating, or stealing (at least not in the conventional sense). Working as a job coach, I could even pass for a good person. I mean, after all, I was doing something positive. That had to count for something. I was just living my life. Where was the harm in that? In the words of Mary J. Blige, all I really wanted was "to be happy." So I was going after what made me happy. Paper. Sex. Stuff. Of course, to see living proof that none of these things did the trick, all I had to do was to look at my rock star. Dude had it all, but he had nothing. Get me? He had tons of cash, phat cribs in exclusive communities, best that the world had to offer right at his fingertips. But his kids were shot to the curb. Dude was on his third or fourth marriage—I can't even remember. And he was still in the paper chase. The sad part to me was that he was as wealthy as some people ever dream of becoming. Yet he still suffered all the pangs of poverty.

Was that where I was headed? I was so confused, I couldn't have told you. I think I landed on true love as my next guess for satisfaction. I mentioned this to Bobbi the next time we talked. She told me no woman in her right mind would want me as I was. Again with the insults. Again she was right. She suggested that I try God. She sent me some Christian books, which I eventually read cover to cover. And she encouraged me to go to church. I did that. And some ten or twelve years later, I'm telling you about it. Don't get me wrong: I had a gang of reservations—and they were totally legit. Not to mention that my past had made me extremely cynical. But finally I had managed to ask the right question. And I knew there was more to life than I had.

3

Da Rules!

Almost everything I had ever heard about Christianity seemed too good to be true. According to the books my moms had sent me (whose titles I can't even remember) and most of what I had heard in church, Jesus could supposedly satisfy ALL my needs and desires. That was cool, 'cause I had a big appetite and I needed and wanted a lot of stuff. The only drawback that I could see was all of them rules! It seemed to me like Christians weren't allowed to have no fun. On top of that, all the Christians I had ever observed seemed to fall into one of two categories: They were either corny, boring, and sportin' some tricky gear, or they were fakin' on Sundays and shakin' it the rest of the week. As a matter of fact, some of the biggest freaks I had "dated" back in the day were women who claimed to be Christians! They didn't act any differently from the unsaved folks. All of the so-called Christians I knew of drank, smoked, cursed, sometimes cheated, gambled, hated life, hated each other, complained about hating life and each other, labored under debt, gossiped, lied . . . you get the point. Even at a young age I figured that Christians weren't supposed to do those things, but it seemed to me that they did them anyway. The only difference I could make out was that Christians pretended that they didn't do those things.

Exposure to such hypocrisy at an early age was really more responsible for my cynicism toward all things Christian than anything else—that and the fact that I never saw anybody who claimed to be a Christian who had it goin' on. Their lives were just as raggedy as everybody else's. They were poor and pretending to be okay with it. They were sleeping around and beating their wives. So what could possibly motivate me to want to explore this joke of a religion?

My own misery—that's what. My need to be satisfied. It was purely selfish. I didn't care about salvation. As far as I was concerned, hell used to be my home address and surrounding neighborhood. I was scared of dying and going there. But I knew I probably deserved it after all the dirt I had done. Now don't get me wrong; it would be nice if at the end of everything I didn't have to go. But I knew I had earned it. I couldn't even front.

I didn't care about the company of other Christians, which in "Christian-ese" is called fellowship. I didn't know any Christians who I actually liked or respected. I didn't know any who I was cool with. Don't front—you know that's important to you, too. Nobody ever wants to kick it with the losers. We all spend our whole lives avoiding them—in junior high, high school, and beyond. No girls want to date them. No dudes want to befriend them. It's impossible to see the merit in hangin' with them—unless you need help with homework or your taxes. In addition to that, everybody knew Christians was some broke niggas. Always giving up they ends to the pastor, who was usually jackleg anyway. Besides, my boys was a'ight and they had they own chedda—most of the time. Naw—I was straight in the "friend" department. I didn't need any new friends.

At least, I didn't think so at the time.

Selfish bastard that I was, I didn't care about helping anybody else for free. I didn't believe in charity. Everything in my world was

quid pro quo—tit for tat, give and take, fair exchange ain't no rob-
bery, all that. So all that stuff about helping the poor, visiting the
sick, feeding the hungry was totally lost on me. I worked with mentally challenged adults. And I got paid for my time.

All a brotha cared about in this life was how he could come
up. The Jesus thing, as I often referred to it, was all about me. And
the line (or should I say Scripture) that arrested my selfish butt
was John 10:10. Speaking to a group of mostly disenfranchised
Jews, who were laboring under Roman occupation—which to my
knowledge was a close cousin of twentieth-century South African
apartheid, and about as humiliating—Jesus dared to tell them that
He had come so that they (the people) could have abundant
life . . . or in some translations "life to the full." Say what you want,
he had guts. That phrase, however, "life to the full," intrigued me.
I had been full before. I had been full of food, full of hate, full of
anger, full of fear, full of lust, full of greed, and (to use a colloquial-
ism) full of sh———. I was certainly full of myself. But never had I
been full of life! At least, not how He meant it. I didn't know what
abundant life was, but I knew enough to know I wanted some. And
given that everything in my life had been a give and take, I knew
I'd have to give up something in exchange—eventually. But I was
content to worry about that later, while I investigated this "abundant life" thing.

What I learned was that abundant life didn't begin after you
died. It did continue after you died, but it didn't start there. And
I'm glad of that, 'cause they woulda lost me right there. No, abundant life begins in the here and now. Life to the full was something
I could have right now. Unlike an insurance policy, there was no
period of qualification. No wait time. No application to fill out.
The catch (and you knew there was one, right?) was that I had to
accept Jesus Christ as my personal Lord and Savior. I figured that
couldn't be too hard. I mean, every rap artist at every music award
show since the late eighties had been doing it, right? Cats was steppin' to the mike sayin' stuff like, "I'd like to thank my manager, my

agent, my record label, and my Lord and Savior Jesus Christ, who gave me the words to 'Lick My Crack.' I dedicate this award to Him. Peace!" Hey—if those guys could say all that in the same breath as Jesus, maybe I could, too. At the very least, I figured it was worth a try.

What I soon learned was that accepting Jesus in that capacity was more than just a phrase or a phase. It was, to use a modern term, a "lifestyle change." I knew something had to be up. When a person accepts Christ, essentially what he's agreeing to is that he will no longer be the boss of his own life. He is handing over all authority to God and submitting to the control of His Holy Spirit. I ain't gon' lie: That gave me pause. I mean, I was the kind of dude who wouldn't even let fools drive my car! And here I was going to give control of my life over to Someone I couldn't even see? At the time it seemed a high price to pay for some abundant life. And I had to really think about that. As you may have guessed by now, I am not a man typically ruled by emotion or impulse. Except for the temporary insanity that was my early twenties, I have always weighed the costs of any decision. So the question before me was, Is this abundant-life thing worth handing over the reins?

I didn't know right away. But at some point I heard it said, probably in a sermon, that if I could have achieved satisfaction on my own by now, I would have done it already. A quick glance over my life proved this statement to be true. So I took the plunge . . . literally. I got baptized. Let me just take a moment to say that you don't have to get baptized in order to be saved. I know of some churches that don't even practice baptism. Baptism is just a public demonstration of your choice to follow Jesus. I was already saved when I got baptized. I had accepted Christ in my heart. That you can do anytime, anywhere. A prayer of salvation can be as simple as "Lord, save me." You just have to know in your heart that in your humanity you're basically just shot to the curb and that you need Jesus to save you from the eternal consequences (a.k.a. life in hell) of your bad choices (a.k.a. sin). To do that you don't even need to come to church. You're just more likely to come to realize that in church because that's where most people hear God's word preached out loud.

So I got baptized. And you know what? I felt different. Not everybody does. That's okay; it doesn't mean that you did it wrong or anything. My wife didn't feel any different after she was baptized. Of course, she had been saved twenty-five plus years when she finally did it. But I felt as though the door was opened to a new life. And I fully intended to walk through it. I felt so great that I went home and smoked a blunt to celebrate! I kid you not. So much for feelings, right?

So now I'm going to church. I'm learning the Word. I'm on my way to abundant life. But before I get there, or so I think, I have to deal with these rules! The rules had kept me away for such a long time. I really had hoped I could get around them. My thinking was, Forget the rules; just give me life to the fullest! What it would take some time to learn was that life to the fullest was in the rules! I know that sounds crazy. But it's true. The very things that seemed to kill my fun were where I would find my life.

Nobody says it better than Jesus Himself as recorded in the book of John. By the way, the gospel of John is a really good book to read if you're a new believer or just curious. Its style is narrative and easy to follow in a contemporary translation, like the New International Version, *The Spirit-filled Life Bible,* or *The Message Bible.* You should find it straightforward enough to give you a good picture of who Jesus is, yet it's confusing enough to lead you to ask the right questions.

In John 12:25, Jesus proclaims that whoever keeps his life will lose it. And whoever loses his life for the sake of the Gospels will gain eternal life. I didn't get it. It sounded like a word problem. But what I eventually got out of it was that basically we all got plans. You got stuff you want to do; so do I. No big. That's normal. Jesus already knows that. What He's saying in John is that if you insist on sticking to your plans, even if you succeed you come up short, because your plans pale in comparison to what He's got in store for you. But if you give up your plans in exchange for His plans, you not only achieve what you hoped to get out of your plans, you get what's behind doors number two and three as well!

That sounds real good, right? But here's the catch. You know I was looking for one, right? The catch is that He doesn't tell you up front what the plan is. He just lays down the rules. It's the ultimate bluff. Except He's not bluffing. But all you have is His promise that He isn't. In other words, He's extending a promise to you without any proof to back it up, except the Bible, which He authored. And you might have to let go of all your stuff and all your plans in order to go after it. Do you see the flaw in that for the average guy? I did. But abundant life kept calling me, so I went for it. I didn't go all out on a limb or anything. I wasn't like, "Okay, Lord, send me to Africa to be a missionary." Nope, wasn't even close . . . still ain't. I just told Him I was willing. I surrendered all my plans, hoping that His really would be better and that He wouldn't clown me.

I kept mine within close reach, though—so that if this thing didn't work out, I wouldn't be left hangin'. The last thing I wanted was to be left hangin', looking like a nut, talkin' about "God's got me!" That was my biggest fear. I guess 'cause growing up in Oakland and Pittsburgh I had seen so many cats on street corners looking crazy, wearing sandwich boards, screaming at people passing by to repent or go to hell. I don't think I'm alone in those sightings. I didn't want to end up like one of those guys. I didn't want my final destination to be selling Bibles on the freeway or something equally as humiliating. But somehow I suspected that the God I had been reading about wouldn't do me like that. I suspected that my calling was different. One thing was clear: If I was ever going to learn what He wanted for me, I would have to do it His way—not mine. For me that was the hard part. Because I had always, always, always done things my own way. Me and Frank (Sinatra) were on the same page.

Understand that I didn't give up everything all at the same

time. I didn't become an über-Christian able to give up weed, sex, drinking, gambling, lying, cursing in a single bound. As a matter of fact, at first I couldn't really see why I should. I thought all of these other Christians must have missed the page in the Bible that says you can still do your thing. A guy can be a good Christian without sacrificing all those things, right? And God looks at the heart, right? Well, I was trippin' and I had some growing up to do. And it had to begin between my ears. I had to learn to think a new way. I had to learn to think God's way.

Don't close the book! It's not as complicated as it sounds. I didn't have to go into any suspended states of consciousness. I experienced no rapturous ecstasy. I didn't have any visions. I just read the Bible, went to church, discussed what I learned with folks who knew more than I did, and prayed. That's all. It's that simple. As a matter of fact, that's still my MO today. Scripture is God's revelation of Himself to humanity. Everything that we need to know about God on this side of eternity is contained in the sixty-six books that make up the Old and the New Testaments. You don't need the Koran, the Bhagavad Gita, or even the kabbalah, for that matter. The reason that most Christians are so ignorant about God and His principles for living is because they never read His Word for themselves.

Reading the Bible isn't like reading any other book, in large part because the Author is alive and immediately accessible. Let me explain. Even though the Bible was scribed by many different people, its sole author is the Holy Spirit . . . or as the Old Testament refers to Him, the Spirit of the Lord. Do you remember the first time you read Shakespeare? Didn't you find it confusing due to the language, the content, and the message? Thank God for your junior high school English teacher who was there to translate and interpret. But how much more insightful would your experience have been if William Shakespeare himself had been there to teach you? See what I mean? When you sit down with the Bible, the Holy

Spirit, who is a Person, is right there to guide you. If you invite Him to help you, He will make it easier to understand His Word.

The problem is, most Christians depend on other people's interpretations of God's Word, those of their pastor, or those of popular Christian and non-Christian authors, rather than bothering to investigate, question, and test it for themselves. That's right, I said *question* and *test*. Despite popular opinion, which is wrong, God does want you to question and test His Word to see if it is true (Psalm 34:8). He wants you to test your pastor's sermons, too. He wants you to test the assertions by popular authors. He wants you to test what I'm writing to you now. (See 1 John 4:1–3.) Everything you allow to feed you should line up with God's Word. If it doesn't, then you've got a choice to make. Whom will you believe? 'Cause the one thing I love about God is He's straight-up with His. Be confused, question, and meditate, but don't try mixing together a little bit of Islam, Buddhism, or astrology with the Word. That ain't gon' work. Challenge Him. He can handle all you got . . . the questions, complaints, and gripes. He ain't scared of you. So bring it. Moreover, He promises to help you. You won't understand everything at once. You probably won't even get through the entire Book at first. But you don't need to. God's Word is so full that pretty much anywhere you start will be a good place.

The reason it's good to go to church is so that you can hear God's Word laid out and explained by someone who's well versed in studying it. Your pastor needn't have gone to seminary in order to rightly divine the Word. I, however, do prefer to sit under one who has. That's a personal preference, not a requirement. I've never found anything in God's Word that states that a degree from anywhere makes someone a better pastor. The Bible, however, does say that we should go to church and socialize with fellow believers. Doing so provides a good foundation to learn God's Word, people to help you understand and apply God's Word to your life, and accountability in case you start trippin'.

The key to being able to do this is to find a church with folks you can relate to. The main reason I started attending Faithful Central was because from the first time I visited, a gang of people there looked just like me! There was a bunch of brothas my age and they all seemed "normal." Well, okay, one or two were a li'l off, but most of them were cool. They were walkin' this walk and didn't seem to be any worse for wear. Moreover, they were real about their struggles. I remember in one men's meeting, one dude was asked by the leader how he was doin' with the sex thing. He said he was doin' okay, but he was helpin' himself out pretty much every night. Other men commiserated with him, which let me know they understood. Nobody fronted like it was repulsive. Nobody gasped and left the room or any of that drama. And you know what? We prayed for dude! That blew my mind! I was like, *This is the place for me. Folks is real up in here.* And the pastor—Lord have mercy! Bishop Kenneth Ulmer and my dawg Travon Potts, who at that time was head over the youth and young adult ministry, called Generation X, came wit' it! They spared no feelings. Pulled no punches. Took no prisoners. They delivered the Word hard and true. I didn't always enjoy what I heard. But I welcome a spiritual enema any day if it will help me pull my head out of my butt.

Speaking of what God's Word says and doesn't say, there's a whole lot on both sides. There are some things that the Word definitely condemns: lying, all forms of fornication (hetero or homo), murder, cheating. There are other things that it commends: helping the poor and the weak, taking care of widows and orphans, telling the truth, speaking to people in love, operating in compassion, living in humility. Neither list is exhaustive. Then there are a lot of things never mentioned by name in the Bible that fall into a gray area. I won't even start on that list. And there are other things that God leaves totally up to us to decide. I won't start on that list either.

It's for the latter two reasons that I don't refer to the code I live by as a set of rules. I prefer to call them biblical principles. The distinction is this: To me rules represent law. Principles represent grace. Given a choice I'd prefer to live under grace. Here's why: According to my understanding, we are all born messed up because of the sin Adam and Eve committed in the Garden of Eden (Genesis, chapter 3). In his book *The Problem of Pain*, CS Lewis refers to all of humanity as a spoiled species. He contends that Adam and Eve's act of disobedience caused "a loss of status as a species." The fall cost all of mankind our "original specific nature." Who we are now is just a really distorted shadow compared to the first two humans. This inherited, sinful condition separates all of humanity from God from jump. But God really, really, really loves us and desires to be reconciled to us. The problem is that He is perfectly holy—free from all contamination. There is no sin in Him. Sin cannot exist in His presence. And He is perfectly just, which means He requires just punishment for the one who sins. So then we have a problem. Under the law, the punishment for breaking the law, sinning against God Himself, is death. However, in His grace, God allows for substitution. The book of Leviticus is full of all the different animals God accepted in the place of the sinner in the Old Testament. He teaches us in the book of Hebrews that without the shedding of blood, there is no forgiveness for sin (Hebrews 9:22). I know this is getting a little deep, so bear with me. Back in the day, if you blew it, you brought your goat or calf or dove to the temple. The priest would slaughter it. Draining out all the blood, he would then sprinkle that blood on the altar. Then he would cook the sacrificial animal, which he and the other priests would eat. I'm oversimplifying the process for the sake of making it plain.

The most significant ceremony was Passover. During this celebration the Israelites commemorated God's freeing them from slavery in Egypt. Read Exodus chapters 11 and 12 for the details. Anyway, every celebration of Passover included the consumption of a sacrificial lamb, which was slaughtered and whose blood was sprinkled on the altar for the forgiveness of the sins of the people. It was a pretty cool setup. Instead of having to die themselves, God made a way for the people to repent and to be able to be clean enough to come to Himself, until the next time they sinned. The problem is, people sin twenty-four/seven. Unless you're willing to live under condemnation, you better have a gang of animals at your disposal.

Okay, so along comes Jesus, the Son of God, the second Person of the Trinity. People of the time think He's some new kid, but they're wrong. He's always been around since time immemorial (John 1:1, 2; John 8:58). Since God knows everything, He knew before Adam and Eve did that they were gonna mess it up for everybody. And He already had a plan in place. So when Jesus stepped out of time and into eternity, He was simply fulfilling what every Old Testament prophecy had said about Him before He came. Don't believe me? Compare Micah 5:2; Isaiah 7:14, 9:6, 35:4–5, 49:1, 53, 60:6; Daniel 9:24–26; Zechariah 9:9, 11:12–13, 12:10; Psalm 22:1, 7–9, 13–18, 16:8–10, and 110:1 to the facts about Jesus' life as found in the gospels of Matthew, Mark, Luke, and John. This ain't the complete list, but it's a good start. The prophets knew because God had told them He was coming, so that the people wouldn't lose hope.

Okay, so up pops Jesus, ready to do His thing. His whole thirty-three years on this planet, He never sinned. He was fully human and fully divine. The gospels all record his passion, death, and resurrection. And Mel Gibson did a dope job of bringing to the screen what Jesus went through for us. You see, Jesus is the final Passover lamb. The significance of His being sinless is that only the purest animals could be sacrificed in the Old Testament . . . a goat without blemish, a bull without defect, etc. Jesus was utterly without blemish or defect. This way He could be the ultimate sacrificial lamb. Get it? The significance of his being a hundred percent divine is that only an eternal being could suffer for the sins of all eternity. His suffering and death substituted for every person who ever had lived and ever will live on the face of this earth. That's a lot of sins to cover! That includes the man who cheats on his wife. The kid

who lies to his parents. The maniacal dictator who commits geno-
cide in the name of ethnic cleansing. The child molester and the serial killer. The greedy person. The judge who takes a bribe. The
crooked cop. You get the picture? His death covers all sins for all
time, making it possible for anyone to be forgiven and gain entry
into heaven; all they have to do is ask.

As I watched *The Passion*, I cried. I cried because I knew that
He caught that beat-down because of the bastard I used to be back
in the day and because of every sin I have committed and will commit since my salvation. I deserve that brutal agonizing death. And
so do you. But Jesus loves us so much that He came to do it in our
place. I gotta admit, I don't have that kind of love in me. If I had
to, I would die for my wife or my children. I might even die in
place of a really good friend. But the hell if I would do it for some
fool who doesn't even want to know me. Whatever, man. All I got
to say is, y'all glad it wasn't me up there. 'Cause all you fools would
be going to hell on the express train. Yeah, that first lash would
have landed and I would have been like, "Hey, hey, hey! Y'all got
the wrong man."

So back to grace. When you accept Jesus as your Savior, you do
give Him control, but you are also saying in effect, "He paid my
tab." You get in on His dime. He paid your debt and then canceled
it. His asking for your devotion seems like more than a reasonable
request, especially when you factor in that His plans are better than
anything you can dream up for yourself (Ephesians 3:20). I don't
know, homie, that sounds like a win-win to me. Let's see. I can either put my sins on Him or I can keep them on me. Hmmm.
Tough choice. You know what it's like? It's like going to a nice club
that's hard to get into. There's a line out the door that wraps
around the block. But you and your boys walk right in because
when you get to the door, you give the name of the person who invited you. That's what heaven's like . . . okay, well, kind of. You get
to the door and you say, "Jesus." And dude don't say nothing; he
just moves the rope. Meanwhile another brother rolls up with his

crew and he says, "Reggie." And the big muscle-bound bouncer steps forward and says, "Back of the line!" Now imagine that this club is not in tropical southern California, but in New York during a winter blizzard. Yeah, standing in line ain't so cute then. And you know what? For some folks, it's gon' be a hell of a long night . . . literally.

But still there are folks who say, "I'm a good person. I'm not a serial killer. I treat people fairly. I don't even cheat on my taxes." Translation: "I don't need to claim Christ because I can get into heaven on my own merit." And a lot of cats feel that way. All I can say is that there are going to be a whole lot of people on the "good person" bus going to hell. Their boarding area will be right next to the "hell in a handbasket" line and the "straight to hell" dropoff. I'm being flip, but really it's really quite serious. See, when you reject the grace that is Christ's substitution on the cross, then by default you put yourself under law or karma, and now it's all on you to make up for all the sins you've ever committed. But the thing is, you can never do enough good to make up for the number of times you have sinned, and that's just the times you know about. Only God knows every single thing you have ever done, including the stuff you've forgotten. Do you really want Him keeping count? He's omniscient! Or would you rather have your record expunged?

The law is set up so that when you break one rule, you may as well have broken them all, because the penalty is the same (Zechariah 5:1–4; Romans 2:12). How hard is it to keep the law? Well, let's just start with the basics. Go one day—just one day— without breaking any of the Ten Commandments. (Read Exodus 20: 1–17 if you need a refresher.) If you succeed (which you won't), all you then have to do is to keep it up for the rest of your life. Oh, but wait. What are you going to do about all those times you broke 'em in the past? What will you offer in exchange for all those times? See how impossible the task is? But hey, if you think you can handle it, you get nothing but love from me, homie. 'Cause I know I can't do it. I ain't gon' even front. But let's just say you could do enough good to make up for all the sins in your life, even the ones you have yet to commit. The Bible addresses this, too. Your righteousness is so far from God's standard of goodness that it's about as useful to Him as "filthy rags," which in modern times equates to used sanitary napkins (Isaiah 64:6). I know that's blistering, y'all. But that's what your goodness is worth to God. So you keep on with that "good person" stuff. Meanwhile, I'll be gettin' my groove on "in the club." Hope you got a nice, warm coat.

So we get that grace is not the same as law. But does grace mean that you can live foul because God will just forgive you? To paraphrase Paul in his letter to the Romans, "Hell, no!" (Romans 6:1–2). That would make God a punk. He is loving y'all, but He ain't stupid! Grace gives the sincere cat, that dude who is really tryin' to do right, all the chances he needs to go legit. That's what grace is about. You don't deserve it. You can't earn it. It's free for the taking. Grace is what enables you and empowers you to live according to God's principles.

So now you're not just tryin' to hustle to keep the law; you're allowing Him to change your thinking and your heart so that you can become the man He purposed for you since before you were born (Jeremiah 1:5a, Psalm 139:15, 16). That takes some doing. And like I said, I ain't there yet. But I'm well on my way. I know I won't be perfected until I see Him face-to-face (1 Corinthians), but in the meantime, these principles have turned out to be the bomb! On the other side of the cross, I thought God was just some ol' crusty fuddy-duddy who didn't want a nigga to have no fun. No drinkin', no smokin', no gamblin', no ho'in', nothin'! But in truth, my "fun" was killing me! In reality, God's principles actually free me. He didn't set them up to kill my party. He set them up so I could prosper and live a life free from drama. His principles are designed to help me avoid all the stupid mistakes that dudes make that end up wrecking their lives and the lives of anyone who comes in contact with them. Before I met J.C., I was a walking accident waiting to happen. Now I'm a man of purpose. I still screw up. But the difference is that now I'm no longer a fool who keeps repeating the same mistakes over and over again. These days I make all new mistakes! And I learn from them.

Living according to God's principles has given me more satisfaction than the life I lived before ever did. Again, it wasn't and isn't a cakewalk. One of the toughest things I had to wrap my mind around was the sex thing. For the life of me I could not figure out why God had such a major problem about folks doin' what comes naturally. I felt the same way about the chronic. It was natural, after all. Actually, I was able to get over the sex thing faster than the chronic thing. But it was rough. I couldn't get with the tithing thing either. How I'm gon' give up my money that I worked hard for to some preacher who probably is buying the same weed he's telling me to give up? For real, that's what I thought. I think a lot of brothas, if they're honest, will admit they feel that way, too. Then again, maybe that's just me. If you feel me, though, keep reading. I'll tell you how He put me up on game on all of those issues. And how, because I'm in line with His Word in those areas of my life, I'm a happier and better man.

4

Her

Back in the eighties and early nineties in my mind and for my purposes, women fell into one of three categories: bitches, hos, or tricks. I agreed with a lot of rappers out there that they were good for nothin' but release. I would say they were good for sex, but that would indicate that there was some mutual exchange. And back in the day, I was all about me. If a female happened to get somethin' good out of being with me, then good for her. But as far as I was concerned, women were there to pleasure Mykel. I loved nobody except my boys. I trusted no one except my boys. And I confided in only a few of my boys. Most of the time I was honest about this with women. I didn't tell a gang of lies, like some guys do, promising the female of the hour that she was the only one or that I loved or even cared about her. I would begin a lot of encounters by saying that I didn't want a girlfriend, wife, etc.; I just wanted to "kick it" (have sex). Meaning I needed to be able to call when I felt like gettin' some, and to be able to leave when I was finished. To my delight, a lot of women were down with those terms. Those that weren't, I left alone.

I don't think any man starts off life as a dog. Contrary to popular belief, we're not just "born that way." For me, at least, becoming a dog was something I had to learn. For the sake of anonymity, let's just say her name was Lisa. We met in high school. She was the popular girl and I was the homie. It wasn't love at first sight, but it did become love eventually—at least on my end. I don't even want to guess what she was feeling. Anyway, we were together exclusively—all the time, until ol' boy came back to town. Ol' boy was David, Lisa's ex-boyfriend, now a college student with a promising career in baseball ahead of him. She dropped me like a hot pot. She went from talking to me five to ten times a day to refusing to return my calls or pages at all. We had spent all of our time together, except for when we were in class, and now I couldn't even find her. I'd go to her house, and no one knew where she was. I'd hit our favorite spots, no sign of her.

Finally, after a week of going ghost on me, she called me back. Her apology sounded sincere. And her promise to return seemed real. She said she and David hadn't seen each other in a long time and they just needed some time to catch up. His family had always really liked her, so she had been spending some time with them. She hadn't told him about me, but she would do so very soon. I wasn't happy about it, but this nigga was sprung, so I went along with it. We set a date for the following night. The next evening when I arrived at her home, her mother and sisters welcomed me as usual. They explained that Lisa had run out real quick, but that she'd be right back. An hour later she still wasn't back. Her mother was getting worried. Her older sister looked pissed. When I guessed that she was with David, another sister confirmed it. I waited a few more minutes in case I was wrong; then I left amidst apologies from her mother and sisters, all begging me to stay.

I was hot! I went home and started blowin' her pager up. Out of sheer stubbornness I paged Lisa every half hour for the next eight hours. I wanted to see just how long it would take her to respond. And wanting her to have no excuse for failing to respond, I didn't move from the phone all night. Not once. Not even to pee. At some point I must have fallen asleep, because the phone ringing at four A.M. woke me up. It was Lisa. She was full of excuses and apologies, but no real answers. I asked her straight up if she had slept with David. Her hesitation before denying it told me all I needed to know. I hung up on her, and at that moment I knew it was over. Even if she hadn't slept with ol' boy, I didn't want her anymore. I had been nothing but kind and respectful to her. I had always treated her well, not because I was so great, but because I cared about her and wanted her to know it. I guess it goes without sayin' that I felt like a dumb ass for having been so nice.

But something more dangerous happened in those hours of waiting for her. I had begun to hate her for hurting me, for humiliating me. Even if she had not been trying to hurt me, she let herself get played. And that thought made me hate her even more. There was one person who I was sure knew and understood what had happened, and that was David. From the minute I saw him his first day back at Lisa's house, he made it clear through his posturing and his fake smiles that he was the big dog and that I was on his turf. Lisa was his and always would be. It turned out he was right. And now he could have her. I couldn't stand the punk. I never could. But my real beef was with her. Lisa was the one who had made the commitment to me. She was the one who had my heart. She should have known better. I held her responsible for hurting me. And I wanted revenge. I didn't want to just go tit for tat. I wanted to crush her. I wanted to humiliate her. It took me a minute, but I finally came up with something.

After giving her a couple of weeks of the cold shoulder, and letting her jock me for a change, I finally invited an eager and contrite Lisa out to lunch at a local eatery. It was her favorite place. For all intents and purposes, this date had the appearance of a reconciliation date. And that was just what I wanted. I had made sure to be extra attentive. I'd used my best manners. I paid her high compliments. I opened car doors and pulled out chairs. I listened intently as she ran her mouth about shopping and school and fashion. I even contributed some to the conversation. I did all that good stuff!

Near the end of the meal, I put on my game face and told her that we needed to talk. She looked hopeful. Then I lowered the boom. I told her that I never wanted to see her ass again. I'm sure I layered in a few expletives as I dumped a bag full of all the little trinkets she had ever given me on the table. To my surprise, ol' girl burst into tears in the middle of the restaurant! Then she did something I never thought I'd hear: She begged me to take her back. People were staring and pointing, but she didn't care. Neither did I. I had strategically picked that place to eat because it was within walking distance of her house and a lot of people we knew ate there. And then I did what any bitter, immature young man would do: I left her there. I can't even remember if I paid the check or not. It didn't matter. I had gotten my revenge. And you know what? It felt great! It felt so good that I wanted to do it again. But instead I just relived it over and over in my mind and told as many people as I possibly could, until another opportunity to humiliate her further presented itself.

The opportunity came in the person of Lisa's archrival, Nina. Throughout their entire relationship since the sandbox, Lisa and Nina had hated each other. Nina presented herself as a friend, but Lisa always knew better. She constantly warned me that Nina was "after" me and would sleep with me in a heartbeat if given the chance. It didn't matter to me, because I wasn't too cool on Nina anyway. She wasn't that fly. She wasn't that smart. As a matter of fact, there was nothing really that special about her at all. Other guys were diggin' her, but like I said, I was cool. Besides, I was loyal to Lisa . . . that is, until she wrecked me.

Word about our breakup spread quickly through our little social circle, and before I knew it Nina showed up on my doorstep—literally. Anyway, I handled my business with her as much as I could, wherever I could, as publicly as I could. She didn't seem to mind.

In fact, she seemed to enjoy it more than I did. Our "relationship" both infuriated and wounded Lisa. She tried to confront me on the phone and in person to tell me what I was doing to her, but seeing her upset only made me happier. As far as I was concerned, she had brought it upon herself. She deserved every bit of what she was getting. So as Lisa wilted, Nina and I celebrated.

Not too long after that I decided to move to Los Angeles. Lisa had continued to pursue me even after things cooled down with Nina. I had gone on to become the biggest ho in my circle. I was hittin' it whenever, however, and with almost whomever I felt like. I had successfully gotten all feelings for Lisa out of my system. Now I was just having fun. Sex had become the recreation of choice. The more vices I combined with it, the better it became. The problem was that in purging myself of feelings for Lisa, I had purged all my feelings—period. I didn't care about much except sex, success, and money. So women became a convenience. In all honesty, they provided nothing I couldn't do for myself with a jar of Vaseline and a *Players* magazine, but at least I had the illusion of company with one or two around. If you had asked me then, I would have told you that I was having the time of my life. I won't lie; I was having a whole lot of fun. I indulged every whim, lived out every sexual fantasy I could conceive of, and had plenty of women who were ready to play.

Somewhere along the line I realized that I didn't hate Lisa anymore. But I was becoming increasingly annoyed with her as she continued to try to get at me. So I slept with her. Even by my standards, it was bad. As soon as I finished, I couldn't stand the sight of her. I had finally lost all respect for her. I remember thinking that she must be the biggest idiot in the world to sleep with a guy who had treated her like I had. I was so disgusted with her, I couldn't even let her stay. I kicked her out. And with that my transformation was complete. I was a dog.

It would be many more years before the Holy Spirit would prick my conscience. Even then, it would be much longer before I listened. I had created a no-win situation for myself. A nice girl would never come near me, unless she was really stupid. So most of the women I dated were players just like me, trying to run game on me the same as I was trying to run game on them. It became a contest to see who could be the bigger dog. I don't have to tell you the kind of emotional Vietnam that environment breeds. Even when I did meet a "nice girl," clueless as she might have been, the worse I treated her, the better she responded to me. When I tried to be respectful and kind, I got dogged and/or used. But when I acted like a dog, not calling for weeks at a time, hittin' it and kicking folks out, maintaining multiple partners, lying about my whereabouts, suddenly my stock would go up! I was more popular than ever, and I was having all the sex I wanted. So I came to the conclusion that women were just hypocrites . . . all of them! In open conversation they were always complaining about a man opening up to them, discovering his feminine side, and treating them with respect and consideration. But when it came time to pick a dude, they always choose the dogs over the decent guys. So I decided I'd just stay on my chosen path and get as much booty as I wanted. In truth, it was the path of least resistance, and I was just straight lazy.

I'd like to tell you now that I met my wife and everything changed instantly. That I became a new man, a reformed man with a godly mind. But that would be a lie. If my wife had met me in my BC (Before Christ) state, she would have hated me instantly and never given me the time of day. God knew that. So He began working on me about a year prior to my meeting her. Little by little, as I continued doing my thing—making cash, buying clothes, drinking, smokin' weed, partyin', and sexin' hard—"doing my thing" became less and less satisfying. It was as though God had pulled back the shiny veneer off my life to reveal termite-infested, dry-rotted pulp. It made me sick. I saw my life for what it was: a long string of meaningless sexual encounters; too many wasted days spent high, drunk, or both, or recovering; a bunch of useless overpriced toys and gadgets—beginning with my car (what idiot leases a BMW when he doesn't even own a home?), my cell phones, pagers, and clothes; and my well-paying but pointless job. I had everything a man in his twenties could want, but I was not happy. I faked like I was when I was with my crew and with females, but in my heart I was bored and miserable. Since I didn't want anybody to know, I kept doing what I'd been doing. But the more clubs I went to, the more I got high, the more I drank, the more sex I had, the worse I felt.

Finally I had had enough and I just quit. I went on strike. I quit going out. I stopped drinkin'. (I still got high—I couldn't let that go just then.) I stopped hangin' with my crew. They thought I was crazy. I remember the night I made up my mind for good. My roommate and I were smoking a blunt in the living room, and I told him that I was tired of the single life, and that the next time God gave me a good woman I was going to be ready for her. He was like, "Yeah, right!"

Like I said, my boys thought I was crazy. They also thought it would pass. After six months of hanging by myself, going to church and prayin' (yes—I had started going at the urging of my moms), God placed in my heart my true desire. When it came down to it, I didn't miss the nameless, faceless sex partners. I didn't miss sittin' around with a bunch of dudes BSin'. This may sound corny to the immature among you, but what I really wanted was a good woman who loved me and whom I could love in return without fear of getting worked.

I had been a ho for a long time and had run across just about every kind of woman imaginable: wealthy and intelligent; dizzy but pretty; angry (but very horny) feminists; Ivy League–educated conservative by day, freak by night; nice girl; nasty girl; fatal attraction head case; needy woman; together-on-the-outside-busted-on-the-inside woman; everything-fake girl; independent, trash-talkin', I-am-black-woman sister-girl; debutante girl; prissy girl; pissy girl; extremely competent, together woman; gold digger; call girl; party girl (a.k.a. ho); superwoman—savior of dogs; and, last but not least, ghetto-fabulous diva. My dating experience had left me with a bad taste in my mouth. Like I said before, I had concluded that most women were hypocritical and stupid. I never fancied myself a male model or anything like that, but I ain't ugly either. I have usually been reasonably well mannered, articulate, and possessed of good taste. Not having been born into wealth, I've been able to do okay for myself. (More accurately, God has just kept me.) In short, I'm just a regular guy. Yet despite my "regularness," women—even the smart, pretty ones—allowed me to treat them so poorly! It seemed no matter how hard they fronted (and some of them were pretty convincing), within the confines of a "relationship" (or something not quite a relationship) most of the women I dated lost all their self-respect and common sense, putting up with treatment that even a pack mule would have walked out on. I wish I could say that my case was unique, except that the dudes in my crew experienced the same thing!

Let me take this opportunity to say that I never hit a woman. I don't believe in that, period! And I wasn't the woo 'em, screw 'em, and shoo 'em brother. I never told a bunch of lies—except maybe to get out of a date. I never tried to sell 'em on the fact that they were special or the only one or that I loved them. That wasn't me. I was honest from the beginning about sex (which was my primary concern) and company—what we called "kickin' it" back in the day. A "relationship" with me was what it was. I was honest about that. And you know what? I had takers on every front. Maybe my honesty was refreshing. Maybe the sex was good. (I can't imagine it was, given what a selfish bastard I was.) Maybe I was a challenge. Maybe my confidence was appealing. I don't know. But quality women, women who certainly should have known better and who deserved more caring men, were kickin' it with the kid—hard. And you know what? I was tired of them. I wanted a woman with enough self-respect to refuse the treatment I gave. What a conundrum, huh? I only wanted a woman who had enough sense *not* to want me as I was.

I think a lot of guys (read: dogs) think that way, even if they don't know it. They want the woman they can't have. They want the one who, by nature of her principles, would want nothing to do with them as they are. But they desire her approval. They want to have her look at them with admiration and respect. And although they may not admit it, or even realize it themselves, they want her to change them.

Recently I was watching a reality dating TV show (what can I say? I'm addicted to most of them). I don't remember the name, but the date starts off with a gang of people and ends with only two after rounds of eliminations. On this particular episode, there was one guy and four or five women competing to win him. Anyway, this dude started off his date with the challenge that he's a dog, hates to be told when to come home, when to call, when he can run with the boys. He stated that he's looking for the one woman who could tame him. He claimed to want a woman who could make him enjoy being "tied down"—his words, not mine. After he issued the statement there was a brief silence in the back of the limo before the date continued on. To my disappointment, but not to my surprise, not one woman got out of the limo. And each eagerly listed her finest attributes (most of which were physical and/or sexual) as reasons that he would want to stay with her. They said things like, "I'll put it on you so good, you'll never go anywhere else," or "I'll love you with all my heart and be everything you need." I was so embarrassed for them all, especially for dude. But his thinking is like that of a lot of cats. Many men assume that the "right" woman will change them. And a lot of women—especially the ones who like "bad boys" or "dogs"—erroneously believe this lie, too.

The women get worked the most, though. Arrogance fools them into thinking that "He may treat all them other hos like that, but not me." Dogs love women who think like this. They eat 'em for snacks. They enjoy taking a cocky, you-just-wait-and-see kind of woman and reducing her to a sniveling, whimpering mess before tossing all her clothes from the night before into the middle of the street. "You knew the game and you still ended up on your back," is the motto of the serious mack. And it's easy to do because no matter how liberated, independent, or turned-out women are, sex means something different to them than it does to most men. For men it can be a welcome activity with no emotional investment whatsoever. For most women, it's not like that. Particularly within relationships, sex is deeply significant for women. It's a demonstration of and a means to an emotional connection. But for dogs it's just f——in'. Excuse my French—but that's really how dogs play it. They will use the pretext of a relationship to satisfy themselves at the expense of another human being. A woman stupid enough to believe that she can accomplish what many women before her (not to mention centuries of organized religion) couldn't falls fastest, hardest, and with the most satisfying thud.

As sad as that is, it's better than the alternative. For the woman in a relationship with a man who expects to be "tamed," for lack of a better word, it's a lose-lose situation. If she loses, she ends up used and humiliated. If she succeeds, she's the B-word for sho'. And the man and all his boys resent, if not hate her. A woman who dominates her man is the ugliest kind there is. In large part she's busted because she has to take on the male role in the relationship in order to get the actual man to step up. And I don't know any straight guy who wants to be with a dude with breasts. God ordained that the man should lead—not co-lead, and definitely not follow.

Now before the feminists among you go ape, understand that I do not care what you think about me. But I do care if you understand God's plan. The man is the head and the woman submits. For the wife batterers among you, to submit does not mean to lie down like a doormat to be trampled on. If anything, submission is a willingness to line up under and support, much the way an entire football team supports a QB.

Now as the head, if you want a woman (especially an educated black woman) worth her salt to submit to you fully, you had better be the man! Notice I did not say "guy." Man. No girls or bustas need apply. If you want your woman to respect and honor you, then you've got to lead by example. And this is the main reason why you need a woman of caliber—'cause you don't want to get played. Meaning, you decide that you are going to do everything the right way, but mistaking your uprightness for stupidity and weakness, she takes advantage of you. You don't want to be loving and honoring while getting used and treated like doo-doo. I've seen it. It's not fly. So choose carefully and wisely.

I wanted a woman of principles. I wanted someone who would hold me to a higher (but not a double) standard, who was my equal, a buddy, a homie, my nigga, my road dog. I wanted someone who had depth—not just education, but intelligence. Sophistication without snobbery. Someone who'd be real with me and who'd let me be real with her. I wanted someone who had good taste, but wasn't materialistic. Someone who was fun but not too goofy, sensual but not a ho, open to accept help but not needy. I wanted a woman I could trust, who would allow me to be emotionally naked, but with whom I'd enjoy some physical nudity, too! I'm just being real. And on the shallow side, she had to be fine. And on the not-so-shallow side, she had to be a sistah. Not that I'm trippin' on interracial dating or anything like that. I don't begrudge any person true love, no matter what race. My personal preference, however, was specifically for a black American woman.

Now, that was asking a lot, given my record. It would seem that I had more nerve than sense asking God for all that in a woman when I was so to'-back myself. And let's not forget my environment. I lived in Los Angeles. Pretty and shallow girls arrive in LA by the truckloads daily. I know because I used to run my own welcome wagon. Aspiring actresses and models are as common as pennies, and often about as deep. So my prospects weren't that great. I knew I was going to need a miracle. And the last time I checked, miracles had only one Source. So off to church I went. In going to church I learned that God, according to Psalm 139, had already chosen my spouse before either of us was ever born. As the man, it was now my job to find her. That was great news! She had been out there all along. I had only hoped that I hadn't already met her and scared her away. But I was pretty sure that wasn't the case. Going to church also made clear to me the importance of prayer. So I began to pray regularly and to read my Bible. My prayers were probably all wrong, and I couldn't understand the Bible for nothing, but I kept trying!

5

Keepin' Ya Draws Up

One of the most difficult principles I had to deal with after I came to Christ was the sex thing. It wasn't so much that I had to stop hittin' it. The sex I had been having had been getting old. I got tired of scandalous hos who were forever claiming that they "didn't usually do this on the first date." (Man, if I had a quarter for every time I'd heard that lie . . .) I was tired of doin' it quick and dirty with women I didn't care about. I had stopped looking at faces. I didn't remember names. I couldn't pretend to care no more. No, I didn't mind abstaining from that kind of sex.

As I said in the last chapter, I eventually went on a fast. For about six months after I got saved, I stopped clubbin' and sexin'. I stopped hangin' with my crew. I just checked out. My boys all knew something was up, but they couldn't figure out what. I didn't bother to explain it because I really couldn't, at least not in terms they would understand. Had I tried to explain that I didn't want easy sex because Jesus had taken hold of my heart, I basically would have faced a group of stares resembling that of the RCA dog. Knowing that I was doing the right thing had to be enough. I didn't need them to understand, nor did I need them to approve. Besides, in a well-intentioned attempt to "get me back on track," that crew probably would have locked me in a room with a stripper or a prostitute or something. So no, I didn't tell them what I had decided.

But what really bothered me about the no-sex mandate was the principle of the matter. God had created me male and with a sex drive. It seemed sadistic of Him to give it to me only to tell me that I couldn't use it. I really wasn't sure I would be able to give this area of my life over to Him. I was thankful He didn't give up on ya boy. At the church I was attending I began to learn about God's plan for marriage and sex. I was surprised to hear that He had one—for sex, I mean. I guess because of how people treated sex as I was growing up, I always thought that God had nothing to do with sex.

God's plan isn't real complicated. You can have all the sex you want, as often as you want, in as many different positions as you can dream up (as long as both partners agree), with whatever props, toys, or costumes you like (again, as long as both partners agree), for the rest of your life, as long as you're married to your partner. See? It ain't that deep. God not only wants us to have sex with our spouses; He wants us to enjoy it, too. I know that for a good minute, preachers and teachers taught that sex was strictly for the purposes of procreation. And certainly that's in God's plan, too. Incidentally, that's also why He hates divorce, because it hinders the raising of godly offspring. But every session in my marriage-prep class, every sermon on sex that I've ever heard Bishop Ulmer preach, every conversation I've had with my own pastor, Reverend Jody Moore, and every passage that I've personally studied on the subject lead me to believe that God designed sex for our enjoyment, too. My marriage-prep instructor, Dr. Kerry Brooks, went so far as to say that sex within marriage is a form of worship.

I began to understand God's plan, but I was still skeptical. He hadn't let me down yet, so I took a chance and attempted to become celibate. Then I met the woman who would become my wife. And I knew my six-month fast had served its purpose. It had cleansed my palate. I really wanted a good woman. I had been working on myself in terms of coming to grips with my bad behavior and making strides toward improving myself as a godly man. I had come to understand and believe that God would not entrust me with one of his daughters if I was still foul. So I put everything I had into becoming the man God wanted me to be. And then He brought me Sheeri.

I really don't have words to describe what the sight of her did to me. We were both at a party at some doctor's house. She had been an invited guest. My boys and me had crashed. It was a pretty bougie crowd with a lot of undercover freaks thrown in. Most of the folks there were doctors, nurses, attorneys, and other professionals who knew each other. Everybody was in casual mode, but clean. It was a pool party, so most of the women were in swimsuits and some kind of cover-up. We rolled in and that was when I saw her. This sounds so corny, but I knew the moment I laid eyes on her that she was my wife. I even told one of my boys, who laughs now when we talk about it. At the time, he thought I was crazy.

I saw her, but she didn't notice me. I'll never forget: She was in a floral two-piece, wearing a matching wrap thing. She was barefoot—and here's the cool part—she was playing Ping-Pong, drinking a beer, and balancing a hamburger on the edge of the Ping-Pong table. She was laughing and having a good time. And she was killin' some fool. I could tell from the way she carried herself and from the way she spoke that she wasn't ordinary. She had quiet confidence and a girlish way about her all at the same time. She had a tight body, but she still managed to be very ladylike. She was womanly, but the child in her was still evident. Her hair was short and she had on no makeup. She stood in stark contrast to the surgically altered, weave-wearing, MAC-laden women at the party. She was hot! My entire crew noticed her. I think many other guys at the party did, too. But it seemed like she didn't notice the attention, and if she did, she took it all in stride. She had that way about her that pretty girls have who aren't stuck on how pretty they are. She was friendly, but not too friendly. She was polished, but not fake.

I don't know how long I stared at her. Good thing I was far enough away that she didn't see me. Then her game ended, and she slid on her sandals, trashed her empty beer bottle, picked up her burger, and disappeared into the crowd. I had to get myself together before approaching her. I knew that I had to make sure that I came at her correct the first time, if for no other reason than the fact that other dudes were hounding her and I might not get a second chance that night.

To make a long story short, we talked for a long while and exchanged numbers at the end of the party. We talked on the phone a gang of times. When we finally went out three months later, I was in love. I knew in my spirit by the end of our third date that Sheeri was my wife. Unfortunately I made the mistake of telling her this, which cut our date short that night. But we had more.

So now the sex thing is really a problem. I love her. I want to marry her. But I have to wait before I sleep with her. What up with that, Lord? After we got engaged it was worse. I had never been so hot in the drawers in my life! I ain't gon' lie. And I have my wife's permission to share this. We fell . . . more than a few times. Thankfully, we had good friends to hold us accountable. We were in the Word and we were determined not to disappoint God. I'll tell you what, though: We got on the fast track to that altar! In the meantime our study yielded a lot of fruit. We learned a lot about God's plans for marriage, and specifically for sex within marriage.

The biggest problem with sex outside of marriage is that it's a really bad habit to develop. God created sex to be between only one man and only one woman within the bonds of matrimony (1 Corinthians 7). I'm sure this is in part because sex is really powerful. It creates a bond between two people that is supposed to last a lifetime. If you consistently have sex with people to whom you're not married, you pervert it. It becomes common, unimportant, plain. The person you engage in it with ultimately becomes disposable. What happens? Guy meets girl. They sleep together. They break up. The cycle repeats. When you finally meet the person you want to marry, sex has lost much of its meaning because you've shared your most intimate physical self with so many other people.

Don't sleep on the danger of the pattern, either. Having sex with people and then breaking up with them is merely practice for divorce. Marriage does not have the power to improve you. Apart from God, no outside influence really does—at least not permanently. Think about it. People are mostly creatures of habit. If you were ho'in' before you got married, it's not very likely that marriage will make you stop. Eventually you will be able to justify a reason to creep. How many guys do you know who get married never having conquered their urge to sleep around? They may make good on cleaning up their act for a little while . . . maybe even for five or six years. But think about it. Marriage is a lifelong commitment. The vows include "until death do us part." They don't say anything about "for as long as I can hold it together." I'm a firm believer that behavior supports attitude as much as it molds it. So if you sleep around, or sleep with only one person at a time in what has become a series of committed relationships, essentially what you're saying is that one person is not enough. If one is not enough now, how is one going to be enough for the *rest of your life*?

Another result of sex is that it connects two people spiritually. Genesis states that man and woman should cleave to each other and become one flesh. Sex assists in cleaving. Have you ever noticed that after you've been sleeping with a person for a while, you start to take on some of their ways, habits, idiosyncrasies, etc.? That's because you're also forging a spiritual bond with that person. Ideally in marriage both of you are supposed to make that bond with the Holy Spirit. God can't bless sex apart from marriage, so guess what? The Holy Spirit ain't with you. So when you got problems, you're on your own.

Sex also takes time to get good at. I mean really good. Anybody can get one off, but to really please your partner, to romance her, to woo him, to make her feel special, to really know him, takes time. And no amount of skill can substitute for this fact. Many different factors, both mental and spiritual, make a sexual experience satisfying. What works one time may not work another. It's dangerous to assume that any old technique will do. Your partner's body should be treasured, caressed, studied . . . not poked and prodded like a dead body at the morgue. Sadly, most relationships today barely last long enough for any exploration to even scratch the surface.

The way most people treat sex today, they might as well be two dogs humping in the street. When we take the sacred and make it usual, in the end we lose out. We become cynical and hardened. What should repulse us entertains us. What should sadden us makes us laugh. What should break our hearts barely gets noticed. Once salt has lost its flavor, it's not much different from sand and much less useful (Matthew 5:13). I agree with what CS Lewis wrote regarding sex in *Mere Christianity*. He likened sex apart from marriage to chewed food that is never swallowed but spit out. You get the pleasure, but none of the real benefits.

Most of us are needing and wanting something unnameable, hoping we can get it from somebody else. At our best we are soul suckers. Worse than that, we are soul destroyers, using other people to get what we need, then tossin' them like trash before moving on to the next mark. I think that's part of the reason that I like books and movies about vampires so much. Vampires just are what they are. They don't front; they make no apologies. Their whole vibe is, "I need to eat. You're an attractive meal." They don't pretend to care or to relate. They remind me a lot of what Paul calls the "old man" (Romans 6:6), in that their nature always wins out. There would probably be a lot fewer sexual exchanges if people were honest about their "old man." Think about it. If the next time you rolled up on ol' girl and she came wit' it: "Hi. I'm Kiki. I have low self-worth and really poor hygiene. In the last year I've contracted chlamydia and genital warts. Currently I'm being tested for the bug. I need you to give me everything my father never did, including direction and value. In exchange I'll do anything you want, including bear your illegitimate child. Once you're nice to me, you'll never be able to get rid of me. Take me home, please?" You'd run like hell, wouldn't you? Or picture some dude rolling up and spitting something like: "Hey. I'm Dex, but everybody call me 'Blunt' 'cause I smoke so much. I have no ambition. I ain't never leaving my mama's house 'cause I got the bomb hookup, unless you want me to come stay at your crib. I'll have all kinds of kinky sex with you, but what I really need is for you to make me feel like a man, because my mama told me I was never gon' be sh———. After I hit it, I'll probably leave and never call because I don't care about you. I just want to get a release, and you're the best-looking girl to give me any attention so far. So what's up?" Yeah—that would go over like a fart in church.

When you think about it, the most common reasons that people give for wanting to have sex is, one, for the high, the sensation, the climax; and two, for the emotional connection, the affection, the feeling of being loved. Almost any vice can be broken down to one of those two reasons. Both of those are needs that God gave us. He gives us desires, which are designed to point us to Him. The problem is that because we're so screwed-up, we go looking everywhere else to get our needs met, except to Him. The Psalmist reminds us of God's invitation: "Open wide your mouth and I will fill it" (Psalm 81:10). God approves of the desire to experience pleasure and joy. God definitely approves of the desire to be loved.

Remember in an earlier chapter, I said that part of my problem with giving Christ control was that I was going to have to learn to do things His way? Well, that's no joke. God wants us to experience pleasure in sex. He designed our bodies so that they would enjoy it. I think that plan is brilliant. How else would He have gotten people to procreate? I have seen my wife go through labor three times. It ain't cute. It's hard, hard work! The term *labor* doesn't do it justice. And yet as soon as the doctor gives her permission, she's ready to go again. God bless her! Yeah, God made sex pleasurable for a reason. Don't sleep. He was the One who brought Eve to Adam naked! And she must have looked good to ol' boy too, because he all but said, "Damn!" He had been alone, naming all them animals. He saw that none of them looked like him. When he saw Eve he knew she was for him. "Bone of my bones and flesh of my flesh!" he exclaimed (Genesis 2:23). He recognized her as his wife as surely as I recognized Sheeri when I first saw her.

Some people try to argue that Adam and Eve weren't married. True, they didn't have a ceremony with the gown, the minister, the string quartet. They went one better. They had God Himself! Think about it. A minister only represents God in a wedding ceremony. If God shows up with your woman, I think you already have His blessing. So kill that.

Don't even try to front like it's okay to get yo' freak on because cats in the Bible did the polygamy thing. God lays down the law in Deuteronomy. He clearly prohibits the king from having many wives. Just because David and Solomon were trippin' don't mean you get to. Know the difference between what the Bible reports and what it supports. The Book only supports the marriage of one man and one woman. As far as polygamy goes, note that God did not introduce that to humanity—a fallen human being did. Interestingly enough it was one of Cain's rock-headed descendants. Remember Cain? He murdered his brother Abel? Somehow his great-great-grandson, Lamech, thought two wives would be the lick (Genesis 4:19). I should also mention that Lamech was the second person mentioned by name in the Bible to commit murder (Genesis 4:23–24). He sounds like a real winner. So go ahead if you must and follow his example. But in order to justify it, you will have to dismiss the entire Bible, including in Matthew 19, where Jesus himself reiterates that marriage is a union between one man and one woman. (Get it? man + woman = marriage. No other formula works.)

The point is that God made sex pleasurable. He wants us to enjoy it, but only in the confines of marriage. My marriage prep instructor, Dr. Kerry Brooks of Anointed Waters Counseling, helped Sheeri and me to understand that sex is really the icing on the cake. The cake is a committed, honest, intimate relationship with your best friend! And I have all that with my wife—and more! Sheeri stuck by my broke ass when I had nothing to offer her except a smile. During our really lean years, I wouldn't have blamed her if she had left me. Things got so bad for us that we had to move in with her mama. That ain't cool, y'all. There was one point when we had no food. We were borrowing cars from friends. And all because I had lost my job . . . again. I was sick of myself. But she never was. She never made me feel like any less of a man because of what we didn't have. She never wavered in her confidence in God. If I was sure that I was pursuing the career path that He had laid out for me, that was good enough for her. And heaven help anyone, including her family members, who tried to criticize me. That happened only once, and that person is still trying pull Sheeri's shoe out of his butt. If her family did have any more beef, they all kept it to themselves after that. 'Cause my boo ain't no joke.

I didn't plan to take her on a trip through hell. And I know she didn't buy a ticket to go there. But she stood by me the whole way and never allowed me to doubt my calling or my God. And divorce? It's not even a word mentioned in our house, because it isn't an option in our marriage. Dr. Kerry Brooks taught us that, too. "Just close that door," he said. Not only has it been closed, but walled over, painted, and now has a mirror hanging in front of it. My wife loves me and is dedicated to my vision and to me. She willfully submits to my authority, which truthfully I don't have to exercise often, 'cause we think so much alike about important stuff.

But now that we're committed, I know Sheeri will always be in my corner. It's pure love, man, genuine and true. Now, I know this submitting stuff has some of you flippin' out, so let me just set it straight for you now. Women who trust God allow their husbands to lead unobstructed, even if he's not necessarily doing a good job. When my wife learned and embraced this principle early on in our marriage, the effect was profound.

Before, whenever we disagreed, we went at it toe-to-toe, almost like two attorneys in court. She'd present her side. Then I'd present mine. She'd rebut. Then I would do likewise. It was crazy. My wife is smarter than I am and a much better debater. That's not what would get me, though. When she was sure she was right about an issue (which was all the time), she'd dig in her heels and go point by point as to why we should handle the situation her way. I kid you not, she'd prepare graphs, charts, lists of pros and cons, typed proposals. She was off the chain with hers. And she would persist until she won. Sometimes I would concede her point of view not because I thought she was right, but because I was just worn out. Those times I stuck to my guns, I paid dearly. Ol' girl would freeze me out for weeks at a time. And God forbid if my decision blew up in my face. I never heard the end of it. And if it turned out that I was right, then she was mad about that, too. It wasn't cool to be me back then.

But then one day a woman named Bunny Wilson came to our church to teach the women about submission. I all but packed my wife a lunch. Sheeri went to hear Bunny, but she did not expect to learn anything new. I don't know what Bunny said in the hour she ministered, but I know my wife came back a different woman. The first thing she did was apologize to me with tears in her eyes for being difficult and rebellious. She confessed that she had been working against me, not with me. She said a bunch of other stuff that I don't remember because I was in shock. But she promised to always defer willingly to my authority even if she didn't agree with my decisions, to show me respect both publicly and privately, and to pray for me daily. To the best of my knowledge she continues to make good on her promise. From that day on the atmosphere in my house has been real different.

By her own admission, my wife experienced immeasurable

peace. For me, it was a little different. In short, it scared the doo-doo out of me. When I realized that my wife was not going to fight me over any more decisions for our family, the seriousness of my role as head of the household became real clear to me. All of a sudden the entire future of my family was on me. Whatever decisions I made, whatever direction I took, that was how we were rollin'. I value my wife's opinions and insight and make few decisions without her input. And let me tell you, man, am I glad she's not only smart, but knows the Lord. But at the end of the day, I make the final call, because I'm the one who has to answer to God for everything that goes on in my house. That's biblical. (Don't believe me? Read the account of the fall of mankind in Genesis.)

Now, if that's not enough to drive even the most confident brother to his knees in prayer, I don't know what is. All I know is that I had to be sure that I could discern where God was leading my family. I understood that my wife's future, as well as that of any children who would be born to us, as well as the future of entire generations coming behind us, depended upon my making good, right decisions in the here and now. Oh, yeah! I got real close to Jesus. And what character I didn't have, I borrowed. I also found a new respect for my wife. A woman who thinks highly enough of you to trust you with her future and that of her children is nothing but a gift from God. She's a precious gift to be honored and cherished at every opportunity. Her willingness to step out of the way and allow God to deal directly with me is not only smart but necessary in a successful marriage. Her stepping out of the way forced me to grow up. And talk about character development. If you ever want to know how to become a better person, stay in the Word and pray about everything that comes before you. God's truth will force you to examine and change your thinking and your behavior. You become a better man almost by default. Simply trying to live right puts you miles ahead of your old self.

Just as my wife's stepping out of the way forced me to mature mentally and spiritually, the same is true of a woman in any serious relationship with a man. A wise woman knows that it's not her job to groom a man and make him suitable for a relationship. I'm a great advocate for charity work, but this doesn't count. Do people help to mold one another? Oh, yeah! By interacting with others the way God intended, we all get the rough edges smoothed out and some of our better points refined. But this is mutual and guided by God's hand. A woman who consciously takes on a man with the intent to change or groom him can't win. And if the truth be told, does she really want to (win, that is)? My wife has often said there are few things as repulsive to her as a man whose wife or girlfriend carries his "balls around in her purse" (her word choice—not mine). She and I agree that no woman truly wants a man she can run. Sometimes women think that they do, but over time henpecked, emasculated men become just as unattractive to their domineering wives/girlfriends as those same wives become to them. See what I'm sayin'? Lose-lose.

A woman worth her salt wants a man who will take responsibility to lead—not a punk who bends to her every whim. According to my wife and her female friends, a man who serves his family in much the same way a good CEO leads a prosperous Fortune 500 company is very, very attractive. A man like this possesses a vision for his family, has outlined a plan to bring it about, and continuously executes that plan to ensure that the vision manifests. That's a powerful brotha. I know from experience that the best CEOs confide in and consult with their seconds-in-command, and rely heavily upon their counsel. After weighing all the options, the CEO picks one, fully willing to bear all responsibility for the outcome of his choice. That's a great CEO and an excellent husband. That's who women should choose and encourage the men in their lives to become. Note I said *encourage* not *train*.

In their defense, many women assume the position of trainer by default. Often the man has not done the necessary work to become a leader. So the job of grooming him falls on the woman in his life. Make no mistake, it is the man's job to be about the business of his own character development—long before he begins his search for his bride. The man must already be in the process of becoming noble before choosing a worthy woman, in large part to ensure his success in winning the heart and earning the trust of his mate. 'Cause again, a woman worth her salt will and does have the good sense to pass up a dog. Many do it every day. I personally am grateful to God that He allowed me to meet my wife only after I had a good head start on my way to becoming the man He created me to be. Otherwise, my wife would have never given me a second look.

Unlike those poor saps who strike it rich and then spend their lifetimes looking for a woman who only loves them for themselves, I know for a fact that Sheeri Mitchell loves my dirty draws. Because there was a time when that was all I could give her. She could have broke me down. But instead she built me up, reminding me that I was not the sum of my circumstances, inspiring me with God's promises for our future. Her disposition toward me has never changed, except to become more determined to see me succeed. It never crossed her mind to think less of me. She tells me often that if anything, I grew in her estimation because of how well I handled myself during our darkest hours. You can't buy that kind of character. You can't fake that kind of loyalty.

Whatever that woman wants, I want to have it ready before she even thinks of asking. I anticipate her every need. I delight in serving her. And you know what? It's mutual. That, my friend, is cake! Our lovemaking is simply an outward expression of our inward desire to serve and please each other. It's not even in the same stratosphere as the self-centered, mutual groping of the unmarried. Sex in the context of a relationship like the one I have with my wife isn't just pleasurable . . . it's a celebration! And we celebrate every chance we get.

The first time Sheeri and I had sex as a married couple, it blew us away. We had (purely by the grace of God) managed to be celibate for nearly a year prior to our wedding. For us, that was a big deal. And when we had sex on our wedding night, neither of us had ever experienced such freedom and pleasure without guilt! It was the bomb! I maintain that there is no sex like married sex. If sex with your spouse isn't jumpin' off, if it isn't the best sex of your life, then you must be doing something wrong. My sympathies to you. I humbly recommend *The Act of Marriage* by Tim LaHaye. The book is so great not just because it addresses the spiritual side of sex—most Christian books do that. But this book gives detailed suggestions on how to make the act itself and everything leading up to it more pleasurable and ultimately satisfying.

Once the euphoria of our first matrimonial encounter wore off, we were both angry. No, not at each other. We wondered how could we have been so stupid as to give away our bodies to people whom we barely even remembered anymore. Sheeri said that she felt like she had been punked. I agree. 'Cause the best sex I had as a single man is no comparison to the worst sex I've had married. That's just true. I concluded that sex outside of marriage was like drinking a strange kind of lemonade. It wasn't that great, but because everybody told you it was, you kept drinking it until you got accustomed to the taste. Then one day you had a glass of real lemonade, and realized that all this time you had been drinking piss! Ha! Ha! The joke was on you! I was so mad at myself. I had given in to the pressure of our culture, of my friends and relatives, all of whom expected and encouraged me to be sexually active. I didn't lose my virginity; I threw it away. And for what?

I don't know about other dudes, but the biggest influence in my life as a young-adult male was hip-hop. The messages from superstars were that real men were pimps. If you wasn't ho'in', then you wasn't knowin'. Now, did hip-hop invent this fallacy? Of course not. It had been prevalent in the culture of rock 'n' roll long before that. In fact, it's almost been nearly impossible to mention rock 'n' roll without its two other cousins, sex and drugs. And before rock 'n' roll? Who knows? I'm sure sexual prowess as a defining trait of true manhood predates recorded history. Hip-hop did not invent the "ladies' man." Hip-hop just renamed him—

"playa," "pimp," "mack," "fly guy," "balla," etc. Do I blame hip-hop for my decisions? No. I made those ignorant choices all by myself. But yes, hip-hop did influence me.

Having no real male role model whom I trusted, I emulated pretty much whomever I thought looked appealing on TV. But even if I had looked to my immediate environment for inspiration, between most of my uncles, my dad, and my stepdad, I wouldn't have seen much difference. They didn't practice fidelity. At least the guys in the music videos looked like me, dressed well, and could dance. It sounds juvenile, because it is. Children, young adults, and adults are highly influenced by the television images they ingest. I ate, slept, and breathed all things hip-hop, including music videos. Music, television, and film are mind molders as much as education or religion. My mind was soft, soft clay, and hip-hop my primary sculptor. Hip-hop videos took black male sexuality to a whole new level . . . at least for me. Brothas was just out there wit' theirs. And the whole world knew we had the goods. No subject was too taboo to sing about or dance to. So the only question to ask was, *How can I be down?*

When I figured out the damage that believing the hype had wrought, I was mad at myself. Truthfully, I'm still assessing it. My sexuality is something that only my wife should ever have experienced. And vice versa. I mourned the loss of something I could never experience: having sex for the first time in my life with the woman I married, and all the unnamed blessings that go along with it. Needless to say I got over it. But it made me determined to teach every young person I knew not to go that route. Even now, we explain to our children that God has a plan for marriage. They don't know exactly what sex is yet, as the oldest is only six, but they already know the phrase, "No ringy—no dingy!"

In the end, the sex with those other women just wasn't worth it. I wish I had waited. I should have waited. Did it really make me any more of a man to sleep around? No. Did it make me a better human being? No. Did it bring me any closer to any of my goals?

No. If anything it did just the opposite. It was a big distraction. And isn't that the enemy's point? He uses sex, among other things, to keep us from focusing on the things God has for us; things that we can get only by living life God's way. And just like so many other men, I fell for it. Well, I know better now. True manhood is not about gettin' your freak on or smackin' up, flippin', or rubbin' down the booty. It's about handling yours. As long as you are doing anything else—including participating in sex outside of marriage, getting high with the boys, or chasing paper at the expense of your soul or your family, then you ain't handling nothing. You just gettin' handled.

I had to unlearn all my bad habits with respect to how to treat women. Because all the women who had made themselves available to me ultimately had no real respect for themselves—despite their claims to the contrary—and I didn't have any respect for them either. I had to learn what God says about how to treat the "fairer sex," and I had to start from scratch. I had a front-row seat in the remedial class. And it didn't end there. I had to reorient my thinking about how to treat all people—men and women. I had never really thought much about anybody other than me. That "playa" lifestyle is extremely conducive to self-focus. Hustlin', you are always trying to "come up" on some cash. Pimpin' (not the profession) is the same. You're always trying to figure out how to come up on some booty. Everything from how you dress to where you spend your time to whom you'll be seen with has to do with getting some. Friends are only as dear as their ability to either hook you up or stay out of your way. The quickest way for a nigga to get ejected from the game is for the crew to find out that he's throwin' salt. The worst part is that because you are so to'-up, you assume that everybody else is, too. You assume that everybody uses everybody, because you do. The motto of the playa is "Play or be played." In that world, girls give it up in exchange for some gear, change, rent, or whatever. Guys exhibit good manners, play the romance card, and tell all kinds of crazy lies—like "I love you"—all for the sake of hittin' it. Sad but true. Ain't no room for love in a world like that. Love is for punks. The worst part is when you roll up on a good woman, you can't appreciate her because you figure she's got an agenda, too. So you play her before she can play you, never realizing that all you're doing is living out a self-fulfilling prophecy.

When I think about all the time I wasted chasing females, all the lies I told, all the women I used, all the drama that ensued, I get pissed off all over again. Had I stayed the course, how much better off, how much farther along would I be today? I can't allow myself to think on it too much. But that's the enemy's goal. By enemy I don't mean hip-hop. I mean the enemy of our souls, our adversary, Satan, Lucifer, the devil. Say what you want, he is real and very active in our world. If you haven't run into him it's probably because you're running with him. For those of you unfamiliar with him, let me explain. Every name he's mentioned by in the Bible reveals more of his purpose: prince of the air, the deceiver, the prince of this world, a roaring lion seeking whom to devour, murderer, father of lies, he who comes but to steal, kill, and destroy. He's the original hater. He hates God, but can't touch Him, so instead he goes after God's creatures—us. He can't do anything to us without God's permission (Job 1 and 2), but God is not the problem. We are. Whether we know it or not, we open the door wide for him whenever we reject God's Truth, by embracing outright lies or even partial lies. And ol' boy lies like a rug. J.C. called him the "father of lies" (John 8:44). That's deep. You got to really be doing some lying for Jesus to call you that. And guess what? He rules in all realms of this fallen world. He can gain authority over the believer only inasmuch as the believer abdicates it through foul living. You live foul when you believe wrong. That's why you've got to run all your info through the Word before embracing it. Only God's Word is Truth. Jesus Christ is Truth personified. So if everything you think, learn, know ain't lining up with the Word on paper or the Word incarnate, then toss it.

You may wonder why the enemy lies. Truthfully he hates us so much that he would murder us all if he could. But since God limits his power, he works hard to deceive us so that we can take ourselves out. The enemy's primary job is to keep us from knowing God. Short of that, he'll settle for keeping us from knowing God's plan for our lives. Short of that, he'll do his best to scare us or discourage us into compromise. And now you know the secret behind God's prohibitions. He prohibits us only from things that wreck our lives—things that kill us either spiritually or physically. For example, God does not say that you can't drink. As a matter of fact, one of the first miracles recorded in the gospel of John is Jesus' transformation of water into wine at the wedding in Cana. What the Word does say is, don't drink to get drunk (Ephesians 5:18). Drunkenness is the sin, not drinking. Why? Think about it. What controls you when you're drunk? Nothing holy, that's for sure. As a matter of fact, I'm sure you know people who use gettin' faded as an excuse to do stuff they would never do sober. Some folks get mean and say crazy things. Others, especially so-called "good girls," get freaky. Some people just cry about their problems. Some get wild; they trash things or drive drunk. Suffice it to say there is no such thing as a good, wise drunk. What worthwhile thing can you accomplish drunk? *Nada.* The best you can hope for is to go to sleep somewhere where no one will take advantage of you and in a position where you won't choke on your vomit.

Getting high usually produces less chaotic results than drinking, but the overall effect is the same. Gambling and any other vice you can name fulfill the same purpose. When under the control of any vice, you aren't capable of operating in clarity and in power. Whatever the vice, if you do it enough, it'll switch up on you. You'll end up with an addiction. Then you won't be able to function sober either. You'll have to do that thing (whatever it is) just in order to maintain. Don't you see? Whatever you submit yourself to, owns you (Romans 6:16). So you may as well submit yourself to the only Someone worthwhile. The enemy has fooled you into thinking you can control your vices, but the joke's on you, brah.

The most famous last words I ever hear from the young men (and sometimes the not-so-young men) that I minister to are, "I got this. You don't have to worry about me." Yeah, okay, playa. Let me just put this in your ear. It don't take much to look up and be fifty with nothing to show for all your fun. And that is how the enemy wins. If he can put enough attractive, pleasurable bad choices in front of you, he can keep you on a treadmill, never getting anywhere until you die or give up.

God doesn't want to kill your buzz. He wants to be your buzz. It sounds corny, but it's true. I never feel so alive as when I'm operating in my gifts and in my calling. Whether I'm brokering meetings, working on writing projects, brainstorming in a meeting, reading my Word, playing with my children, or just chillin' with my wife, I am satisfied by the fact that I am moving in purpose. I don't need drink or bud. My best high can't compare to my most hectic day. I am driven. I am motivated. Most important, I know that what I'm doing counts for eternity. I know that someone else—maybe someone I'll never meet—will come up because I'm taking care of His business. Consequently, I try my best not to engage in any endeavor that I don't see His hand in. Talk about freedom! Talk about abundant life! My life has become a gift. The extreme satisfaction and real joy that I have on the regular are only things that God can give you. All that other stuff? Smoke and mirrors, dawg. Only God can reveal to you the plans He has for you. But you gotta ask (Jeremiah 33:3).

At the heart of the matter is whether or not you will trust God with your sexuality. Do you believe He's got a plan for you? Do you believe, even if it doesn't necessarily make sense to you right now, that you should wait? Don't go by your friends. They're all stupid anyway. Go by His Word. Do you really want all He has for you? Do you want His plan for your life? Then don't f—— it up, literally. How can He trust you to handle prosperity, wisdom, riches, knowledge, and all that other good stuff when you can't even keep li'l man in your pants?

Have you figured out that sex apart from marriage leads to a lotta drama? Know anybody who has a baby's mama? How's that working out? Paid for any abortions lately? Know anybody with herpes? Genital warts? AIDS? I don't mean to beat a dead horse, but again . . . God doesn't share His principles with us to stop our fun. He gives them to us so that we can live our best lives drama-free.

Open your mouth. Let him fill your belly with good things. Things that will bring life, not death. Hope, not despair. Excellence, not mediocrity. The easiest thing to master is your body. Take control over your impulses. Don't let what's between your legs cheat you out of your blessings.

Lastly, consider this: Your body is not your own. It was bought and paid for with a high price—Jesus' precious blood. God's ultimate plan is for your body to be the temple, the dwelling place of his Holy Spirit. Can you imagine that? The same power that raised Jesus from the dead is available to you! That's why it's so important to offer your entire body up for God's use, not for sin. Whatever you allow in ultimately rules you. You don't think so? Know anybody addicted to gambling, drinking, porn, smoking, sexing, overeating? They opened the door. What began as a naughty little habit grew into a big, ugly beast. Now they're whipped. As human beings we have no choice. All of us are controlled by something. Some people are run by greed, vengeance, anger, depression. How much better to be controlled by God's Spirit? Imagine what you could accomplish in this short, short lifetime if that were the case for you. We're only here for a moment. If you allow God the opportunity to work through you, you'll be amazed at the results. If you want help in this or any other area, just ask. He's always available.

But believe me, if you can't go that route just yet, if the nut has got you by the nuts, I feel you. I'm not kidding. I truly understand. I started having sex when I was fifteen. It took eleven years before I could or even wanted to stop. But then again, I didn't have a book like this to read. My story doesn't have to be your story. My mistakes don't have to be your mistakes. My wife shared with me a quote she heard in her weekly Bible study: "A wise man learns from the mistakes of others. An average man learns from his own. A fool learns from no one." Which are you?

6

Root of All Evil . . . Yadda, Yadda, Yadda . . .

So here I was, saved and really walkin' for a solid four years. I was a good, faithful, loving husband. (Yeah, I was and still am sprung on my wife, with her fine self.) I had ditched all the old janky crew (y'know 'em, the ones who turn into crabs in the barrel when it looks like you about to come up or make something of yourself) and replaced them with some real homies, all of them doin' thangs—you know what I'm sayin? One of my boys was makin' his way in the music world, tryin' his hand at producing. He was only gettin' a few nibbles, but he wasn't giving up. Another was deep off into education. He was the youth pastor at my church and was making plans to start his own boarding school for young black kids in the 'hood. He wanted to teach them the important stuff about business and academics, in addition to living a Christ-centered life. But anybody who knows about life in the ghetto understands that the hardest thing for a kid to do there is the right thing, unless he at least has a stable home environment that supports what he's learning in school and church. So my man had plans to combine all three—Jesus, school, and home—to give young cats a chance to at least taste potential. My other dog was tryin' to get his foot in the door in entertainment. He had been working retail for years and was literally sick of it. His health was in jeopardy because of the stress of his job and his long hours. He had high blood pressure and all its cousins—hypertension, high cholesterol, and a bunch of other high somethings. Anyway, he needed out. He would have quit while he looked around for something, but he had a wife and two kids to support, and nobody could blame him for stickin' with the weekly paycheck. My other homie worked in human resources at a production company in Hollywood and hated it. At heart he was and is a writer. And going to his daily grind was zapping him of every ounce of strength he could muster up. None of us were hard-pressed, except dude with the high blood pressure. We all attended the same church. We all worked in youth ministry together, mentoring teenagers. All of our wives were friends. All of our children played in the sandbox together. We weren't rolling in cash and trinkets, but we weren't broke either. At least not until I lost my job.

When I met my wife I had two jobs. I always had a minimum of two jobs and some side gig (legal or illegal, depending upon the time—BC or AD). My wife was no slouch either. She was as brilliant as she was greedy. She liked clothes and toys, so even when she worked full-time for the district attorney's office in San Francisco as an investigator, she took a second job at the Adrienne Vittadini boutique because she wanted a discount on designer clothes. See what I mean? She rationalized that since she was single and childless, all she'd be doing with her free time was hanging out or spending money anyway, so she might as well get paid for her time. That's partly why I married her: I knew no matter what, my girl was gon' have a nigga's back if push came to shove. And please believe it when I tell you push came to shove when I lost my gig.

Here's how it happened. Like I said, I had been working two jobs. I was an assistant to a well-known international mega rock star and I worked as a behavioral specialist coaching developmentally disabled adults. My second job was much more rewarding to me in a lot of ways because I taught life skills to people who really needed them and wanted them. Thinking back, that job paved the way for working in youth ministry and mentoring teenagers. As anybody who has ever worked with teenage males knows, there are few groups who need more life-skill coaching than those guys, and few who act as stupid—no offense, y'all, but you know I'm right. But anyway, about this time I got the bug to pursue entertainment on a higher level.

I had been on track back in the day. Like a lot of brothas, I had been part of a group. We actually got signed by Tommy Boy, but our wack-ass manager went back behind our backs, botched the deal, and got us all booted. Oh well, whatcha gonna do? After that, I started producing Greg Mack's Afternoon Drive Show on Los Angeles's KDAY back in the late eighties and early nineties. And I was starting to get the itch to work in music again—this time from the executive side.

The itch was actually planted after attending a singles conference hosted by my church. We went away from Inglewood to the seaside community of Ventura. And there by the sea I listened to Bishop Kenneth Ulmer explain in great detail the difference between vocation, avocation, and ministry. I had never thought that a career in entertainment could ever be considered ministry, but here was this educated, sanctified man of God telling me so. He shed light on an area that I think many Christians struggle with: separating the sacred from the profane. I was sure that a career in music, with all its backdoor politics, meetings in strip clubs, and after-hour rendezvous, must fall into the category of the profane. But Bishop Ulmer assured me that if God had called me to an area, then He had already gone before me and made a straight path. And since I had no other passions (apart from J.C. and my wife), I concluded that God could have been calling me back to entertainment. I discussed my epiphany with Sheeri, who was then my fiancée, and after securing her support—which she gave willingly—off I went.

After doing my research, though, mostly informational inter-views with some would-be HNICs, I realized that the only way "in" was through a slavish internship, which meant I was probably going to have to quit one of my very well paying jobs to work for free. I didn't mind so much because the dream was alive. And I was convinced that I was walking in God's purpose. But then it oc-curred to me that my wife-to-be might not understand so well.

Now before you he-man jungle brothas start trippin', let me just set you straight. If you are married and want to stay married, if you have respect for your woman and want her to be happy and, more important, on your team, don't make the mistake of pullin' that chest-beating routine, spouting all that testosterone rhetoric. If my relationship with Christ has taught me nothing else, it has taught me how precious a good woman is—and how rare. And any fool who been screwing or screwing around with hos knows what I'm talkin' about. So don't trip. Before I make any decision, I talk to my queen. Not for permission but for counsel. My wife is smart, wise, and full of insight. Discussing stuff with her is like consulting a team of experts. And she will be honest with me—especially if she disagrees. A yes-man she is not. She's Condoleezza Rice to my George Bush. But the best part about a woman like my wife—that is, a woman who really loves Jesus—is that she is submitted. She will let me know her opinion—which I always want. But the final decision is always mine. Whatever I say, she's wit' it. However we rollin', she's on board. Support like that is priceless. And because she's like that, I'll work my butt off so I can give her whatever she wants. And the best part about Sheeri is that no matter how hard I mess up or how messed up the situation gets, she is not mad at me and never withdraws her support. She knows that I take my role as head of household very seriously. She sees me praying and she prays with me. I don't act recklessly, especially not with my family's fu-ture at stake. And she knows this. Her confidence is not so much in me as it is in God and my relationship with Him. So whatever decision I face, we discuss it first. And whatever decision I feel the Lord is leading me to make, I do it and she's right behind me, cheering me on.

So as I was saying, I knew my wife well enough just to be straight with her. She thinks she's a tough girl, but to her credit she is fair and loving. When I explained to her that I would have to give up one job to work another one for free, she said (and I will never forget her exact words), "Baby, if that's what you believe God is leading you to do, then you better do it." I don't think even she knew what she was agreeing to. I know I didn't.

Fast-forward two years, one baby, several internships, and some pitifully paying gigs later and I was standing on the cusp of a new life. I'd been consulting for the now-defunct record label of a prominent NBA star and had been assured that I would be brought on full-time for a hefty sum. On the eve of getting my check, I got fired. No explanation. No known reason. Just, "Sorry, it didn't work out, brah." I will spare you the details, but I was pissed. Not one to rest on my laurels, I picked up another gig in a few weeks. This one came with pay off the bat, but dude was real shady. I knew this, so I was up-front about mine. We negotiated enough pay that I could quit my fallback job for the rock star, which, by the way, was a pain in the butt and kept me away from my wife and my son at night. Besides, this new gig required travel and some extended hours here and there, which would interfere with working for the rock star. At this new job, I worked a semipopular reggae artist and managed to get him some spin on the charts. We booked some shows and got him some appearances. All was well and I was paid regularly. I was paid so well and so regularly that I told my wife that she could quit her job as a literary assistant to pursue her dream of screenwriting and being at home with our eleven-month-old son. Life was great, and we were prospering.

Then the bottom fell out. Suffice it to say that ol' boy really jerked me. After paying me regularly for months, suddenly he was

late with the ends. "No worries." He explained that he had temporary cash-flow problems but they'd be over soon. He promised to
hook me up shortly with regular pay, plus extra for being so patient. This "hookup" date just happened to coincide with my wife's
last day of work. Well, he didn't come through on that day, so I
picked up my wife and went straight to his house. Even though his
Lexus was parked out front for the world to see, he wasn't answer-
ing his door, nor his phone. So we waited . . . and called . . . and
waited . . . and called some more. And just that quick I found myself going back to my old way of doing business. There was a time
when if a nigga was late with my money, I'd be waitin' for him in
the bushes with some type of metal, be it bat or gun. And like
Pablo Escobar, my philosophy had been "silver or lead" with one
minor modification: Give me my silver or taste my lead.

I found out later that ol' boy had absconded with the funds and
was hidin' out in Jamaica. I never found out just how shady he was,
but I'm pretty sure there were more sinister characters than me
looking for him. But I was still pissed. Here I had worked my butt
off on some wack reggae artist on this busted label. I'm sittin' in a
borrowed car (long, long, long story) with my wife, who just quit
her job, and my baby in the backseat, and this fool is vacationing on
eight thousand dollars of my pay? Oh, you know a nigga was hot,
don't you? But I couldn't let myself go there. I was saved now and
pretty sure Jesus wouldn't handle the situation that way. Not to
mention I had a wife and son at that point and I couldn't risk doing
anything that would take me away from them. You feel me? So
there I was—pissed off, but feelin' impotent as a ninety-year-old
with no Viagra in sight. And I found myself wondering, *What happened, Lord?*

If I was pissed, then my wife was furious! She was cursing up a
storm. I had never heard such filth come out of such a pretty face!
She was hot! Not at me, mind you, but at ol' dude. And get this:
She was pissed at God, too! Can you believe it? She was mad at

God! And she let Him know it! She pulled no punches. For the next hour, she told him in no uncertain terms what she thought of Him. She questioned His methods; she called Him out on every promise she could think of, and when her memory failed, she pulled out her Bible and started underlining the Psalms and Proverbs, saying things like, "What about this one, Lord? Does this apply to us?" She demanded to know how He could let this happen to us. She was actually mad at Him for what was happening to me!

It messed me up. I have never heard anyone pray like that before or since. I thought she had lost her mind, except she was making perfect sense. She vented all of her frustration over our situation and our relationship with Him in that conversation. And you know what? I was scared for her. I remember thinking that if she didn't shut up, a lightning bolt was gonna come out the sky or something and blow us up. And when I tried to calm her, she went off even more. "Don't try to tell me how to talk to God, Mykel. He knows where I am." I won't repeat much else of what she said, because that's personal, but the gist of it was this: She reminded God that He said that He loved us, was our provider, that He was our protector, and He was our shield. She reminded Him that we diligently served Him week in and week out and earnestly sought to do His will. We had followed what we were sure was His leading in our personal and professional lives, and yet we were still not only not prospering, but we were getting screwed over and over. Every time we found ourselves on firm footing, the bottom seemed to fall out. What was up with that? Should we just chuck the entertainment thing and go get jobs at the post office? She declared that she was fed up trying to remain faithful, and that if God wanted her to be in a different place, He'd have to come get her. Then she broke down and cried.

And in my heart, so did I. I understood her pain and anger. I felt they were justified. But her honesty really affected me. And six months later, savings depleted, checking account empty, credit cards maxed out, still unemployed, as I stood in line at the welfare office waiting to be approved for food stamps, I finally got around to venting those same frustrations.

All I knew was what God had said in His Word. He said He'd take care of me. He said that if I sought the kingdom, everything else would be added (Matthew 6:33). He said that I didn't have to worry about food, clothing, and shelter. He said that if I asked anything in Jesus' name it was mine (John 14:13). He said that if I delighted in Him, He would give me the desires of my heart (Psalms 37:4). I was sure that I had been following His leading at every turn. And it wasn't like I was asking for outrageous, frivolous stuff. I just wanted to be able to earn a living in a field I was convinced He had directed me to. So I had to ask Him, "What da deal, man?" I had done everything I knew to do right by Him. And all I had to show for my efforts was an empty bank account, a shoeprint on my butt, and one very angry and discouraged wife. But I did know this: Either I had misunderstood something or God was lying. Since I knew the latter was not possible (John 17:16), I concluded that the former must be true. So I began my search to find out what had gone so wrong. Sheeri eventually came around and joined me. The search for the answer would send me deep into the consciousness of the Christian community, where I would discover and uncover not only misconceptions about money and wealth, but myths and outright lies.

"Money is the root of all evil." How many times have you heard that wack quote? Probably your whole life, right? Do you know that it's a bald-faced lie? People who use it often do so to make a point that money and everything connected to it is bad. The worst part about it is that they claim that that's what the Bible says. Wrong. The Bible says that "the *love* of money is a root of all kinds of evil" (1 Timothy 6:10). As long as you don't love money, you're not in a bad place. Another favorite quote used by Bible thumpers comes from the gospel of Matthew, chapter 19, verse 24. It says it's "easier for a camel to enter through the eye of a needle than for a rich man to enter into the kingdom of God." Sounds pretty impossible to be saved if you're rich, right? Well, this time the quote is correct, but it's extremely misleading when taken out of context. Read on.

16 Now a man came up to Jesus and asked, "Teacher, what good thing must I do to get eternal life?"

17 "Why do you ask me about what is good?" Jesus replied. "There is only One who is good. If you want to enter life, obey the commandments."

18 "Which ones?" the man inquired.

19 Jesus replied, " 'Do not murder, do not commit adultery, do not steal, do not give false testimony, honor your father and mother,' and 'love your neighbor as yourself.' "

20 All these I have kept," the young man said. "What do I still lack?"

21 Jesus answered, "If you want to be perfect, go, sell your possessions and give to the poor, and you will have treasure in heaven. Then come, follow me."

22 When the young man heard this, he went away sad, because he had great wealth.

23 Then Jesus said to his disciples, "I tell you the truth, it is hard for a rich man to enter the kingdom of heaven.

24 Again I tell you, it is easier for a camel to go through the eye of a needle than for a rich man to enter the kingdom of God."

25 When the disciples heard this, they were greatly astonished and asked, "Who then can be saved?"

26 Jesus looked at them and said, "With man this is impossible, but with God all things are possible." (Matthew 19:16–26)

Did you miss it? The key to this account is in verse 21, where Jesus tells the rich young man to sell all his possessions, give to the poor, and follow Him. Lots of folks use this part of the story out of context too. They claim that the only way you can truly follow Jesus is to give up all your cash and prizes and go serve the poor. But understand, Jesus didn't give these instructions to everyone He encountered, just to this guy.

I know the first time I examined this account the first thing I wondered is why ol' boy didn't stop with the "love your neighbor as yourself" part. Why did he have to press? And another thing to notice is that he came to Jesus—not vice versa. He sought out Jesus . . . presumably because like a lot of rich cats, he had it all goin' on, but knew that he was empty. Do you know fools like that? They got everything they could ever want and they are still hollow? They're the ones who commit suicide and the world wonders why. This young guy was smart. He knew that his life was missing something. So he went in search of what it was missing. He just wasn't prepared for the answer.

But check this. Like I said before, Jesus didn't make this request of everyone, just this guy. Why is that? Don't sleep, God is omniscient. He knows everything, even stuff you don't know about yourself. Jesus knew that the most important thing to this dude was his money. So that's what He asked for. If the young guy had a prize collection of cats, you best believe that J.C. would have asked for Fifi and her friends. This is an important clue to God's character. He wants nothing in the way of you and Him. He wants all your love. Fools come at me all the time with how unfair they think that is. That it's selfish for God to try to possess people. To which I answer that He doesn't seek to possess us. That's the devil's job. God loves us and wants us to love Him back.

Imagine if you had a fine girlfriend, who just had you sprung. You're like Beyoncé, just crazy in love, right? And you found out that she was in love with someone else. Ol' girl was with you, but you have discovered by readin' her diary, or something stupid like that, that she really loves someone else. You'd be messed up, right? True. You might try 'n get her back, if you lived in a romance novel. But more than likely you would kick her sorry butt to the curb. Why? Because you ain't no fool and you want your affection returned in kind and exclusively. And if baby ain't with it, then bump her, right? Well, if you got that much sense, how much more sense does God have? Is it clearer now? Jesus gave the rich young ruler a choice: Love your money or love me. The young guy chose his money. So J.C. didn't sweat it. He let it go. See?

This was one of the first Scriptures I went to when I started seeking an answer for my "misfortune." I had to ask myself, Did I really love God more than money?

I grew up in Oakland, California, and if Oakland is nothing else, it is a town full of hustlers. Everybody is getting their hustle on. Some are legit and some not so much so. Did you know that Oakland is considered to be the "pimp capital" of the United States? Supposedly there are more pimps in Oakland than in any other city in America. That's a dubious title, I know, but it shows you that fools in the Town (natives call it the Town) will do whatever it takes to get paid! And I was no different. The only thing was that after my conversion, the means of my hustle had to be one that brought glory to God or was at the very least legal. But in my heart, I was still puttin' in work. I was a hustler, a paper chaser. I grew up working-class poor. And for as long as I could remember, I have always wanted the big house in the wealthy neighborhood, the bomb car, vacations around the world, private schools for my children, enough money so that neither I nor anyone I loved would know lack. And to me this didn't seem evil or even bad. As the man, I felt I should want to provide well for my family. And to the best of my knowledge God agreed with me. But the question still nagged me: "Do you love these things more than you love Me?" And in my heart of hearts I had to admit that at best it was a tie. At best I loved wealth and all its trappings at least as much as I loved God, and probably more sometimes. I had been doing all the "right things." I had been religious—going to church, working diligently in ministry, serving. Yo, I had even become a deacon! If anybody was holy, it had to be me, right? And you know what? I think that's how a lot of Christians fall off.

God gives only His best and He expects nothing less of us. Now, He understands that our best is shoddy, so He knows our best won't measure up, but that's why He allowed Christ to die as a substitute for us. So really the only thing we have to give Him is our hearts. And our best is really our whole heart.

Like a lot of Christians, I had fallen into the practice of pimpin' God. I thought that if I tithed, gave offerings, was a good little Christian, did my best not to curse, get drunk, or get high, loved my neighbors, loved my enemies, and so forth, that God had to bless me the way I thought I should be blessed. In exchange for my loyalty, God was supposed to hook a nigga up. I have even heard pastors preach from the pulpit that if you need a blessing, then sow a seed, as though God operates on some kind of money- or works-exchange program. Behave and your life will be smooth. Tithe and give offering and you'll be rich.

That kind of thinking is beyond busted. Let me tell you why. For one, God's love cannot be earned or lost! There is nothing you can do to make God love you and nothing you can do to lose God's love (Romans 8:38). Think about it: If you could earn your life into a better place, you'd have done it by now. You wouldn't be so to'-up in whatever area where you suck. Part of being human is that we just need a hand up. And we don't need to work for God's love because He gives it freely. He wants us to achieve worthwhile goals. He wants us to mature into the person He originally planned for us to be. He wants us to be joyful. He wants us to be at peace. And yes, He wants us to prosper in all areas, including in our finances. What better testament to the world of God's goodness than the prosperity of His people?

I know Christians who designate areas of their lives as "God areas" and others as areas they take care of themselves. Sadly, finances often fall into the latter. They rationalize this division by saying that God doesn't care about something as trivial as money. Makes me ask, God has numbered the hairs on your head, but not the dollars in your wallet? A roach can't drop dead without His permission, but He don't care if you're broke? That sounds straight crazy to me, and way out of character. God cares about how much money you have. He also cares about what you do with it.

Now, don't get me wrong. I'm not on the prosperity-gospel thing. I'm not selling some "name it and claim it" or "blab it and grab it" crap. I think that's just as bad as pimpin' God for tithes. God cannot be manipulated. Simply because you speak a blessing doesn't mean that God must give it to you. He is not some heavenly bellhop at your beck and call. He is not a genie in a bottle, waiting to do your bidding. He's God. He is sovereign and perfect. That means He does what He wants when He wants and it's all good. You, on the other hand, can say none of those things about yourself. On your own, you can't even pray right (James 4:3). So it's very likely that the stuff you're namin' and claimin' ain't even close to what God wants you to have. And since He cannot contradict His own nature to answer *your* prayers (read: demands), you gets nathan. God can and often does answer no to our prayers. When He does, you can bet it's because He knows something you don't.

God wants to be in control of every area of your life. But He won't take control. You have to give it to Him. And if you don't, He will let you keep doin' your thing until you finally mess up enough to realize that you need Him. I believe that's what He did to me and my wife. She was on the same page I was. She was going tit for tat with God, keeping score, as it were. But the problem with our thinking was that we were doing the right things to get God to bless us, not because we loved God so much that we just wanted to please Him. I mean, we told ourselves that we loved God above all else, but really we were all about getting paid. I'm not saying that if God had prospered us financially back then that we would have turned away from Him. But I know for a fact that if we hadn't undergone such suffering and misery, we would not have been up in His face as much, in the Word as diligently, praying as fervently, nor as often. Consequently we wouldn't know Him as well we do now and we would not be as mature as we are. Let me be clear: God was not punishing us for wrong thinking. He was merely getting our attention and pruning us. I am convinced that financial prosperity is an integral part of His plan for us. But just like I would never give my six-year-old keys to his own car, God would never give me anything that I wasn't ready for either. My wife and I would need much more preparation and pruning in this area of our lives before God would begin to trust us with more. But He has been faithful. As we have proven ourselves better stewards simply out of our love for Him and our desire to please Him, not to get more out of Him, He has allowed us to come into more and more ends. But that begins with the attitude, not the stuff.

So then why do so many Christians seem to be so broke while so many hip-hop artists, executives, and entrepreneurs who glorify such lowbrow living are so rich? I've got three main answers for that question. For some Christians, the work that God requires of them requires little to moderate cash flow. I have it on good authority that the lifestyle of a missionary in the Congo is substantially cheaper than that of a family of five living in New York. Remember I said God meets your needs? Well, some folks just need less than others.

Another reason that some Christians live modestly is because that's all they desire. Some people want only an apartment, maybe a house, some kind of car, and a steady job with a regular income. And trust me, I'm not dissin' those folks. It's only a sin to live small if God is calling you to something bigger. But wherever you are, you can be useful for the kingdom. Some people simply want less than others.

Now, me, I'm a capitalist at heart. And thankfully I had already committed myself to Christ when I learned that being a Christian didn't mean being broke. But I have to say that it sure seemed so at first. It seemed like every time I turned on the TV, Christians were begging for something. And every church I went to had some kind of building fund. And the tithe . . . I won't lie. It took me a good minute to understand and agree with why God was entitled to 10 percent of my hard-earned cash. I don't mean to sound irreverent, but that's where I was. I'll go deeper into that in subsequent chapters. But for now, let's go back to where I started.

I was deep off into hip-hop by the time I came to Christ, right? And as you well know, hip-hop artists and front guys aren't known for their frugality. They believe hard in blingin' and, if need be, slangin' to get them ends. Like I said, I was a hustler with a somewhat shady past, and I too was all about the Benjamins. "How do I get mines?" was pretty much my only concern for a good portion of my young-adult life. So what happened? On the front end I wanted to be rich. Again, I wanted the flied-out crib in the bomb neighborhood, the nice car sittin' on them thangs, the trinkets, the gadgets, and all the bells and whistles, right? Then I came to Christ. He wore my butt out and made me examine my heart. And you know what? I still want all of those things . . . and I am unashamed. The difference is that now I don't want those things more than I want God. And now I understand that the cash, the riches, and the stuff aren't mine to do with as I please. It all belongs to Him. I just get to watch over it for a minute or two till I pass on to glory or pass it on to the next few generations. And my job is to "keep doing business" until J.C. returns.

Don't believe me? Read the parable of the talents in Matthew. In this parable Jesus explains to the disciples that a rich guy left town for a while and gave his servants some cash to invest. Some invested wisely and some didn't. One guy buried his money in the ground . . . stupid. When the boss came back, he rewarded them according to their return on their investments. One guy made a 100 percent return. Another guy made a 50 percent return. And the last guy, the guy who buried his money, made *nada*. So the master takes the money from the loser and gives it to the guy who made 100 percent, and rewards him with his own kingdom. Jesus finishes off the parable by explaining that the folks who have will get more, while those who blow it get what little they have taken away.

Now, as with everything Jesus said, of course there is a spiritual explanation. Some scholars believe that He's saying that those who truly embrace Him will be rewarded with even more godly wisdom and spiritual gifts, while those who reject Him will lose what little spiritual insight they barely have. But there is also a lesson here that applies to stewardship, and it is this: When we take care of what God gives us, He is more inclined to give us more. When we can prove ourselves responsible, He rewards us with more responsibility. This is a kingdom principle and applies across the board. Money is no exception. If we can show ourselves trustworthy with financial resources, it then makes sense that God would be inclined to reward us with more. It has definitely proved true in my life.

So what does it mean to be responsible? Responsibility covers many areas, but the basics are attitude and operation. What is your attitude toward money? Do you worship it? Do you believe that it has power? In your mind does it make the world go 'round? Do you give more respect to people who appear to be paid than to those who don't seem to be? Do you expect better treatment from society as a whole the larger your paycheck? Have you ever uttered that hopeless phrase, "If I just had more money, I'd be happy?" Do you worry over money? Do financial concerns stress you out? Do you live in fear of losing your job? Do you keep your job simply because it pays your bills? Do you work for money? If you answered "yes" to any of these questions, then you very likely have an improper attitude toward money.

On the flip side, how responsible are you with your money? Do you maintain a budget? Do you know how much you spend a month on utilities, clothing, food, or entertainment? Do you know how much you spent today, and on what? Do you keep your receipts? Do you go over them daily, weekly, monthly, yearly? If you had to produce physical records of your spending for the last year, could you? Do you regularly record your expenditures? Do you balance your checkbook daily, weekly, monthly? Do you reconcile your checkbook against your receipts? Do you save or invest your surplus cash monthly? Do you even have surplus cash? Would you even know if you had surplus cash? Do you plan for larger expenditures? Do you pray over your finances? Do you resist impulse buying? Are you living free of consumer debt? If your answer to any of these questions is no, then you probably have bad money-management habits too.

Let me ask you this: If you owned a business, which of your employees would you entrust with a million dollars? The one who steals? The one who never steals, but constantly miscounts and often loses his receipts? Or the one who always balances the cash drawer perfectly and keeps his receipts in order? Yeah. That's what I thought. Well, God is way smarter than you are. If you never keep track of how much you spend or of what you buy, if you never tithe, always bounce checks, are constantly dodging your creditors and neglecting to pay off your legitimate debts, why would God trust you with more money? I believe that many Christians suffer financially because they are bad stewards of their resources, namely of their loot.

I know this family who bought a house a few years ago, then turned around and sold it at a hundred-thousand-dollar profit. Smart move, right? Six months later they were broke and had no idea where the money had gone. They had no idea the money was gone until checks started to bounce. They never reviewed their bank statements. They never balanced their checkbook. They just kept writing checks and withdrawing money. Closer examination showed that they had no money-management skills. The problem was they had never had that much money before and didn't know how to handle it. It was gone before they knew it, and all they had to show for it was some clothes, a car, and some gadgets. How sad is that? They had the means to create wealth and they spent it on junk. Of course, they could get financed to buy another house and sell it at a profit later, but who's to say they wouldn't repeat their mistake? Broke people stay broke because they do the things that broke people do with money. Wealthy people get wealthier because they do the things that wealthy people do with money. Get it? It's not rocket science.

But here's the thing: To live in this world costs money. God is not ignorant of nor indifferent to that fact. If there's anybody He wants to have resources it's people who have His heart. People who want to advance the cause of the kingdom. But if none of His people have His heart, then He'll use nonbelievers to advance His cause. I believe that God is interested in feeding the hungry, clothing the naked, providing for widows and orphans. I believe that He would go beyond that too. I believe He would give scholarships to needy college-bound students, provide housing for the homeless, provide debt relief and education for the financially ignorant, fund ministries that help to rehabilitate and train ex-cons. I've named just a few things, but I'm sure God has many plans. Yet His people miss the opportunity to serve in these areas because they have wrong attitudes about money and even worse habits regarding its management. There are ministries waiting to be birthed or that have been birthed but lie dying for lack of funding. And before you ask, yes, God could just go ahead and implement all of these great ideas without us. But He has always chosen to work with His people, not apart from them. I don't know why, but the Word and history show that He chooses to involve us in His plans. Wouldn't it be great if we could position ourselves to join Him?

So on the other end, what about those seemingly immoral peddlers of hip-hop? Why are they so well paid? The truth is, God can bless whomever he pleases, and he needs to ask no one's permission. Also, only God truly knows a person's heart, so hold off before you judge. True, you can judge the tree by the fruit, and some of hip-hop's fruit looks a little suspect. Songs about doin' it this way and that, sexin' up and down, buyin' more bling, slangin' and doing whatever to get paid, ho'in' and gettin' high. A lot of hip-hop's fruit is far from sanctified. And still, on occasion, some is truly uplifting and edifying. What I find interesting is that some of its biggest names grew up in Christian households. Have they rejected Christ? Are they on the fence? Truly only God knows. In the meantime, I imagine hip-hop icons can expect the same amount of grace that God affords the rest of humanity as He waits patiently to get their attention. I do know one thing, though: Hip-hop boasts some of the savviest entrepreneurs since the age of the robber barons, as well as some really generous philanthropists: P. Diddy, Russell Simmons, Sean Carter (Jay-Z), Chris Lighty, Mona Scott, Master P, E-40, Todd Shaw (Too Short), Ice-T, Eazy-E, Ice Cube, Will Smith, Damon Dash, Scarface, Snoop Dogg, and Dana Owens (Queen Latifah). The Body of Christ could learn a lot from these young men and women. All of them have mastered their craft and have successfully branched out into at least one other business medium. They are risk takers and have been able to do well with a little and as a result have amassed more. To the best of my knowledge, none of their families are wealthy by tradition. Most of them come from working-class, professional, or even single and/or poor parents, but not from generations and generations of money. Yet with their talent and preparation, they have been able take advantage of opportunities presented them and are changing not only the face of music, but the entire landscape of domestic and international business. No doubt on at least the financial front, they have all been good stewards.

7

Leave Ya Pockets Like Rabbit Ears

So I joined this community of believers at Faithful Central Bible Church in Inglewood, California, and just like with anything that feels this good, I'm waiting for the other shoe to drop. I have lived my life by a certain code, which tells me that at their core, people are just wack most of the time. No need to bother depending on them because they will let you down. Don't trust 'em with nothing because they will stab you in the back or the front—sometimes literally. And under no circumstances should you ever be stupid enough to accept anybody or any situation at face value.

So I'd been sitting under the dynamic teaching of Bishop Kenneth Ulmer for about six months, and to be honest, I was feelin' him. Over the course of my time at FCBC he has shown himself to be the real thing. He grew up in Saint Louis, Missouri. He attended the University of Illinois. He pledged Kappa Alpha Psi as an undergrad. On top of that he went on to acquire his master's and doctorate degrees in theology and a doctor of ministry degree from United Theological Seminary. Ol' boy got a head on his shoulders, and I can respect that. But the best part about him is that he's human. A sermon of his feels more like an intimate conversation you'd have on the fly with your favorite uncle. He drops some knowledge on you, makes you laugh, and challenges you to change all at the same time. And he's a brotha fo' sho'. He's smart, articulate, and funny. And he is definitely old-school black man with his. One of my boys calls him Bishop Cat Daddy, because he's mad cool. It would be a shame to die and leave this earth without hearing him preach at least one time.

Beyond his oratory skills, Bishop inspires the common man because he is really walking this walk. The Christian lifestyle is really tough to maintain in the culture at large. He readily confesses his struggles both past and present, and openly questions God's Word in order to provide his flock with the most accurate understanding of the Bible he can manage. And he's so cool. Did I mention that? You just want to kick it with him. He's one of those dudes that if you were his age you'd be his homie. But he's your pastor! It's the best of both worlds.

Even with all of Bishop's good traits, I knew that one day I was going to stumble onto something that was gon' make me reconsider my views. It didn't take long. About six months in, at the end of one service, he announced that the following week he was going to begin a series on tithing. FCBC is no different from any other church in that they take up a collection at some point during the service. I had certainly noticed, but never thought much of it. After my grandmother's experience in Pittsburgh, I knew I'd just as soon offer up my right arm as hand over my hard-earned cash to any preacher. I didn't care how cool he was or how many letters he had behind his name; homeboy wasn't gettin' my scrilla. And that was that.

I went to church the next week anyway, more because I wanted to hear how Bishop could possibly try to justify my handing over my money than because I was willing to listen. I sat though praise and worship, which if I recall correctly was particularly moving that day. I didn't let it faze me though. I was ready. I held Bishop in high esteem, but I had to admit that he was just wrong on this point. I had read some in the Bible about tithing, and I just couldn't see why it was necessary. Well, needless to say, Bishop broke the Word all the way down that day and in subsequent weeks. I came away with a better understanding of why I should tithe, but with an equal amount of determination that I would not . . . ever.

As I look back, I realize that my grandmother's experience with the preacher in Pittsburgh had affected me more than I was aware. In many ways it had laid the foundation for my mistrust of churches in general, but in particular for pastors and tithing. Why did we have to give? Where was my money going? Who was it benefiting? And why on earth did God need my money? I mean, He's God, after all. If He wanted some money, couldn't He just make some? Or better yet, why would He have to shop? Couldn't He just make what He needed? I mean, He was the One who said, "Let there be light," and we all know how that turned out. So why couldn't He just say, "Let there be new church vans," or something like that? This is the same God who raised Jesus from the dead. He parted the Red Sea. He shook down the walls of Jericho. Why not just make what the church needed miraculously appear? I could not wrap my mind around it. What possible need could the Almighty have for 10 percent of Mykel Mitchell's paycheck?

I had all these questions and many more. Bishop's teaching went a long way toward helping me to understand. One thing he has always done, however, is to warn his listeners never just to take his word for it. One of the things I like about FCBC is that they encourage personal study of the Word over study of someone else's opinion of the Word, no matter how well-informed that opinion is. There is no substitute for reading the Bible yourself. If you don't get something, you must ask questions—not just of those more learned than you, but of God Himself. After all, He breathed out the Bible. He's still alive. He wants you to understand it. So if you don't get something, go to the Word. Ask the Holy Spirit to help you understand and then read with spiritual eyes, expecting to comprehend. Sometimes you get instant enlightenment. Sometimes you don't. But Jesus promises that if you ask, "it will be given to you; seek and you will find; knock and the door will be opened to you" (Matthew 7:7–8). It's pretty much a win-win situation. The author Himself will interpret His manuscript for you! That beats Cliff's Notes hands down!

So that's what I did—and did I get answers! Years later, the Holy Spirit is still teaching me . . . not so much because I'm a slow learner (which I certainly can be, except where money is concerned), but because God's Word is so deep in this area. The Bible has so much to say about financial matters. Anyway I've learned enough to be convinced that every believer should tithe. Here's why.

First of all, God commands it. "Bring the whole tithe into the storehouse!" God commands in Malachi 3:10. To hold back the tithe is to rob God. It's no different from sticking a gun in His face and screaming, "Put the money in the bag!" I don't know about you, but I don't ever want to be in that position. Why does God see it like that? Why is mishandling the tithe so offensive to Him? Part of the reason is that from day one God has been interested in having intimate relationships with people. Genesis says He walked in the garden with Adam. He was a friend to Noah. He wrestled with Jacob. He communicated with Joseph through dreams. Moses actually came face-to-face with Him (the only person to ever do so and live). Through Moses, God gave the Hebrews His commandments to help them to live a productive, peaceful life in the new land they would inherit. His motive with all of humanity has always been to reveal more of Himself that we might know, love, and have a relationship with Him. God is always interested in showing us how to do things His way. Given the fact that He's perfect, omniscient, and all that other good stuff, it's a good bet that His way works better than anything you or I can think of.

I like to think of his relationship to us as similar to that of a car manufacturer to its car. Land Rover makes the Range Rover. When you purchase one, you get a lesson in four-wheel drive on the lot on a man-made mountain. You get an owner's manual, a warranty, and a full automotive/body shop at your disposal, along with a bunch of other perks. If you want your Rover to run its best, then you should follow the directions in the owner's manual regarding maintenance and operation. You should use unleaded gas, change the oil every three thousand miles or so, and go in for engine maintenance as the schedule or dashboard lights indicate. If anything goes wrong, you can take it to other mechanics, but truthfully it's better to bring it into a Land Rover–certified mechanic, who is most often found at the dealership.

It's the same with God and us. He created us. He knows full well how He intended us to perform and function. He knows what works best. He has given us an owner's manual, which covers everything from relationships (marriage, parenting, friendships) to finance (running a business, dealing with employees, managing money) to life situations (confronting wrongdoers, handling disappointments, rollin' with success). You get the picture. There is pretty much no topic left uncovered either directly or indirectly in the Bible. When we're having problems, we can go to other sources—shrinks, counselors, or friends. But it's best first to turn in prayer to the One who created us and to read His Word. Given that He wrote every moment of our lives down in His book before one moment came to pass, He's got a better idea than we do of what lies ahead and what we need in order to come through it successfully (Psalms 139:16). So it makes sense to seek Him out and to listen to what He has to say.

With God, it's all about the relationship. Everything He does or allows is motivated by his love for us. He even disciplines us out of love. Like any other being with sense, He would like us to return in kind. He wants our motivation for all that we do to be out of love for Him. Like anyone with self-respect, He's got standards of how the relationship needs to work. And you know what? Given what He offers, His requirements are very reasonable.

I learned that God doesn't want our money. First off, it isn't ours to give. It's His money. I know that sounds crazy, but let me explain. You may work a job and get a paycheck. You may own your own business, real estate, or other investments, which provide a return. But all those things belong to God. "The earth is the Lord's, and everything in it, the world, and all who live in it" (Psalms 24:1–2). Everything belongs to Him. That we do not acknowledge this fact makes it no less true. The company you work for, the investments you hold, the business you run are the means through which He chooses to provide for you financially. But don't sleep; He is the one doing the providing. Corporations downsize. Stocks plummet. Small businesses fail every day. But don't trip. If any of your sources of income ever go belly-up, the Lord is able to provide for you some other way. Most of us just refuse to recognize.

It's tempting to boast that you are self-made, but that's simply a lie. If you've ever admitted to being lucky in your life—even once—then you are not self-made. You can't control luck. I don't care what New Agers say; you can't make good things happen to you or for you. So many things play into making you who you are and placing you where you are today. Certainly your deliberate choices play a part—choices such as to pursue a college degree or to start your own business or to marry and have kids. But the events you can't control weigh in just as heavily, maybe even more so. You had no say into which family you'd be born. You had no choice in whether your father would be a postal worker, a crack addict, or a brain surgeon. You had no say in whether your parents would divorce or die during your childhood. You did not choose your race. Even the way in which your brain developed was never up to you. The fundamentals of your personality were predetermined and/or shaped by forces you couldn't even comprehend or affect. Even the opportunities presented to you were created by someone else. You may have prepared for them, but you couldn't call them to you. I know for a fact that there are a whole lot of dudes sitting in prison whose manuscripts will never see the light of day, even though they are far better writers than I will ever hope to be. There is a gang of rappers who could run rings around the best of the best, but they will never make it out of the ghetto. That's just real, y'all. And if you want to know the truth, I could just as easily have been writing my memoirs from prison, but for the grace of God. There are so many variables in any given life that no one can brag about his accomplishments apart from God. So shut up already.

Every good deal you ever got or "lucky" break that ever came your way was ordered and/or allowed by God Himself. That's true of the bad stuff, too, so don't get it twisted. Everything you got, God either gave it to you or let you have it. So "your" money is not yours; it's His. He's just lettin' you hold it while you're alive. That makes you a steward, not an owner. And like any other master, don't think He won't hold you responsible for what you do with it when the time comes to settle up.

Another reason God does not want "your" money is that He doesn't need it. He's infinite and eternal. What could He possibly need from your sorry butt? *Nada*—that's what. There is one thing that God wants from you that He can't get from anyone else, though. That's your love. He wants you to love Him first and above everything else. The first and greatest commandment upon which the entire Old Testament is based is "Love the Lord your God with all your heart and with all your soul and with all your mind" (Matthew 22:37). God wants you. But like any respectable person, He wants you to give yourself willingly, understanding all the benefits and sacrifices involved in the relationship. He will never force you.

That's where tithing comes in. God created people, so if He knows anything, He knows that we are prone to loving money. Yet He specifically tells us over and over again throughout the Old and New Testaments not to love money. Why? Think about it. People who love money kick rocks. They do anything to anyone in order to get it. And they are never satisfied. When you are greedy, your appetite is like a cup with a hole in it: You can never fill it. No matter how much money you have, you want more. No amount can make you happy or content. It's like being addicted to crack. There can be no happily-ever-after as long as you love money. Loving God, on the other hand, produces all the satisfaction you ever dreamed of and more. He promises that when you seek Him first, He'll make sure that you get all the other stuff you need. He will fulfill your desires with good things and you won't have to break your back to keep them. 'Cause if He provides it, He'll maintain it for you. And should He decide not to, then you don't need it anyway. You can live in peace either way, once you are convinced that His love will afford you only the very best life has to offer.

When you tithe, what you are saying is that God is more important to you than money. You are saying that out of sheer love for Him and appreciation for His many blessings, you symbolically give back into His hand a portion of what came from His hand in the first place. You give Him his "cut" purely to honor Him. The cool thing is that God promises to reward you for your diligence in this area. Tithing is one of the few areas where God actually invites us to test Him! In Malachi 3:10, God challenges, "Test me in this . . . and see if I will not throw open the floodgates of heaven and pour out so much blessing that you will not have room enough for it." God extends this promise to the Israelites, who at the time were straight punkin' Him. He had been loyal to them for generations, while they did their own thing, slippin' and dippin', coming back to Him apologetic—only to fall away and come back again. Finally He just lights them up in Malachi. He tells them through the prophet Malachi that they've been wack and that they need to get on their J-O-B. Then, as though to encourage them, He challenges them. "Do it and see if I don't hook you up" is basically what God is saying. Okay, I'm paraphrasing, but you get the point. Since God does not change, his Word still applies today to anyone who will take Him up on it.

Now before you go crazy, notice that the issue is not to tithe so that you can get. That would be wrong. That would be pimpin' God. If I know anything about Him, I know this: God will not be pimped. So get it right from jump. You give to God because it's a requirement He has put in place. You give out of love for Him. Out of gratitude to Him for your very existence in the world He created, you tithe—*cheerfully!* You tithe for the same reason you praise God: He deserves it. He is worthy of it.

During the opening ceremonies of the 1996 Summer Olympics in Atlanta, my wife and I sat transfixed as we watched Muhammad Ali light the torch that would signify the start of the games. In the advanced stages of Alzheimer's disease, he trembled violently as his hand pressed the torch to the giant Olympic torch. Sheeri and I had both grown up in families where Muhammad Ali—or Cassius Clay, as both our grandmothers had insisted on calling him—was not only well liked, but nearly revered. As a black American he represented so much to every generation in both our families. As a national hero, a civil rights icon, and a formidable athlete, he is the object of our personal affection and respect. Sheeri and I were so proud of him that we actually stood up and applauded when he successfully lit the giant torchère.

Later the Holy Spirit would speak to my heart: "That's how I want you to feel about me." I understood. If I could admire a man who had only indirectly affected my life, clap for a man whom I have never met, offer my respect to any man, period, how much more so should I offer everything I have to the God who sacrificed His own Son to save my worthless behind? There's no comparison. That is the attitude that should be at the heart of our tithing. God says, "I want you to give." In response, I say, "Yes, Lord!" Doing anything for God is such a privilege. Just so we're clear, He don't need us. He chooses to work through us to accomplish His plan for humanity. In return for our genuine affection, He pours out his blessing—because He chooses to, not because He owes us.

What's important to remember is that God's pouring out His blessing is not necessarily the same thing as His meeting our needs.

In chapter 6 of the gospel of Matthew, Jesus patiently and thoroughly explains the futility of worry. He asks rhetorically in verse twenty-seven, "Who of you by worrying can add a single hour to his life?" He goes on to explain that we shouldn't worry about what we'll wear or what we'll eat, because God provides those things for us. He charges us to "seek first His kingdom and His righteousness and all these things will be given to" us, too (Matthew 6:33). Now, the first time I heard this verse, I thought it sounded crazy. If I don't handle my business, then who's gon' handle it for me? It sounded so pie-in-the-sky, so corny and unrealistic. I remember thinking that philosophy might work for folks who don't mind living under cardboard boxes in the scary part of town, but I'm tryin' to do bigger things. You know what I mean? So at first I just dismissed it as fluff.

I eventually came to understand that Jesus isn't encouraging us to be irresponsible. He's not telling us to sit on our butts singing "Kumbaya" all day long, cup in hand, hoping someone will give us some change for lunch. He is definitely *not* saying that. In fact, His charge to us is just the opposite. In the parable of the talents, found in Matthew, He commands us to keep doing business until He comes the second time. What Jesus is saying is, don't worry about your needs being met.

Now, that may not mean much to you if you've never had a real problem. But if you've ever been next to homelessness, bordering on bankruptcy, or about to get ya lights cut off—then you understand worry. True worry consumes all your thoughts and sometimes your dreams, too. It takes you over as you struggle to come up with a solution to a situation that you can barely wrap your mind around. Your situation doesn't have to be life threatening, just life altering. A kid who finally gets into the college of his choice, but can't afford to go, can obsess over millions of ways to solve his problem as easily as a senior citizen, who realizes too late that her Social Security benefits and retirement combined aren't enough to meet her minimum monthly bills. Worry can eat away at your peace, your hope, and your health. Most of us worry over things that haven't happened yet and over which we have absolutely no control. Therefore worry is as pointless as it is destructive. No amount of worry can change what will happen. No amount of worry can prepare you to handle the unknown. Jesus knew this. That's why he commands us not to do it.

Out of His love for us, God created us. Out of that same love He provides for our every need. A bird can't fall from the sky without His permission. How much more important than a bird are you? The problem with the way God does His job is that when He's doing it to our satisfaction, we don't even notice that He's doing it. Think about it. What if your all your needs being met tomorrow depended on your thanking God for meeting them today? Yeah. Many of us wouldn't even wake up tomorrow. That's how much God does for us. He meets needs on the regular that we don't even know we have. My family and I do a lot of daily freeway driving. Every day we pass at least one or two accidents. My wife is very careful at bedtime to remind our children to thank God in prayer for getting us (and everybody we know) home safely one more time. I have no idea how many hazards God protects me from daily. And you know what? I don't wanna know, 'cause that might be a little much for a brotha to handle. But daily I just offer up a blanket thanks because I know He does so much more than what I see.

Also, when God handles business in a way that pleases us, we take credit for it ourselves! That's crazy. We will give credit to ourselves, to "being in the right place at the right time," or, worst of all, to luck. I can't stand that. We're not that great or that skillful, and "luck" doesn't exist in a world ordered by God. If you want to know the truth, we couldn't wipe our noses without God's help. Anybody who has ever suffered any form of paralysis or chronic pain can tell you, when your legs don't work or your back goes out, no amount of intelligence or self-will can fix either of them. Anybody who has ever suffered through the flu can tell you that while you're lying flat on your back, praying to luck makes no difference.

It's only when God does His thing in a way that troubles us that we suddenly pay attention. After 9/11, so many people demanded to know where God was: "If He is supposed to be omnipotent, then why didn't He prevent the attacks?" In defense of God's character I had only two things to say. First, the attacks *were* thwarted to some degree. We know at least one of the planes did not hit its target. So, praise God, it wasn't as bad as it could have been. Second, who do you think has been covering our butts for the last two hundred or so years? It's my understanding that foreign terrorist threats were much greater in the 1970s than any other time in our history, but we didn't experience even one attack on our soil during that decade. And when you consider our nation's history with brown people the world over, that's pretty amazing. Say what you want, but God deserves some dap for that. Many people claim that our intelligence sources not having been as good as in decades past contributed to the success of the 9/11 attacks. I don't doubt that. But the best human intelligence goes only so far. We just need to come up off some praise to God for protecting our sorry behinds this far. As people in other nations can tell you, it could be much worse on the regular. So stop playin' and give God His props.

So what's the point? It's this: God meets our needs all the time, simply because He loves us. We don't deserve it. We didn't earn it. He's just that gracious. And when you consider how much we kick rocks, that's a lot of grace. In Matthew 6, Jesus doesn't chastise us for having concerns. As a matter of fact, he encourages us to bring our concerns to God directly. "Give us each day our daily bread," is what He instructs us to ask (Luke 11:3). God cares for us. He hurts when we hurt. We live under God's benevolent covering. It's for this reason in particular that we shouldn't worry. God's got our backs. All He wants is our hearts. Matthew 6:33 instructs us to rearrange our priorities. Put God's concerns first and let Him take care of yours. "What does God care about?" you may ask. I have yet to hear it better worded than in Micah 6:8, which reads, "And what does the Lord require of you? To act justly and to love mercy and to walk humbly with your God." James 1:27 goes into more detail: "Religion that God our Father accepts as pure and faultless is this: to look after orphans and widows in their distress and to keep oneself from being polluted by the world." That's pretty straight-forward. It ain't easy, but it is clear.

I'll give you an example from my own life of how God hooked me up. Sheeri and I were working on a deal between two parties. The first party offered us a legitimate finder's fee, standard in its industry, for bringing the second party to the table. Everything was straight until a third party, who worked for the first party, came to me in secret demanding a cut of my finder's fee, threatening—albeit very politely—that the deal would not go through unless I agreed. I figured that's just how it had to go. Besides, a percentage of something was better than 100 percent of nothing. Without praying about it or talking it over with my wife, I agreed. Later as we began to pray about it, we both became uncomfortable with the idea. It wasn't so much that we had to share the fee. It was the way and the reason we had to share the fee—in secret and because of someone else's greed. To say that this third party was already paid is an understatement. I know for a fact that this person was pullin' down at least seven figures annually. We decided to forgo the fee altogether. Let me tell you, it was a six-figure fee and we weren't having the best year financially. And even if we had been, I wouldn't turn my nose up at that kind of cash. At any rate, we were sure that we had made the right decision because of God's confirming peace. If you have never experienced it, I really cannot explain it to you. Suffice it to say we were cool. But before we could inform any of the parties of our decision, the deal fell apart and the person demanding the kickback got let go. We were disappointed that the deal flopped, but months later the first two parties renegotiated the terms, reached an agreement, and—get this—my fee quintupled and I didn't have to pay any kickbacks off of it. You can't tell me nothing about my Jesus. Because Sheeri and I were willing to let go of the cash (which we really could have used, y'all) in order to obey the prompting of the Holy Spirit, God hooked us up! We sought the kingdom first. God made good on His Word. You can't beat that.

I'll give you one more example before I close shop. This one involves giving. When Sheeri and I met, she was pushin' a little red Miata. It was cute but small. That was no problem, though, because it was just the two of us and I had my own ride. When things started to get tight, we let go of my car. It was inconvenient to share a ride, but not impossible, until we got pregnant.

We decided to sell Sheeri's car, which was paid for, and use the cash as a down payment on a new one. Perfectly logical. We put an ad in the paper and waited . . . and waited . . . and waited. We could not understand why we got not even one inquiry. Our ad ran out and we placed another. Still not one call. And we were asking well below blue book.

Then Sheeri came to me one day and said that in her prayer time the Holy Spirit spoke to her heart. I ain't gon' lie; sometimes I just hate to hear her say that 'cause I just know that what's going to follow is gon' press me. So she tells me that she's pretty sure that the Lord wants us to give the car away. You know I looked at her sideways, right? I think I said something like, "Are you sure, Sheeri?" Clearly she was. And peep this: She knew who we were supposed to give it to as well. I wasn't excited about it, but I did give her permission to go ahead. In my spirit, I was sure she had heard from the Lord.

So we got the person's number. Sheeri called and offered the car. The person flipped out! It turns out he had been living in Los Angeles for almost a decade and taking the bus because he couldn't afford to buy a car yet. There was screaming and shouting and all kinds of praising as homeboy made arrangements to pick up the car the following week. I was not prepared for how it made me feel. I don't think I had ever given anything at God's prompting in my life. And I had certainly never given away anything along the lines of a whole car. It felt great! I wanted to find some more stuff to give away. I can't tell you how it moved me to see the gratitude on the face of that guy who took the car. I was so grateful to God that He let me be a part of something that could so positively affect someone else. I vowed then to do it as often as He would permit me.

Okay, so there we were—carless. We were expecting a baby and living in Los Angeles, a metropolis not known for its fine public transportation. And I sho' as hell didn't want to be that dude on the bus with the stroller and the car seat. Much love to anyone who has to go that route, but I was not trying to hear that. What happened next I still have difficulty believing. Someone gave us a car. I kid you not. A friend's elderly aunt owned a classic Mercury Cougar and gave it to us. She and her husband had two cars, but used only one. They seldom went any farther than their neighborhood grocery store. And since her hip-replacement surgery, she had stopped doing much driving altogether, so she gave us a car! No hassles, no worries. I still bug out at that. Yeah, it was older, but it was clean. And older cats loved it! Every time my wife or I drove somewhere, someone—usually a man over sixty—would stop us to admire it. It was crazy! A friend pointed out that we had given away a car with two seats and got one with four. And talk about a tank! That car was made of metal, not fiberglass. I had no problem toting my little man around in that.

God had shown us yet again that if we trusted Him, took Him at His word, and obeyed Him, He would make sure that "all these things would be given" to us as well. Don't sleep on this. If He will do it for me, He will do it for you, too. Those are only two stories from my life. Between me and my friends, we got a truckload of stories like that, most of them involving tithing. In what areas do you have difficulty trusting in the promises of God? Do you even know any? In what areas of your life are you being tempted to compromise in order to advance or to meet your needs? I bet that if you went to God and asked Him to meet your needs in order to keep you unpolluted, He would answer you. If that's your situation, you really have nothing to lose. The worst He can do is nothing, which would leave you in no worse shape than you are now.

All of that's to say, once I got that God didn't want my money, but my heart, my devotion, my will, it became a small thing to give up the cash. I see that His requirements are quite reasonable. It seems like I'm giving up something, because I am! But really the resources, the cash, the people, the stuff in my life aren't mine anyway. They are His. And whatever He wants from me—my cash, my time, my effort—He's got it. I'm sold out, y'all. He's been too good for me to front. The way I feel about my God is similar to the way I feel about my wife—only more so. My wife has given me so much, so willingly, and so completely that anything that nigga want is hers. She has earned it just for stickin' by me when nobody wanted anything to do with me. And as much as I love my girl, she ain't got nothing on my Jesus. Yeah, it's like that. If you don't know that kind of devotion, ain't much else I can say, except I'm sorry for you. But if you ever figure out that you'd like to, just know He's only a short prayer away.

8

The Big Disconnect

I knew I had said something wrong because my moms, who was never without words, was silent. She was washing dishes with her back to me. Then she turned around and, after drying off her hands, answered my question. I don't remember what her face looked like as she spoke. I don't remember her exact words either. I just knew that the information she shared that day completely flipped my world.

She told me that the reason I didn't look like Stan or my brothers was because Stan was not my father. Stan was my stepfather. She went on to explain that my real father was a man named Bill Mitchell who lived in Sacramento and was a professor at the university there. I don't remember much else, because my eleven-year-old world just stopped. Suddenly so many things were clear to me. I understood why I could not relate at all to Stan at times. I understood why I was so different. This information was as freeing as it was devastating.

Later, all of the questions would come: "What's he like? Where's he from? Why did he leave? When did he leave? Why hasn't he contacted me? What does he look like? When can I meet him?"

Many of my questions would be answered, although I never have found out why my dad never tried to see me growing up.

Eventually I did meet my biological pops. We teetered on and off in our attempt at a relationship, and we have only recently begun to have a consistent relationship. By now I have forgiven him for his absence in my life, which I've come to learn wasn't entirely his fault. I have outlived my adolescent anger and my young-adult fury. I just don't expect anything from him as a father. I only know that I want my children to know him, because he's a cool and interesting person, not to mention their granddaddy. It is also important to me that they have the piece of the puzzle that I had missed. In not growing up with my father, I never met his parents or his grandparents. I decided that would end with me. So my pops and I reconnected and began again.

When I was a kid, growing up without a dad was the norm. Yeah I had a stepdad, but he left my mom while my brothers were still young. Since I had my differences with him, it really didn't bother me too much. But his leaving really devastated my brothers. If nothing else, my stepdad's leaving only made me and my brothers more like all the other kids around the way. Almost nobody we grew up with lived with their fathers. A lot of kids had never even met theirs. It was just like that. For a long time I thought it was unique to Oakland. I would find out later just how wrong I was.

At college, I discovered that many of my black peers had the same experience. Years later, in a Generation X Bible study, my wife and I connected with several black young adults who, like us, grew up without fathers in the home. We were a group of fifty or sixty black twenty-to-twenty-eight-year-olds, and most of us either didn't know our dads or didn't have relationships with them. We all wanted to know what had happened. How was it possible that an entire generation of black men just checked out? Some dads left for other women. Some left in a fury. Some just walked out the door and never came back.

As I got older and worked with more and more black men my

age, I found that most of us had the same story. It was rare to find a brother in my generation whose pops had stayed. Of the few I have met whose dads were home, only two can say that their dads were really present. That is, they did all the *Brady Bunch* stuff dads are supposed to do with their sons, like camping, hiking, attending their Little League practices, going to their football games, listening to music with them, teaching them the facts of life. The rest of us were left on our own, or, to borrow a phrase I've heard Bishop Eddie Long from Newbirth Missionary Baptist Church in Atlanta use, we were "scratch babies." We had to learn everything from scratch. We didn't have the benefit of positive male role models who would pour into us their wisdom about finances, women, politics, the arts. We pretty much had to come up with those things on our own.

One of the things that was uniquely our own was hip-hop. My generation was in grammar school and junior high when we first heard those mesmerizing beats and fluid lyrics. We embraced the sound, invented the culture, and developed it into what it is now. Of course, it is ever evolving, but its roots live in us. Like many young men my age without fathers, I lost myself in hip-hop. I found myself in hip-hop. I ate, slept, and breathed it. And the fact that men my father's age hated it made it that much sweeter to me. At last I had something that was all my own, created by men I could relate to. And in those lyrics I learned pretty much all that I wanted to know about gettin' paid, gettin' laid, and becoming a man (such as it was). I found my own gospel. I found my own code that came complete with its own community of fellow believers.

Like I said in an earlier chapter, my parents' generation hated all things hip-hop. They criticized our clothes, our hair, our morals, and our music. I can't even tell you how many times I have heard rap referred to as "nigga mess." Truthfully, the fact that "grownups" disliked it didn't bother me as much as the fact that they refused to respect it. And of course, being black, they were and continue to be very vocal about it.

Hip-hop—and rap music in particular—has many worthwhile qualities. Those of us who love it recognize it for the art form that it is. Oral tradition has always been prevalent in African culture and in the slave culture that eventually gave birth to African-Americans. That a younger generation would pick up on this historic thread and thrive from it shouldn't surprise anyone. I've heard ignorant people say that anyone can rap. BS. It takes a lot of skill and polish to become a good rap artist. And more important, you've got to have a story to tell. Sure, lots of cats rap about shallow things, like having sex all the time, making a lot of money, and doin' a lot of shootin', but even to do that requires skill. And that's one thing that the hip-hop community never lets slide. If you get dap from the rap community, you must be a'ight. Hip-hop heads can spot a fake a mile away. And once outed, the perp gets no love. Folks who appreciate the genre recognize the prowess required to excel. That's why, when critics slam it as degenerate noise, they get no ear from us. And that's not to say that hip-hop deserves no criticism— it does have its flaws. But heads won't listen to critics of it once they find out that they have no respect for the art form or its origins.

That attitude toward hip-hop's critics transfers readily to baby boomers and to their predecessors as well. Gen X's attitude toward the Old Guard is basically "F—— you, then! If you can't respect us, then bump you. We got this!" Hip-hop is so ingrained in us that it's difficult to separate us from it. So to dismiss it is to ignore us. This attitude, coupled with the sad fact that so many of hip-hop's first children—Gen Xers—grew up without fathers and have little experience relating positively to older black men, lays the groundwork for what I refer to as "the big disconnect." I lived most of my life without any real input from any older man whom I respected. Honestly, that would have never really been a problem until I got saved and started going to church. In my usual day-to-day, I didn't deal with any older cats, except maybe in traffic or at the grocery store. On my job there were a few, but they were very far removed and left the office upkeep to me and my peers. I didn't have any friends who had fathers that I could kick it with. I didn't go to any clubs where older men hung out. I didn't play any sports, like golf, where I'd run into any of them. So my life was pretty much free of the older black man. And you know what? That was cool with me. I had met only one whom I actually liked and enjoyed spending time with. He is my wife's uncle on her mother's side. He's all the things that an older man should be. Uncle Arthur is solid, easygoing, an intellectual, a gentleman, a professional, an engaging conversationalist, and a really good listener. In short, he's mad cool. After meeting him for the first time, I thought to myself, *I'm sitting at dinner with Cliff Huxtable!* He wasn't the last really cool older black man I would ever meet, but he was one of the first. And the sad part is, I didn't meet him until I was already twenty-six.

So anyway, I didn't have no love for the older black man. But like I said, that didn't matter. Even at church for the first seven or eight years I was there, I didn't really have to get to know any of them. My new-members class was taught by a young cat. My ministry of choice was Generation X. And once I began to serve, both my wife and I became active in . . . you guessed it, youth ministry. Teenage boys and young-adult males are still my favorite group to kick it with. They are hardheaded, but blunt and transparent. I appreciate that. So everything was going fine until the associate pastor at my church asked/demanded that I become a deacon. It sounded kind of stuffy to me. But I respected him, and, truth be told, I was honored. So I began the yearlong process of qualification. I didn't even know how much doo-doo I was in for. Truthfully, the process wasn't that grueling. It was kind of like pledging a frat. But the focus was more on becoming and living out servitude as Jesus did. It was humbling, but I didn't really have a problem with that either. My problems began once I passed the yearlong qualification process and became a deacon. Most of the men who went through the process—there were about twenty of us—were in our twenties and thirties. The majority of the deacons, however, were well into, if not past, their fifties. In a way I felt like I had been duped. I went through the process with men my age, but then had to integrate myself with a group of men who were old enough to be my father or grandfather. Not good.

If my group was less than excited, the older deacons weren't feeling us either. I quickly learned that there was no love lost between them and us. And that a group of them wasn't really feelin' the associate pastor who was the one who made the appointments for the group. They referred to him as a "young cat." (Mind you, he was in his late thirties and conservative by most standards.) Here we were in our cornrows, baggy jeans, Phat Farm gear, brandishing chains, pierced ears, and tatted arms and backs. Some hated us, and they showed it. With the exception of a few, none of them ever called me by my name. A lot of them behaved as though we younger dudes were there to serve them, instead of us all working together to serve the church. They resented any improvements to the ministry we suggested, balked at any ideas we submitted, and talked around us at meetings. Not one to stay where I wasn't wanted, I came very close to quitting. But for the conviction of the Holy Spirit and the support of my wife and encouragement from the associate pastor, I would have. I came to realize that, as a group, I hated older black men. I hated the way they looked at men my age with distaste and suspicion. I hated the way they referenced us—usually as thugs and punks (unless we came suited and booted). I hated the way they refused to acknowledge us as men. I hated the fact that they treated us the same way whites treated them back in the days of segregation. I thought they, of all people, should know better.

My wife witnessed my ordeal serving as a deacon and began to pray fervently for me. One night she sat me down and shared with me some insights she had. I wasn't in the mood to listen to what a jerk I was being. I didn't want to hear about what a big baby I was, but her persistance got my focus off myself. She believed that she had some understanding of why our generation experienced so much static with our parents and their kind. She reminded me of a report we had both watched on the Discovery Channel. Apparently, somewhere on a plain in Africa, there was a herd of wild adolescent bull elephants who had been put down because they were killing rhinos. The report said that the behavior was highly uncharacteristic of bull elephants, which were usually more peaceful and definitely not killers. The researchers on the project came to the conclusion that the problem with this particular herd was that all of the older males had been prematurely killed by poachers. Therefore the young male elephants had no one to teach them how to act like elephants. In lieu of role models, they had simply gone wild. My wife drew the conclusion that lots of men in my generation (at least those in our church) had grown up without the influence of a father, so like me, they had pieced together role models from different examples, real or imagined (like superheroes) and arrived at their own brand of manhood. It wasn't necessarily wrong, but it was nothing like the men our fathers predicated themselves upon, so they simply couldn't relate to us, and we couldn't relate to them.

Then she made it personal. She concluded that because of my own anger toward my absent father and my intense dislike for my stepfather, I was working at a dual disadvantage. Those older deacons at church embodied everything that I was sure represented my father and my stepfather. She concluded that I wasn't open to trusting or liking any of them in the first place, so when they began to behave their age, I could offer no grace. She ended with her usual, "That's all I have to say."

In retrospect, I understand that she was telling me in a really nice way that I was handicapped when it came to relating to older black men. I wasn't sure I fully agreed with her then; nor am I sure now. But I have gotten to a place where I've been able to forgive both my father and my stepfather. And I do have a couple of older black men in my life whom I consider friends. I've come a long way, but I do admit I'm a work in progress. My relationships with older black men don't come easily. I wonder how many other dudes out there are like me: can't relate, don't want to and don't care. Truthfully, I can't say that I don't care. I understand that I am deeply indebted to every generation that came before me. At the time of this writing, the Civil Rights Act is barely approaching sixty years old. I remember that every time I vote. My children attend a predominantly white Christian school. I think about my mother and my mother-in-law, who never attended anything but all-black institutions—and not by choice. I sometimes think about what life must have been like for those first Africans who were taken from their homeland and forced into the most brutal form of slavery the world has ever known. I think about it so often that I actually wrote a screenplay about it with my wife. Am I, as Maya Angelou boasts, their hope and their dream? Would they be proud of me? Would they be proud of men like me? Would they understand and approve of the former crack dealers–turned–rap stars–turned–business moguls, like the late Biggie Smalls, Jay-Z, or 50 Cent? Or would they view them as thugs and punks, like so many older African-Americans do today? Honestly, I don't know.

What I would most like from older black Americans, especially those who lived through Jim Crow and the civil rights movement, is for them to remember that my generation and all the ones that follow are simply exercising the freedoms for which they fought so hard. They fought against racism in America so that Sean "P. Diddy" Combs could own and operate his own record label, signing and developing the acts he likes best. They suffered beatings at the hands of white mobs so that Russell Simmons could own his own credit card company. They labored against oppression so that Jay-Z could buy the New Jersey Nets. I wish they could see that my generation embodies the freedom—economic and social freedom—that they strove so hard to secure.

We're not supposed to do our thing their way. We're supposed to do it like we do it. Our way isn't necessarily bad. In most cases it's just different. Besides, our stories are what they are because of what the generation before us either did or didn't do. Without a drug-addicted, absent father, Sean Carter would not be the man he is today. Without the mother who was shot to death in the street and who dealt drugs before him, 50 Cent's story would be very different. Our way of doing what we do, the stories that we tell, aren't necessarily new, but our response to them is uniquely our own. We embody the legacy left to us by the generations before us. So though our choices may not meet with the approval of the old guard, we didn't create ourselves in a vacuum. We draw from our experiences with or without fathers; we draw from the places in which we grew up (affluent or otherwise); we use the education we acquired (whether from the street or from university) to become the generation of forward-thinking men and women we are. In many ways we are but an extension of those who have come before us. It would be nice if older, more conservative folks would just recognize. We can't make older generations respect us, but it sure would be nice if they did.

At the same time, what I wish my generation and all those after it would acknowledge is that by virtue of the fact that they are still here, our elders deserve our respect. That doesn't mean that we have to agree with everything they say or do or how they do or say it. In the same way that we want them to respect how we do it, we gotta make the effort to understand the "why" behind their "how." We should learn from our elders, both from their failures and from their triumphs. Maybe they weren't around to set an example, but their absence can serve as a lesson to us who are now fathers ourselves: We know what not to do. Some of the best dads in my age group are the ones who were raised by their single moms. My wife maintains that most of the men she knows who were brought up as I was have no difficulty respecting women's abilities at home or in the workplace. She maintains that when you grow up watching your mother work (sometimes multiple jobs), pay bills, nurse cuts, attend football games, and drive you to school dances, all by herself, it's hard to think of women as inferior to men.

But those who have come before us can offer us sage advice,

and we can draw knowledge from the situations our fathers left us in. Those still living have wisdom unequaled by any of our peers. Sure, there are some fools among them, but if you watch long enough, you can even learn from a fool. People my age and younger need to humble ourselves, sit at the feet of our elders, and give them the courtesy of our ears. They have so much to say. And so much of it is good. Doing so will not only help us better understand them, but ourselves as well.

As difficult as the road has been, my attitude toward older black men has changed a lot. I can say without hesitation that every positive change has come as a result of embracing Christ. Naturally the church should be the one place where old and young come together in harmony to embrace Christ. That should be the case, but the biggest problem with the church is that it's full of people! And people are stubborn. The best any of us can do is to let God's Word truly penetrate our hearts until it affects the way we think and then the way we act. That takes time. Still, I am hopeful because I am not the same man I was ten or even five years ago. And I know that as long as I stay in God's Word, I'll only continue to improve.

Much of my deliverance came when I realized that as jacked-up as my dad's absence was and as mean as I found my stepfather to be, none of it could have happened without God's permission. I learned that not one thing happens in this entire universe and beyond that God does not control. Although He does not enjoy letting "bad" things happen to us, He allows them. And here's the hard part: They are always ultimately good (Romans 8:28). I know that sounds like BS, but it's true. Anything bad that has ever happened to you or me is for our good. How we respond to it is the key. God wants us to come to Him in all situations. Nothing is too small. Nothing is too big. He cares deeply about everything. That doesn't mean that when disaster strikes He expects us to jump for joy and remain unaffected. But He does want to get us to a point where we know enough about Him to trust that whatever He's letting happen is a good thing, even if we can't possibly see how that's true.

The best example I have from my own life was the time I had to take my then-three-year-old son for his immunization shots. When he was an infant it was no big deal, because before he understood what was happening, the doctor had stuck him and we were out. But by three he had developed a healthy fear of needles and people in white coats. This time, when he realized what was happening, he ran into my arms. I embraced him. Then I held him fast while the nurse stuck him. The look of confusion and pain in his eyes nearly made me cry. He was sure I had betrayed him. He had run to me for protection, and I had not just allowed the nurse to hurt him, but I held him down while she did it. I knew he was mad at me, because it took him a while after we got home before he would hug me. He let my wife hug him and pick him up, but not me. The worst part was that I had no way to explain to him that I did what I did because I love him. I knew that the pinprick of an inoculation was nothing compared to contracting smallpox (or whatever he got vaccinated against that day). I couldn't make him understand. So I just had to let him be mad at me in his three-year-old way until it passed. We're the same way with God. Like children, when bad things happen we whine, "Why me?" "What did I do to deserve this?" or in my case, "Why did he have to be my jackleg daddy?" "It's not fair!" we cry. "I deserve better than this!" we complain. Like a loving parent, when we're hurt, confused, angry, disappointed, weary, exasperated, God wants nothing more than for us to come to Him with our problems. He invites us time and time again in Scripture to pour out our hearts to Him. If we take every injury to Him, not only does He promise to do something about it, He promises to do what's best for us. He delivers rest, comfort, peace, and joy . . . sometimes in the least expected ways. Unlike me in my situation with my son, God has no trouble showing us the purpose behind His actions (or seeming nonactions). He will help us to understand inasmuch as it's possible for us to do so, if we go to Him. If we ask, He even promises to tell us how to proceed (James 1:5)!

I know a Bible-study leader who maintains that all the answers to every question we have can be found in God's character. In the same way I know my wife well enough to know if what someone says about her is true or not, I know enough about God to know that whatever the circumstances look like, He's going to be true to His nature. If a man came to me and said, "Your wife was trying to holla at me," I'd know from jump that was a lie or ol' boy was drunk, because my wife (don't take this wrong, honey) is not a "friendly" person—especially where men are concerned. She refers to her disposition as politely distant. I would say that where men are concerned, she borders on unapproachable. That's just how she is. That's how she's been since the day we started dating exclusively. And she has only grown less approachable in the years since we've been married.

In the same way, when disaster strikes and I'm tempted to think that God must not love me, or that He is just incapable of changing my situation, I purposely recall His past behavior in seemingly dim situations. I remember how He has never failed me, even when I had given up on Him. I read His word and reiterate His promises until I am convinced that He's working out His good plans for me. I talk with other believers who have weathered storms, some of them with me. And in recalling what He has done for me in the past, the promises He has made in His Word, and the revelation of His character both in the Bible and in the person of Jesus Christ, I basically stop trippin'.

But don't think I came out of the box like that. It took some time and really crazy situations to get my attention. But once I understood that God caused all things to work together for my good, it wasn't long before I had to address the issue of my pops. Why would God give me a dad who bailed? Why would He give me a stepfather I couldn't understand? Why would I live in such a grimy town, under such poor circumstances that hustling would prove to be the best available option? I went to God with my questions, and I stayed in my Word and in His face until I was satisfied. Let me say on the front end, I didn't get no big voice like Moses did. I got no literal flashing signs coming down from heaven with explanations. No angelic hosts delivered me any messages etched in stone. I didn't get any of that. What I did get was the counsel of wise older men who showed me based on Scripture what grand, amazing plans God had for me (Jeremiah 28:11). Those who came before me may not have known or cared what God had to say, but that was on them. What would become of me was entirely dependent upon my response to the Lord. I won't bore you with the details, the revelations, the insights the Holy Spirit hipped me to. But suffice to say that by the end, I understood that I needed just as much mercy as anybody for the crap I had done and would do in the future.

In recognizing my own need for mercy and forgiveness and the fact that God freely gave it, I realized I wasn't in a position to withhold it from anyone else, no matter what the transgression. That was the first part. The second part came a li'l bit later and is still coming. On this side of thirty-five, I now understand how God has used every single adversity I have ever experienced to shape me into the man I am today. Many of them I wouldn't have chosen for myself. But on this side, I'm glad I went through them. And the best part is, I was never alone. Looking back at some really dangerous, potentially life-threatening situations, I see how He protected me from stuff I didn't even know I needed protecting from at the time. I know now He spared me for a reason and has used every disadvantage to my advantage. He's so bomb, He even used the stupid stuff I inflicted upon myself to make me a better man. Part of the reason I appreciate my wife so much is because of all the to'-up females I used in my past. I wouldn't recommend that method in order to find your wife, but that's where I was, so that's what He used. My penchant for hustling in illegal realms has translated into an incredible head for business and a sound business ethic in legitimate circles. Those are just two examples. Trust me; my life is full of them. But all that to say, God knew. Just as the Psalmist proclaims in Psalm 139, before one day of my life was lived, it was already written down in God's book. That's true of the good times as well as of the bad. He's got me and He's got you, too.

So how does this relate to the big disconnect? Well, my generation and the ones before may never see eye-to-eye. What's done is done. My dad will never be able to go back to my childhood years and be a parent to me. I'm not thrilled about it, but I can live with it. What I can do is to make sure that the curse of absent fathers ends with me. God willing, none of my children will never ever know what life is like without their "papi" actively involved in their lives on the most personal and intimate level. On a larger scale, I refuse to dismiss manhood because it doesn't come in the form I've become accustomed to. I am determined never to put down the products of a generation or culture purely on the basis of personal taste. I reserve the right to fail to agree, to object on biblical merit, and to simply dislike, but I will always seek to understand and to connect first. Unlike many of the men of the generations before me, before making "withdrawals" of criticism and scorn, I will invest time, patience, and energy—so that never will there be another herd of wild bull elephants destroying the countryside. Not on my watch, anyway.

9

Just Another Trap

I'll admit that when I first heard the news about the murder of Matthew Shepherd, I didn't pay much attention. After growing up in Oakland and then living for a time in south central Los Angeles and the projects in Pittsburgh, Pennsylvania, I'm sad to say that news of murder doesn't shock me anymore. It bothers me; it saddens me; but it never shocks me. After all, I am convinced that human nature is evil at its core. I believe that if people could do better then we would have done so by now. As advanced as we are technologically, we are still enslaved by our nature. That's why crime, racism, abuse, rape, greed, hate, extreme poverty, extreme cruelty, and every possible addiction thrive among us. When the evil that is in us finds its way to the surface, I am seldom surprised.

I had learned from some friends that Matthew Shepherd was gay, but what I learned from subsequent news reports and articles was that he had been murdered *because* he was gay. That changed things. Murder all by itself is crazy enough, but this man had been singled out because his attackers didn't like his sexual orientation. Again, I wasn't shocked. It was just sad. I grieved for Matthew Shepherd, who would never grow old, have his own family, start a career, or see another sunrise. I grieved for his mom. As a new parent myself at the time, I couldn't even wrap my mind around ever having to bury my son. A parent should never have to bury a child. That just ain't right. I grieved also for the young men who committed the crime, so sure they were right that they never showed any remorse. I felt sorry for young men whose hearts were so hard that it seemed they couldn't acknowledge the extent of the damage they had done. From the news reports I saw on TV, it seemed like they had no remorse at all.

Then a few days later I saw the footage of the protests outside of the funeral home where Matthew Shepherd was being waked. I had been doing something in the house that day when my wife called me to the television. I ran to see what was up, but all she could do was to point to the television screen. We both bugged out as "Christians" who had assembled across the street from the funeral home chanted hate slogans and carried signs that read, MATTHEW IS IN HELL, and GOD HATES FAGS. "Can you believe this, Mykel? He's dead! What the hell more do they want?" Sheeri screamed before tears exploded down her cheeks. She wondered aloud how they could protest in the name of Jesus. I, too, wondered how God could possibly get any glory from their activity that day. I wondered just how those people thought they were advancing the gospel of Jesus Christ. Of course, I knew the answer: They weren't. But it worried me that non-Christians would see the footage and think that those people represented us all. The last thing I remember my wife saying through her sobs was, " 'Fags.' God doesn't even use that word."

The first time I had heard her make that statement was on a date long before we were married. Somehow our conversation had drifted onto the topic of a gay man that I knew. She asked me how I felt about homosexuals in general. It seemed an innocent enough question. I told her that I was pretty sure I had a cousin who was gay, but I didn't associate with him much. I told her that for the most part I just didn't get it. I could not understand how a man could look at another man and get sexually aroused. I explained that I just couldn't relate. At some point in the discussion, however, I made the mistake of referring to gays as fags. Sheeri cut me off quick. She blasted me for being an ignorant hypocrite, reminding me that if I trip when white people call us niggers, then I shouldn't call gays fags. She went on to say that God doesn't use that word and a bunch of other stuff that I don't remember too well, because my thoughts had drifted into "I don't hear you" mode. I'll be honest; Sheeri is kinda sexy to me when she's pissed off, and I got distracted with my own thoughts. Besides, I really didn't give a flip about gay people or their problems.

But God would change that. Within the course of a year, He would bring three men into my life who would become my very good friends. At one point or another, they all pulled me aside to share that they had been engaged in the homosexual lifestyle and were in the stages of overcoming it. Their confessions messed me up on so many levels. Each shattered any unfounded prejudices I may have harbored against gays. One guy is such a dude's dude. He's not hard like a thug, but he ain't nobody to mess with either. In addition, he's always been a favorite of the females. Women love his model good looks, his attentiveness, and his humble confidence. He just didn't fit the profile of the type of guy I thought would have been with another man. All three of these men went on to successfully abandon not only the gay lifestyle, but also the gay mind-set as well, which, given the enormity of their struggle, is a testament only to the power of the Holy Spirit. One of them, whom I can name, Kevin Giles, went on to write and self-publish a book about his experience called *Gay but Not Happy*. Kevin has always been painfully candid with me about his struggle to overcome what he and many Christians refer to as the "spirit" of homosexuality and about the rejection he experienced in the church while doing so. He and my two other friends helped me to understand something about homosexuality that I had not before: It's just one more trap of the enemy—no worse and no better than any other.

For those of you who seek to justify homosexuality or the gay and lesbian lifestyle, you gets no help over here. You have no ally in Mykel Mitchell. I fully accept the Bible's condemnation of homosexual activity. Scripture abounds with examples of God's rejection of the gay lifestyle. Given that I willfully accept the Holy Bible as the final authority in my life, I agree 100 percent with its assessment of all sin. In the book of Romans, the apostle Paul explains that both lesbianism and homosexuality are shameful desires.

> Even their women exchanged natural relations for unnatural ones. In the same way the men also abandoned natural relations with women and were inflamed with lust for one another. Men committed indecent acts with other men, and received in themselves the due penalty for their perversion (Romans 1:26–27).

Paul writes that once God abandoned these people, their lives then became full of every kind of wickedness. His list includes: "greed . . . depravity . . . envy, murder, strife, deceit, and malice" (Romans 1:29). He goes on to characterize these people as backstabbers, haters of God, insolent, proud, boastful, inventing new ways of sinning, disobedient to parents, refusing to understand, breaking their promises, heartless, and unforgiving. These people know how God feels about their behavior, but they don't care. In fact, they encourage others to follow suit (Romans 1:30–32). These and other passages very clearly present the biblical view of homosexuality. Having said that, here's the part that I feel many Christians overlook: Contrary to what those nuts at Matthew Shepherd's funeral proclaimed, God does not hate homosexuals. Nor does He condone the murdering of gays or hatred against them. And anybody who says differently is not a follower of Jesus Christ (1 John 4:19–21).

What God hates is sin. All sin. I have searched and searched, and nowhere in the Bible have I found that some sins are more acceptable to God than others. God hates all sin, but He never hates the sinner. Over and over the Bible shows God to be a holy God.

He is free from all contamination. There is no shadow in Him. There is no deception or filth. Sin cannot exist in his presence. He despises sin. However, the book of John also reveals that God is love. He is the very essence or personification of love. God loves perfectly everything He created. In the words of my six-year-old son, "He created everything and everybody." So for God to hate His own creatures, His own creation—even though they sin—is inconsistent with His very nature. So one more time: God does not hate sinners. God hates sin. All sin. All sin stands in the way of our relationship to God. All sin keeps us from living out the lives for which God created us. All sin prevents us from becoming the people God intended for us to be.

The apostle Paul, in his letter to the Church of Corinth, includes what I like to call the sin roll call. "Don't you know that those who do wrong will have no share in the Kingdom of God? Don't fool yourselves. Those who indulge in sexual sin, who are idol worshipers, adulterers, male prostitutes, homosexuals, thieves, greedy people, drunkards, abusers, and swindlers—none of these will have a share in the Kingdom of God" (1 Corinthians 6:9–10 New Living Translation). It's important to see that Paul not only condemns homosexual sex, but all sexual sin, along with other sins that many people who are not homosexuals commit all the time. He gives all of the listed sins the same weight. No one is any more or less offensive to God than the others. All disqualify those who indulge in them entrance into God's kingdom.

My personal problem with the Church at large is that it tends to treat homosexuality as some unforgivable sin, but winks at many of the others Paul mentions and that are detailed throughout the Bible. I wish that all Christians found their own sins as disgusting or repulsive as they find homosexual behavior.

I have been working on my relationship with Jesus Christ for a little over a decade now. What always gets me is how Christians often misrepresent Jesus to the world and to each other. It is true that Jesus will come back again to judge the living and the dead, but we who are alive now have ample opportunity to know Him as our loving servant-Messiah, who willingly gave up His life so that we could experience all that this life and the next has to offer. Yes, God does have standards. Any relationship does. Healthy people look for relationships where respect, honesty, and loyalty are reciprocated. Well, God's got at least as much sense as you do. He says, "If you want to get with Me, then I need you to at least attempt to live by My principles." He wants us to talk to Him (prayer). He wants us to listen to Him (reading the Bible). He wants us to encourage and walk with each other (fellowship). It really isn't all that complicated. He loves us, knows absolutely what's best for us, and wants us to experience it.

In the same way He desires to heal a burn victim, a man who is addicted to pornography, a woman who can't control her impulse to steal, God desires to heal the man or woman engaged in the gay or lesbian lifestyle. It's too bad that Christians seldom present this side of Jesus to the world. I apologize particularly to any gay man or lesbian who has met condemnation where there should have been grace, or who has encountered hatred where there should have been love. My hope is that you will give Christ the opportunity to show His love for you individually and that you will respond to this invitation to live a new and improved life.

So what relationship, if any, does this have to hip-hop? It has been my experience that hip-hop, being dominated by and having grown out of African-American culture, has a similar view of homosexuality as that of the black Church. Hip-hop is slightly more progressive in that gays and lesbians who are authentic to the culture meet with slightly less antagonism than they do in the Church, but the underlying sentiment in many ways is the same. Gays and lesbians are not embraced or necessarily welcomed as part of the community. I find this interesting, however, because hip-hop so readily flaunts every other vice. A man who sleeps with multitudes of women is championed. People who flaunt their wealth through excess are applauded. Women who bare and grind their bodies are desired (if not necessarily respected). Gangstas who boast about murdering achieve icon status. Folks who get high draw sly smiles and even a few laughs. But gays and lesbians are often alienated, discriminated against, and even targeted for violence. Lesbianism is more fashionable, for lack of a better word, but only in as much as heterosexual men find it arousing. But on the whole, hip-hop and the Church seem to share the view that homosexuality is unacceptable, while seeming to tolerate every other sin.

If the Church and the hip-hop community are barely tolerant of gays and lesbians, then you know they outwardly reject the cross-gendered. The term *unnatural* never seems to get tossed around more than in reference to those who cross-dress or who have changed or are attempting to change genders. Now, talk about sticky territory. To my knowledge I have never met anyone who cross-dresses or who believes (s)he was born the wrong sex. I have no clinical or academic background in dealing with such individuals. I just know a li'l scripture. I know that God never makes mistakes. God creates people to be either male or female. I have heard of cases where people were born with both sets of genitalia, and in rare cases with both male and female chromosomes. In the case of the former, sometimes the person's genitals were altered in opposition to their chromosomes. Meaning sometimes the penis was removed despite the fact that the baby's chromosomes were XY, or the vaginal opening closed when the chromosomal signature was XX. I have nothing but compassion for any person who has experienced this. People who fall into the abovementioned categories are the *only* people who have legitimate grounds for gender confusion. Notice that I said gender confusion, not a choice in sexual orientation. Once gender is determined, the sexual orientation is to be heterosexual. The Bible offers no alternative. If you are a person who has been unable to determine his/her gender, I humbly submit that no one can truly help you but God almighty. He created you. He knows who He created you to be. Seek Him diligently in this area of your life until you have His peace. Settle for nothing less. Ask Him to lead you to people with experience and knowledge in this area, who embrace His standard, not the world's. Pursue Him until you get an answer to this very important question. Then depend on the Holy Spirit not only to embrace the answer He gives you, but also to live accordingly.

Just as I know that God never makes mistakes, I also know that the mission of our adversary is to kill us. Barring that, he seeks to confuse us in every area of our lives. He desires to twist the truth so that we cannot get to it or even recognize it when we see it. Confusion at such a basic level as sexual orientation in a person's life has the potential to cripple if not to destroy him or her.

God does not create us gay, transgendered, or in the wrong bodies. The Word does say that we can be born with inherent weaknesses, which the Bible calls iniquities. We are born into sin, but we are never born in error or by mistake. God has a perfect plan and mission for every single soul on this planet. He does not seek to frustrate His own efforts. For the man or woman who faces gender confusion, who questions his or her sexual orientation, the only definitive answer can be found in Christ. Just like you would go to the owner's manual if you were experiencing difficulties with your car, you should go to God if you are experiencing difficulties in your life. You may not enjoy what you hear, but it will be the Truth. And it will be real.

Most of the gay men I know tell me that they knew they were gay early on in life, many from the age of five or six. I have heard the same is true of the cross-gendered. I never argue this point because each person's experience is his or her own. However, I would challenge that recognizing that something about you is different is not confirmation that that difference is from God. We all are born with weak areas in our lives. Science is only just now catching up to confirm that sometimes people can be genetically predisposed to steal, to drink excessively, and to overeat. I know that there is re-search going on that seeks to confirm that homosexuality is also rooted in genetics. It wouldn't surprise me to find out that a person could be genetically predisposed to be gay. That would only line up with God's Word that we are all born in sin.

My problem with the argument that presupposes gay genes is that people use the predisposition as a validation of the gay/lesbian lifestyle. It's not okay to commit crimes, it's not okay to drink to excess, and it's not okay to be gay—no matter what genes you have. Remember my standard is God's Word, which says all of those things are sin. And just so you don't think I'm biased, het-erosexuals don't get off scot-free. God created people to be hetero-sexual, but simply because we feel like having sex doesn't mean we have the Lord's permission. He set guidelines for this too. No sex apart from marriage!

The point is, our feelings do not dictate what's right. The Bible is really clear on the subject. "There is a way that seems right to a man, but in the end it leads to death" (Proverbs 14:12). Time and time again I have heard homosexuals and the transgendered cite their feelings as grounds for their choices. But feelings are fallen. Anybody who has ever taken high school psychology knows that emotions are the most primitive part of the human animal and often the least developed part of any personality. Feelings can fool you. They are useful, but ultimately they are to be dominated by our wills. Sometimes late at night, my feelings often urge me to in-dulge in a box of hot Krispy Kremes and milk. But that's a bad idea for so many reasons. First off, doughnuts at a late hour work in op-position to the body I spend time tryin' to tone. Second, I'm se-verely lactose intolerant. But there are nights when I am certain that because my desires are so strong (they be callin' me, man), al-most to the point of being overwhelming, they must be right. Ex-cept they're not. They're just real strong. There are men who earnestly feel as though they should beat their wives and girlfriends, but their feelings are wrong. Prisons are full of people who felt like committing murder. They were wrong to follow their feelings. I hear that doing heroin makes you feel great, but at what cost?

You may be in the same place with your desires. You may strongly desire to have sex with people of the same gender. You may strongly desire to change your gender because you are certain that you were born the wrong sex. I don't discount your desires, nor do I discount how early you first became aware of them. I am simply saying that just because they are strong doesn't mean they are right. It's very possible that you are deceived. In fact, I'd count on it.

God is consistent. He never gives us desires only to mock them. He would never make you a man when He really meant for you to be a woman and then condemn you for your desire to become a woman. He isn't sadistic like that. He places His desires in us so that He can fulfill them (Psalm 37:4). He fills us up with good things (Psalms 103:5) so that we can experience the abundant life He promises through Christ. But He won't do it if you don't ask. He stands at the door knocking, but He will never force His way in. He waits for your invite. So know that if your desires (whatever they may be) contradict God's character, then they don't come from Him. Let me rephrase that: *If your desires do not line up with God's character or His Word, then they don't come from Him.*

If you experience confusion anywhere on any level in your life, go to Him directly. Ask Him to send you folks who will be sensitive to your situation or struggle, not gawkers who will ostracize you or gossip about you. It may take a while, but be encouraged and don't give up. He is intimately acquainted with every detail of your life and waits for you to call on Him. Even if it doesn't feel like He's with you, doesn't see you, or can't hear you, He is, does, and can. The Bible promises that if you ask, seek, knock, God stands ready to answer, be found, open the door. If you draw close to Him, He will come close to you. This is good news for those of us who feel that we are all alone with any of our issues. The Word says that Jesus was tempted *in every way* when He walked among us on earth (Hebrews 4:15). So even if no other human being alive right now can identify with your struggle, He can. Will you go to Him? Will you go to Him on behalf of that person in your life who won't or can't?

If you are someone who is engaged in homosexuality or lesbianism, know that God does not hate you. He hates what you do, no doubt, the same way He hates thievery or prostitution, but loves the thief and the prostitute. He loves you. If you could guess how much, you would be embarrassed for Him. He knows you intimately, better than you know yourself. He knows what paths led you to be where you are right now and He understands. More important, He has provided for you a way out of that lifestyle if you'll take hold of it (1 Corinthians 10:13). If you are happy where you are and don't care about what God thinks or what the Bible says about how to live your life, then there's nothing I can say to you. But if you do care about the eternal consequences of homosexuality, or are concerned about someone who is engaged in that sin, then know that homosexuality is no different to God than heterosexual sex outside of marriage. God does not differentiate between greed, hate, gossip, scheming, swindling, lying, or any other sin you can come up with. We're all in the same boat. We have all sinned and fall short of God's glory (Romans 3:23). So we all need Jesus. If you reach out to Christ, He will equip you to fight the battle against the sin that hinders you—whatever that sin is. And the best part is that you don't have to lie to kick it with God. He already knows your heart and your struggles anyway. And remember He is love (1 John 4:8). His love for you is better than anything you have yet to experience. Come to Him; He won't reject you. He will embrace you and love you "as is." He will love you into a better version of yourself, if you will trust Him enough to give Him a shot.

10

The Problem
of Forgiveness

Yo . . . It's some white boys tryin' to rap!" my next-door neighbor yelled on the way out the house one Saturday morning.
My first response showed my disbelief and disgust. "Damn!
They can't let a nigga have nothin'!" As far as I was concerned it
was Elvis all over again. It seemed like every time black folks came
up with something new and original musically or culturally, some
white dudes always had to come along and copy it. And what's
worse is that the white imitators always make more money than the
black originals—and with less talent! America seemed to love the
white copycats, but left the black artists filing for bankruptcy. I was
pissed, and so was every other head I knew. But that was how I first
heard about the Beastie Boys.

Needless to say, I had to hear for myself just how wack they
were, so I caught the number 40 bus over to Leapold's in Berkeley
to listen. As I stood there judgmental as hell, willing myself to hate
the white rappers from the East Coast, one of the first beats I heard
was "No Sleep till Brooklyn." It started and I was really pissed.
They even had phat beats. But I just knew their lyrics would be
booty. So I waited. And waited. And waited to hear something that

I hated. I listened to the next track and the next. And to my shock, it was kinda hot! I can't front; it was different but good!

But what did this mean? Had white boys figured out how to rap and now would be taking over hip-hop? Over and over my friends and I debated the pros and cons of hip-hop going mainstream. Up until this point, much like R & B, it had been for us and by us . . . no imitators, no infringers, no fakes. And if the truth be known, even after the Beastie Boys, it didn't change much—despite the rise and fall of the likes of Vanilla Ice and Marky Mark and the Funky Bunch. Like myself, most of the hip-hop community embraced the Beastie Boys for their talent, their message, and, above all, for their authenticity. In the end, what won me over was the fact that they weren't white guys trying to act black. They were white guys who loved hip-hop and could rhyme. They seemed to eat, sleep, and breathe hip-hop. And they had a respect for the genre that manifested itself in honoring the source—black urban America. They weren't some ignorant suburban kids just trying to make a quick buck. They were and remain true hip-hop heads who just love the music. White or black, you can't be mad at that.

And so it was that hip-hop brought me my first brush with multiculturalism. Because of the Beastie Boys and their music, I actually saw white people in a new light. There were some I could relate to. There were some who shared my interests. I didn't know it at the time, but in a way I had hope for this world for the first time.

I was old enough to have studied the civil rights movement of the sixties and smart enough to realize that it hadn't worked, at least not in my neighborhood. From where I stood black people were still broke and white people were still rich. We were confined to the ghetto, but they had the run of the whole world. They could do pretty much whatever they wanted, but we were always getting harassed by the po-pos. Discovering hip-hop's appeal to nonblacks gave me something in common with people who were aliens in my world. It made them human.

I had grown up in a home that had some pretty bigoted views

about the world—especially where whites were concerned. Whites were the enemy. They were the oppressors of blacks. They were devils, liars, and corruptors. They were two-faced. They pretended that the United States was a democracy, that we were all equal, but chafed if we moved into their neighborhoods, got into college ahead of their children, or earned promotions they coveted. It was said of the northern United States that blacks were permitted to move up, but not near. Of the South, it was said blacks could move near, but not up. I was taught to neither trust whites nor fraternize with them. The thing is, most of these views were shared by all the black folks I knew, so I never really thought that anything was wrong with them until I examined them in the light of the Bible. Since my community was primarily black, I didn't really interact with people of other races, so there was never any evidence to prove our prejudices incorrect. For the most part, white people were viewed with suspicion. White friends—who were few and far between—were to be heavily scrutinized. And under no circumstances was I to ever bring home a white girl. It would almost have been better to bring home a boyfriend, given my family's bent on the matter.

My limited experience in church was no better. Whenever I did go, which was rare as a teenager and rarer as a young adult, the institution was all black. And despite the proclamation that we were all one in the body of Christ, all I ever saw of the body was the black part. So without really being aware of it, I figured that this "oneness" was either only applicable by race and/or was a total lie. Not to mention that a lot of the black Christians I knew personally were some of the most prejudiced people walking. Many of them had been survivors of the segregated South, had lived through the civil rights movement, but had seen little change in their daily lives. And so they continued to protect themselves as a lot of blacks did and continue to do—by keeping to themselves and talking bad about whites. And since no white people were making overtures of friendship toward them, their views were seldom challenged. I have a couple of uncles who married Jewish women, but they were certainly the exception in our world, and not even close to the rule.

What I didn't see in my community or in the church, however, I did see in my music. Early on I noticed that hip-hop didn't just attract black kids. Whites, Asians, Latinos—everybody was listening. Realizing this forced me to accept that hip-hop didn't belong exclusively to me. It was bittersweet. On one hand I thought the commonality was cool. On the other, I feared that hip-hop would lose its uniqueness—that it would become watered-down and eventually die out. That hasn't happened, in part because the hip-hop community is very true to itself. For the most part, if an artist is good, then he sells. If he's wack, then he falls off. The fact that true hip-hop heads cross all ethnic, racial, and cultural barriers and both genders astounds me. It would seem that hip-hop managed to do in one generation what Christianity has been trying to accomplish for centuries.

We remain a nation divided among color lines—particularly along black and white. Four hundred years after slavery and nearly half a century after the civil rights movement, we still can't pull it together. Racism takes many overt forms. There's the Klan and their splinter groups, who preach hatred and violence against all nonwhites. There's racial profiling and white flight. There's the fact that blacks statistically make less money than their white counterparts for the same work in the same positions, and receive more severe sentences for the same crimes committed by whites. Racism takes subtler forms as well. The fact that black babies have a higher mortality rate than white ones. That public schools in black neighborhoods are inferior in almost every way to their counterparts in white neighborhoods. The fact that property values in black neighborhoods are statistically lower than those in white neighborhoods. And that few churches can boast of a racially mixed congregation.

It's really too bad. And I know racism in any form breaks God's heart, because He is a God of reconciliation, not division. He has purposed for His people to come together in His name and to carry out His work in the world. Only we can't do that because we're sick with sin that we refuse to acknowledge. The Church should be leading the way in racial reconciliation, showing the world the truth of the hymn, "They'll Know We Are Christians by Our Love." Instead we are the best examples of racial segregation in America.

My family and I now attend a predominantly black church. I say *predominantly* because presently there is one white member. Our pastor, Reverend Jody Moore, desires for his congregation the same end that his father-in-law, Bishop Kenneth Ulmer, desires for his flock—that it would reflect the ethnic and racial diversity of the very first Church at Pentecost (Acts 2). That's gon' take some doing. I've listened to the people at our church and at Faithful Central. Not to mention I attended Grace Bible Church, which is nearly all white, for two years in between. Based on my limited observations and interactions, I've concluded that people don't have to *be* bigots in order to act like bigots. That is to say that people can hold inaccurate and outright wrong views of one another without harboring any evil intentions toward one another. If this is true of individuals, it's certainly true of races.

As close as I am to my wife, there are times when I misunderstand her. Usually we straighten out our differences quickly, but only after a bad attitude or some poorly spoken words reveal that a problem exists. If no one speaks on it, the problem can grow real big, real fast. Most of the time when we examine the cause of an argument, we find that it's rooted in a misunderstanding. The quicker we address the misunderstanding, the quicker we get back on track. I often compare our relationship with each other to a high-speed train, whose end destination represents our joint purpose in life. When we squabble, the train slows down. When we fight it stops. Derailments represent periods of time when we've stubbornly refused to apologize, forgive, and reconcile. I'm thankful those are few and far between. When they do occur, however, we usually do our best to make them as short as possible so that we can realign the cars, get back on track, and resume our course.

If race relations in America were a train, not only would it be derailed, but there would be cars, parts, and people sprawled and rotting all over the countryside. We're in a mess of trouble, with no hope of getting back on track if we keep up our current attitudes and practices. America will never approach its full potential unless we address the need for racial reconciliation.

I am convinced that God would do more with us as a nation if we were truly united. We'd have fewer domestic problems, we would be much more effective in the world, if right here at home we followed the two great commandments: to love God with all we possess and to love our neighbors as ourselves. If our nation is ever to heal from its painful past, the Church in America will have to lead the way. All over the country there are churches that are developing racial reconciliation ministries, whereby they are attempting to bridge the gap between all races, but particularly between blacks and whites. I pray they succeed.

I believe that God seeks to reunite His Church so that the work of racial reconciliation in America among other things will become possible. If we want to join Him in this work, then we must do our part. In order for black people and white people to come together on a large scale to worship and to serve as one, we'll all have to admit guilt, repent of sin, and seek forgiveness from God and from one another. That's a tall order—forgive.

Let's start with the greatest offense, slavery. You can't talk about black-white relations in America without first addressing the problem of slavery. We can all agree these days that the slavery practiced in the antebellum South was a detestable evil. I have heard people say that the Bible doesn't express an opinion either way. I disagree. Apart from the "love your neighbor as yourself" admonition directly from Christ, of which slavery and many other current practices are clearly violations, the Bible does speak directly to the issue of slavery.

For the most part, the slavery practiced in biblical times wasn't as brutal as the various forms practiced in the eighteenth and nineteenth centuries. It usually came about as a last resort for repaying debt. The way it worked was something like this: You borrow a ton of cash from me, but when it's time to pay up, you don't have the cash. So we work something out. If you don't have anything that I can exchange for cash, like livestock or property, then I take you or a family member to be my slave to work off the debt. Once the debt is worked off, the person is free to go. It sounds straightforward enough. But human nature being what it is, you know there were abuses, right? Of course there were. No need to go into that here. The point is that this type of slavery is obligatory, but is understood as part of an agreement from jump. In a sense it is volitional, though not necessarily welcome. At some point, two parties entered into an agreement with each other. The Bible reports it, but doesn't necessarily support the practice. God's goal is for all people to be free in Him.

Some folks get stuck on Paul's letter to Philemon and on the passage in Romans where he encourages both Philemon and the readers of Romans to be the best slaves they can be. What Paul is saying in both documents is simply that in whatever station in life you find yourself, behave in a manner that glorifies the name of Christ. Work as though God is your boss, not man. In his letter to Philemon, Paul also commands the slave owner to forgive the slave and to treat him as a brother in the Lord.

The form of slavery to which Africans were subjected was nothing like the kind to which Paul refers. My ancestors were abducted, mutilated, brutalized often to the point of death, and stripped of all human rights and dignity. By law, we weren't even people. I believe the book of Amos addresses the abuses of slavery to which black Africans were subjected. In Amos, God pronounces His judgment upon Israel and surrounding nations for their detestable practices. He promises all kinds of horrors will befall every nation named. For two of the nations, Gaza and Tyre, the Lord pronounces death and utter destruction. "Because she [Gaza] took captive whole communities and sold them to Edom [a neighboring country], I will send fire upon the walls of Gaza that will consume her fortresses" (Amos 1:6–7). "Because she [Tyre] sold whole communities of captives to Edom . . . I will send fire upon the walls of Tyre that will consume her fortresses" (Amos 1:9–10). From these verses in or out of context, it's clear to me that God does not approve of the capturing and selling of human beings.

Okay, slavery was a to'-up practice. It remains a huge, nasty stain on America's history. Its effects are so far-reaching we may never know the full extent of the damage. For that reason alone, we must all repent.

Already I can hear the protests from both parties. From whites I have heard the complaint that they are not guilty of crimes committed by their forefathers against African slaves. Blacks would argue that although no white person alive today actually owned slaves or perpetrated the sin of slave trading, whites continue to benefit from slavery and its lasting effects on American culture, while blacks still labor under the negative effects. Moreover, many black people I know just want heartfelt acknowledgment from whites that slavery was wrong, evil, and never should have happened. The kind of apology they rightfully expect should be in the same spirit as the condolences offered to a friend who loses a loved one. You may not be responsible for the loss, but you acknowledge that it was a terrible thing and offer both your sympathies and assistance in recovery.

For white Christians, however, the "I didn't do it and therefore have no reason to accept responsibility" argument is busted at best. Scripture is full of examples of the innocent repenting on behalf of the guilty, Jesus being the ultimate example. "Father, forgive them, for they do not know what they are doing" (Luke 23:34). He spoke these words while on the cross. The people He interceded for were the very ones who wanted Him dead. If ever there was an innocent, pleading on behalf of the wicked . . . In the books of Ezra and Nehemiah, both men go before the Lord to apologize on behalf of Israel for various atrocities committed against Him. When Ezra arrives to visit the Israelites who have returned from Babylonian captivity, he finds that they have intermarried with the pagan women of the land. This is an offense not because of racial differences, but because of the contaminated religious practices of the pagan people surrounding Israel. From what I understand, God did not want the bloodline from which the Messiah would come to be defiled by intermarriage with nonbelievers because Israel's worship of and relationship with Him would then be compromised. He also didn't want the Israelites to be absorbed into other cultures and die out altogether. At any rate, when Ezra heard about the intermarriage, Ezra 9:3 states that he tore his shirt and coat, pulled out hair from his beard and head, and "sat down appalled" until the evening sacrifice. I think it's safe to say he was pissed and probably disappointed. Ezra later prays to God on behalf of the exiles. In verses 6 through 15 he confesses Israel's sins as though they are his own, including himself among the *we* and *us* in the prayer. His prayer is very moving and a great example of group confession before God. The incredible thing about Ezra's prayer is that he included himself among Israel's rank even though he wasn't even a participant. As a matter of fact, he wasn't even present! He leads the people in repentance, then institutes some radical reforms to cleanse the land.

Nehemiah does likewise. In the first chapter of the book that bears his name, before his first trip to Jerusalem to rebuild the wall, the man of God prays day and night. In verses 6 and 7 he confesses the sins that "we Israelites, including myself and my father's house, have committed against you. We have acted very wickedly toward you. We have not obeyed the commands, decrees and laws you gave your servant Moses." Did you catch that? "My father's house." When I read that, it blew me away. He confessed the sins of his ancestors. The principle that applies here is that in the body when one sins, we all sin. Nehemiah knew that. So should we.

Even if you agree that I've made a case for white folks to confess and repent of slavery on behalf of generations past, you may be wondering what black folks have to confess and repent of. After all, we were the victims of slavery. We were the ones torn from our homeland, stripped of our dignity, and subjugated into what is arguably the most brutal form of slavery ever known to mankind. What do we have to confess? Easy. We must confess our anger, retaliation, and unforgiveness. The thought of slavery and its resulting racism, which still lingers today, can and should make black folks angry (actually it should make everyone angry). But we must move on from there. We can't afford to linger in the past, to demand recompense and then to maintain resentment. We must abandon teachers who demand that we pollute our souls with hatred. We must retire rhetoric that divides and refuse to pass it, along with any slurs, on to our children. We must not only open ourselves up to the possibility that we can be reconciled to whites, but we must seek it at every turn as a first step.

I don't think all blacks linger in the past and nurse resentment and bitterness toward whites. But many of us do. These sins certainly seem justifiable. When someone offends you, you are justified in expecting that things should be made right. When the offender not only fails to do so, but seemingly flaunts his apathy regarding your wounds, it's understandable that you would become resentful. When he then blames you for the wounds he inflicted, while denying his culpability, that's enough to make any sane person bitter. This is how white America appears to many of the black people that I know. Like I said, bitterness toward and resentment against whites is certainly understandable, especially when you view American history through the eyes of black folks. But as understandable as they are, holy and acceptable to God they are not. As long as we allow them to fester among us, we will never become the noble people God created us to be. We will never ascend to our proper place in history. We will never be able to embrace those white brothers and sisters in the Lord, who sincerely seek reconciliation. And we will never be able to please God.

I understand the reluctance on the part of both whites and

blacks to venture into the territory of racial reconciliation. For both sides, opening up makes us extremely vulnerable. If whites make the overture and blacks refuse, or if blacks avail themselves of the possibility but whites drop the ball, either side risks rejection. The whole racial climate could end up much worse than it already is. The question remains how such a monumental task could ever be accomplished, and under what conditions.

My blueprint for any quiet revolution is Jesus of Nazereth. He came with a plan. After some preparation time, He began to teach. He yoked up with some like-minded dudes who were open to His message and teachable. He taught them, lived with them, loved them, and led by example. Then He sent them off to handle their business. What began with One grew to thirteen, and now look at it.

Possibly without being aware of it, hip-hop has certainly imitated the pattern of the early Church. It began real small. Now look at it. I guess any great idea follows this pattern. Wouldn't it be cool if the Church could grab it and run with it?

So far I've been speaking in big concepts: races, churches, movements, revolutions, etc. But certainly there's a role for the individual. Your band of disciples could be your friends, your community, your church, your relatives, or, in my case, your children. In any case, you would still need to begin with yourself. In order for the whole forgiveness thing to work, you've got to be saved first. You can only forgive inasmuch as you are forgiven. If you are not saved, then your sins still count against you. If you are a believer, however, then you're off to a decent start.

Let's each of us examine our consciences before the Lord, asking Him to reveal our prejudices and discriminatory habits. We ask Him to show us, because left on our own we're bound to overlook or justify our wrong attitudes and behaviors.

Next I'd suggest healing on the community-church level, primarily through service. If yours is a black church, pray to God about opening up dialogue and fellowship with a white church. If yours is a white church, do the same with a black one. My wife has brought it to our pastor's attention that our former, mostly white church hosts a summer camp every year for young people from the city. The host church is pretty small and is always in need of counselors and other kinds of helpers. My wife has asked if Praise Tabernacle would volunteer to serve Grace Bible Church at their camp next summer. Talk about a learning experience for everybody involved. A Pentecostal black church with a median age of thirty-three, serving a conservative white Grace church with a median age of fifty—you do the math. It would seem that the two groups would have nothing in common. But that's not true. We share the most important element, Christ. We all believe He is Lord. We desire to please Him. I expect nothing but good things. That's not to say that camp would be easy. That's not even to say that camp would be a success in conventional terms. But don't sleep on the coming together. That's monumental.

When people come together we discover how similar we are. We learn that we all want to live in nice neighborhoods without crime and vandalism. We all want to minister to the lost. We discover common hobbies and favorite sports teams. We demolish stereotypes. We demystify, as well as appreciate, our differences. We discover our shared humanity. Instead of "those people" we become Christina and Terry, Ben and Latwanas. We give and remember names and faces. We extend friendship and share faith. We intersect lives, experience concern for one another's problems, and pray for one another's needs. I have been in assemblies where men and women of different races and cultures come together with a common focus. If it's powerful at a rap concert, imagine how much more powerful it would be in Christ. That's just beautiful to me, man. And guess what? It's available to you, too. Look around, see where you can be of use, then get to work. Offer your arms and legs and any other abilities in the name of Jesus. Don't try to lead. Don't roll up tryin' to run nothin'. Just show up and serve diligently, without complaint, doing "all for the glory of God" (1 Corinthians 10:31).

I can tell you from personal experience, it's real hard to dismiss someone you have to serve. And it's even harder to do so once you've prayed with or for that person.

My heart's desire is to witness reconciliation on a national level in my lifetime. I am so down with Dr. King's dream. And I'm ready to put arms and legs to it. How great would it be for a pair of Christian leaders, say President George W. Bush and Reverend Jesse Jackson, to participate in a foot-washing ceremony, like the one Jesus carried out at the Last Supper, in order to promote racial healing in our land? If each man, representing his respective race before the Lord, would humble himself, apologize (to God and to each other) for past and present atrocities committed by both sides, ask forgiveness (from God and from each other), and extend forgiveness, I bet our nation would go a long way in healing itself from the damaging, lingering effects of slavery.

Before America's problems are political, economical, social, or racial, they are spiritual. Our past sins have opened the door for the enemy to reign free in our nation. Many of the issues we face as a nation—high crime, rampant drug use, school shootings, thieving corporations, teen pregnancy, high divorce rates, and even terrorism—are a direct result of our consistent abandonment of biblical principles. God's Word is not just a blueprint for the individual or for the family; it's the blueprint for a nation. The entire Bible chronicles God's history with Israel. It reveals their mistakes, successes, and failures. As Paul writes in 1 Corinthians 10:11, "This [the written history of Israel's relationship with Jehovah] is for us." God gave us the Bible for more than just a little bedtime reading. Through it, He speaks to us. He reveals all that we need to know in order to live successfully. Its contents are applicable to man, woman, community, and nation alike. Biblical principles applied in any society work, regardless of culture. They work because God, who transcends culture, who created the people of every culture and the culture itself, does not change. If what He told Israel and the Church worked back in the day, then it's still good now.

In the Bible, every time Israel got in trouble, they knew what to do. They returned to God, repented, and sought His forgiveness, which He always gave. If America wants to overcome its woes, then it must follow Israel's example as set forth in the Word. We must humble ourselves and seek the Lord. We must confess our corporate sins and individual sins and ask His forgiveness. God promises that if we do so, He will forgive us, heal our land, and restore us (2 Chronicles 7:14).

Living out God's Word breaks every form of spiritual bondage to which humanity is subject. The way to defeat racial hatred is through loving people of other races. The only way to overcome a spirit of unforgiveness and to break its hold is to forgive. Forgiveness is not admitting that you are wrong or that the other party is right. Forgiveness simply says that our relationship is more important to us than our pride. It says that we've had a derailment, so let's get back on track, because our destination is the most important thing of all and we can only arrive together. Yeah, forgiveness says all that.

I maintain that if forgiveness has the power to heal an entire nation, imagine how powerful it can be in the life of an individual. Forgiveness sets a person free. It breaks the hold of the past and allows you to live in the present. When you forgive, you cancel a debt. It may be a debt legitimately owed, but canceling it means that you don't have to be concerned with collecting it anymore. It's as great a feeling for the debtor as it is for the person owed the debt. Unfortunately it's a hard place to get to without a relationship with Christ. Truthfully it's even hard with Jesus. Somebody wrongs you. You want it made right. But that's usually not the case. Sometimes what's wrong can't be fixed, ever. So you just have to suck it up. That's hard. It's kind of a catch-22. The only way to forgive is to be forgiven. But the only way to be forgiven is to forgive. All forgiveness comes first from God. We love because God first loved us (1 John 4:19). We are capable of forgiving for the same reason.

In Matthew 18:21-35, Jesus breaks down how forgiveness works in the parable of the unmerciful servant. I'll paraphrase. This broke dude owed his boss the modern-day equivalent of something like a billion dollars. Scholars say it was more than the guy could ever make in a lifetime. When the boss told the broke dude to pay up, broke dude didn't have it. So the boss ordered him, his wife, and his kids to be sold to pay for the debt. But broke dude went all the way there. He screamed and cried and begged, promising to pay back everything. The rich boss was so moved that he just straight canceled the debt. Just like that, broke dude got a blank slate. But I don't think he really understood that. Because as soon as he was released, he hemmed up an even broker cat who owed him something pitiful, like a hundred dollars. This other guy also begged for mercy and time to pay back his debt. But broke dude wasn't hearing it and had him thrown in jail. Is that busted or what? Well, apparently broke dude's boss thought so, too. Because when he found out, he snatched broke dude up and had him put in jail, too, but not before he chewed him out for being such a punk and refusing to forgive the other guy's little debt, the way his boss forgave his giant debt. Jesus concludes the parable with a warning. "This is how my heavenly Father will treat each of you unless you forgive your brother from your heart" (Matthew 18:35).

The more I study this parable, the more convinced I am that the servant just didn't get it. The debt was canceled. He didn't need to collect because he was free and clear. I agree with David A. Seamands, who writes in his book *Healing for Damaged Emotions* that the servant must not have really believed that he didn't have to repay the money he owed, so he was still trying to collect. On the other hand, it's possible that the servant, out of pride, was just hell-bent to pay off his boss. Because he wouldn't allow himself to receive charity, he was incapable of extending it. I know people like that. They are so hard on everybody else because they labor under some imaginary and unreasonable standard of perfectionism. They try never to make mistakes. But sooner or later they make one.

Then they spend years beating themselves up for it. Because they never receive grace, they never give it. And when someone else makes a mistake—watch out! They never let him forget it. It's annoying as hell. I don't know anybody who enjoys the company of people like that.

The point that Jesus makes in the parable is that whenever we refuse to forgive another we're guilty of the same offense. Our refusal to forgive anyone is obnoxious to Him. It's an affront to God when we, whom He has forgiven so much and whose sin debt *He died to pay*, then turn around and refuse to forgive other people, regardless of our reason. Jesus died for every sin, not just the ones you find acceptable. So who are you to say that His blood isn't good enough to cover the offense against you? Whatever happened to you, it's covered. Get over it. He doesn't approve of unforgiveness in unbelievers, but He cuts them slack because they're ignorant. Coming from the believer, though, unforgiveness is a stench in God's nostrils.

True forgiveness isn't necessarily an emotion, although it may be accompanied by many. The best description of it I have ever heard came from a book called *The Doctrine of Prayer*. In it, TW Hunt states that forgiving someone is like going to court. You gather up all your case files against your offender and lay them before the Judge. In doing so you basically tell the Judge that because you know His attributes and characteristics, you trust Him to make a fair and just judgment, because He knows absolutely everything there is to know about the case. Then you leave it. Every time you're tempted to peek at one of the files, remind yourself to give it back and to tell the Judge again that you will abide by His decision, whatever it may be, even if it doesn't seem fair or doesn't satisfy your need for retribution. Repeat this as often as necessary, until you are free.

I like this analogy because it shows that forgiveness is an act of will and that it isn't necessarily accomplished in one fell swoop. Like anything else worthwhile, it is a process that takes time. The other thing this illustration reminds me of is that, as much as I'd like to think I am, I'm not the Judge. God is. Only God has proper perspective on any situation, including our grievances. He even provided the payment for the perpetrator, Jesus' death on the cross. As I stated above, if we refuse to forgive another person, we're basically saying that Jesus' sacrifice wasn't good enough. The problem with that is that it boomerangs back on us. Jesus Himself taught us to say to God, "forgive us our debts, as we also have forgiven our debtors" (Matthew 6:12). I like that wording. Any sin is a debt that demands repayment, just like in the parable. Jesus' sacrifice, however, settles all accounts. If you say that it doesn't cover some offense done to you, what you're really saying is that offending you is worse than sinning against God; hence you are more important than He is and you have a higher standard of righteousness. You're also saying that Jesus' sacrifice doesn't cover your offenses either. That's a lot to be saying. Now keep in mind that you've got a ton of sins that you aren't even aware of. Because all sins are committed against God first, then others. And He takes all sin very personally. Do you still think that you have room to hold a grudge? If it helps, just imagine that God harbors one against you. Then ask yourself if that's a position that you really want to be in.

There are a ton of other benefits to offering forgiveness that I won't go into. Read the Bible to find out more. One point about unforgiveness that you should know is that when you refuse to forgive, you put God in a position not to hear your prayers. That means anything that you utter or desire in your heart, He ain't hearing it. It's like He says to you, "Talk to the hand."

So what now? If you find yourself in a place where you're able to forgive anyone who has offended or hurt you, then don't waste time. Do it now. If you aren't there yet, tell God that. Trust me, He already knows. Then ask Him to help you. If you don't even want to be able to forgive because you're still too pissed, hurt, crushed, tell Him that, too and ask Him to help you. Regardless of who has done what to you, whether they are individuals, communities, races, or nations, Jesus covered it on the cross. Give Him a chance to heal you. You could use the freedom and the peace. And so could everyone around you. Remember, the quicker we get these cars back on the track the quicker we can get this train movin' again.

11

Holier than Thou

The moment I had dreaded was approaching. Peabo Bryson, the R & B singer, was about to finish his set. I've never been a big fan of his, but my wife really digs him, so this one Christmas I bought tickets to see him and a group of other artists perform a concert at the Cerritos Center for the Performing Arts. Cerritos is a quaint little city in southern California about twenty minutes south of Los Angeles. The evening had been nice so far. We'd heard James Ingram, Sheena Easton, and a couple of other crooners knock out jazzy renditions of some classic Christmas songs. My wife was having a good time, and that made me happy. I was feeling the Christmas spirit. That is until Peabo finished his set.

I had never cared much for brah-man, because I'd always felt he'd been unnecessarily hard on hip-hop, and on rap in particular. He barely acknowledged it as music, let alone an art form. I knew he had a mouth on him, and used every platform as an opportunity to clown heads. So I was ready. But so far he hadn't done it. It was the end of the show, and he had managed to end his set and to thank all the fans for coming without one foul word about rap. I was impressed. I wondered if he had experienced a change of heart, or had been persuaded to see rap's value.

The audience was on its feet, and all the artists were just about to take their final bow when Mr. Bryson lowered the boom. Just before the lights went down for the final time, he addressed the audience one more time. "And please ladies and gentlemen," he said, "support the arts and programs like this one, so that next year we won't end up having a Snoop Doggy Dogg Christmas." The audience, which was mostly middle-aged white people, roared with laughter and heartily applauded their approval. My wife stifled a grin while pointedly staring straight ahead. She was amused by the incident, but at least she didn't clap. I remember feeling deeply annoyed, but not surprised, thinking, *That nigga's got some nerve.* It was only decades ago that the general populace criticized R & B, jazz, and rock 'n' roll, claiming that they had no real value either musically or morally. It wouldn't be the last time I heard rap music get bashed in public. But it was the first time I vowed to defend it in an open forum if I ever got the chance.

Hip-hop's critics often cite it as the new social evil. There is some merit to this charge. With many messages glorifying violence, sexual promiscuity, misogyny, drug trafficking, drug use, and a general disrespect for authority, hip-hop—particularly gangsta rap—has gotten a li'l bit crazy. Clearly hip-hop could stand to refine its presentation on all fronts: the half-naked, gyrating females, the profanity, the conspicuous consumption, the seeming amorality. Hip-hop is hard to defend sometimes. Its profiteers could stand to focus a little more on legacy than on cash. Not that I am opposed to profit. I just wish that hip-hop's trendsetters would consider that the images they project, the messages they put out, and the behavior they encourage affect so much more than just themselves.

With the advent of Kanye West's *College Dropout* album, Jay-Z's *Black Album,* and the subsequent rebirth of Sean Carter, not to mention Ma$e's return to the game, I'm hopeful that rap will continue its trend toward championing more life-giving values over morally questionable ones. But if it doesn't, it would remain no different from other types of entertainment. It needn't be singled out for any offense greater than those found in rock 'n' roll, film, or television. Somehow it seems that lyrics soliciting murder for hire seem to offend less when accompanied by a wailing guitar rather than by an 808 beat. But, speaking as a devoted lover of the genre, it would just be nice if more of hip-hop's most influential front people conspired to raise the bar a little higher, if for no other reason than for the sake of the next generation coming up.

What really gets me is that many of hip-hop's critics overlook its positive messages, which include but aren't limited to: female empowerment, questioning history and tradition, learning to think on a new level, exploring your beliefs, demanding more from yourself and from your environment, and embracing entrepreneurialism. These same critics also manage to ignore the millionaires hip-hop has birthed—men and women, most of whom are Gen Xers, who passionately seek to improve and empower their disenfranchised communities of origin.

The bottom line is that hip-hop in and of itself is not evil. It's simply a medium that can be manipulated to spit positive or negative values. As with any other medium, hip-hop reflects what's in demand. People enjoy titillation. They always have. And hip-hop delivers. Hip-hop can go either way. How well it does sometimes depends more on the quality of the music itself than it does on the depth of the message. Kanye West has proven that if the beat is phat and the rhymes are tight, you can even get fools to scream out "Jesus Walks" in the club. All heads want to know is this: Is the music good? Does it flow? Is it authentic? These are the questions asked of a new song, a new artist, or a veteran. The deeper the better. But deep is not a prerequisite. You can groove just as easily to Lauryn Hill, Talib Kweli, or Kanye West as you can to Lil' Kim or Missy Elliott, depending on your bent. Authenticity is why Eminem, even though he's white, can find the very credibility that now eludes Ja

Rule. Hip-hop heads are savvy. They can spot a fake and dismiss him just as readily as they can zero in on the real thing and embrace it. One thing that earns respect is the telling of your story. 50 Cent's freshman project is a violent account of life through his eyes. But it's his account. It's his "testimony," to put it in Christianese. No one can take his experience from him. And the best part—aside from the lyrical and musical quality—is that it's real. His story deserves just as much attention as that of any American president. He and his contemporaries are the very stuff of which America is made. Who among us doesn't love an underdog who went from rags to riches?

My challenge to the sanctified folks is to look past the package to see the man. You don't have to affirm the likes of Eminem and 50, but at least you could hear them out before you condemn them. You may be surprised by what you learn. They're not just icons, but real men, with real struggles. So many folks enjoy their music because they can identify with them. In one respect they are Everyman. For those of us in the business of ministering to the world, it would behoove us to at least make an attempt to understand what people in the world embrace and why. We're not called to agree, just to understand and to relate.

What surprises both critics and fans once they get a glimpse inside the lives of rap stars is that they live like normal people. Most want a peaceful existence with one wife and some children in a safe neighborhood with good schools. Few rap stars actually continue to live 'round-the-way once they "make it." Those who do often end up dead or in jail. You might think that the Glock-carrying, filthy-mouthed, saggin' gangsta who gets chauffeured home from his urban venue to his all-white neighborhood in the suburbs would lose credibility with his fans. But one part of the American dream that hip-hop's entrepreneurs have embraced is the "move up and move on" mentality. They not only embrace it, but they embody it. And their audiences buy it by the truckload. It's okay to be rich and to enjoy it. You can stay true to your roots as long as you just don't forget where you came from. And truthfully, you can remember the ghetto you grew up in even if you live in an exclusive gated community in Beverly Hills. Often the pros and cons of each make you better able to appreciate both locales all the more.

The same is true of an authentic walk with Christ. No matter how mature you become in the Lord, or how godly you appear, regardless of how much Bible knowledge you amass, it's impossible to get stuck on yourself if you always keep in mind where you came from. Remembering the gutter God dragged you out of makes you appreciate the sanctuary that much more. Sometimes people— especially younger dudes in the world—look at me and think I'm just so holy because I don't drink, smoke, or curse (that much) anymore. They marvel at how I can still be fienin' for my wife after nearly ten years of marriage and have remained totally faithful to her since we met over twelve years ago. Some of them confess to me that they "just couldn't do it." My response is always the same: "Neither could I." I'm far enough along in my relationship with Christ to appreciate how much better my life is with Him in it. But I'm not that far removed from my old habits to remember why they held my interest for so long. I remember what it was like to get out of the wrong bed with some girl I didn't even know. That's why every morning I wake up next to Sheeri Mitchell is a good one. I remember what it was like to give a woman, pregnant with my baby, money to go to the abortion clinic. That's why I embrace my three children every chance I get. I remember what it was like to live on the run, peepin' around corners, hidin' my ends in paper bags under staircases. That's why I'm smilin' even when the line at the bank is ten people deep. I haven't forgotten what it was like to stand in line at the welfare office, barely holding on to my dignity as social workers talked down to me and regarded me with contempt. That's why every time I write out a check for my tithes I sometimes literally weep for joy. I remember who I was and where I was headed. And I am utterly convinced that all good things in my life are purely God's gifts to me. I don't deserve any of them and I could never say I earned them. If anything, I earned just the opposite. I earned prison time, loneliness, emptiness, misery, and death. That I have a loving, devoted wife; beautiful, healthy children; a flourishing career; some ends; not to mention joy, peace, and hope is purely God's grace and mercy in action. I can't brag about nothing. My whole existence is charity!

I tell you what, though—the minute I forget that, I'm toast. As soon as I buy into my own hype, I render myself useless to the kingdom. I'm cleaned up now, but I know what lurks in the basement of my soul. I know the evil I am capable of, and so does God. Refusing to forget makes me a better minister of the Gospel. As long as I realize that I am nothing without Christ, I'm less apt to look down on other people and better able to serve them. I don't trip off brothas on lockdown, who are addicted to drugs, who are runnin' game, who gangbang, who smoke, or who chase that paper. How can I? They're me! I might be in a different place now, but at my core I am no different. I can relate to all the drama they go through on the regular, and I give up nothing but respect. I understand the struggle, and I don't come shakin' my finger in their faces. That's not to say I don't come with the Truth, but I don't have time to be fake or highbrow. Frankly it takes too much effort.

Long before I became a believer, *fake* was the only word that came to mind when I thought of the Church. I held fast to the notion that the Church was full of jackleg preachers trying to take my money; undercover freaks pretending to be holy; and lots of old, mean people who stayed in church all day long and left meaner than when they came. Where did these views come from? Mostly from the experiences I had growing up—that and the opinions of the adults and people around me. I know many people who actually agree with the message of the Bible. They just can't get past their experiences with Christians in order to become one. I was one of them. The image that many nonbelievers have of Christians is that we're supposed to be loving, but we're elitist. We're supposed to embrace, but we reject. We're supposed to be prosperous, but a lot of us are devastatingly poor, mentally, emotionally, spiritually, and financially. In short, the world sees us as fakes and hypocrites. And you know what? They're not entirely off.

If you claim to value honesty but lie every time you open your mouth, then you don't value honesty. Does what you say match up with what you do? Are you always fakin' like you "the man," but living like a punk? Do you profess to be a Christian, but refuse to stop sexin'? Then I, like Paul, question not only your commitment to Christ, but your salvation as well. I maintain that there are many people out there who call themselves Christians who not only behave in no way like Jesus, but who don't even know anything about Him or His teaching! My contact with many of those people led to my disregard for Jesus' message, my dislike of Christians as a whole, and my distrust of the Church. My perspective changed only after I met some folks who were serious about their walk and who expected me to be serious, too. But it would be a while before I met those guys.

I remember my first time going back to church after a nearly fifteen-year absence. The Holy Spirit had just begun speaking to my heart about my behavior and attitudes toward Him and toward the life He had given me. I debated for weeks whether or not it was possible to renew my commitment to the Lord without actually having to go into the church building. Finally, after the Holy Spirit had stood on my neck long enough, I agreed to go. To tell you the truth, I became determined to go. I had finally gotten to the place where I realized that my life would never work the way it should without Him. So I went. And I was feeling pretty good about my decision.

I rolled up in the sanctuary in my version of my "Sunday best." Keep in mind, I was doing me. So I wore a fresh white Hanes beefy tee, my new jeans, and my new all-white Nikes that I had just bought for the occasion the Saturday before. I knew enough not to wear my matching baseball cap into the sanctuary (a hat on a man is a sign of disrespect in church), but it was waiting for me on the front seat of my 325i. So I rolled up, excited I was coming home. I had heard that the pastor could really deliver a good Word, and that this church had a lot of young people like me, so I wouldn't stand out too much.

Into the sanctuary I stepped, and who was waiting for me at the front door but the devil himself. Now, understand that it wasn't the guy with the pitchfork and the pointy tail, but I know this sister had to know him well, 'cause he used her to get to me that morning. She was an older black woman, perhaps in her late fifties or early sixties. I don't know what she was doing so close to the entrance; she didn't seem to be greeting anyone or directing any traffic. Anyway, ol' girl took one look at me—a long look, mind you—up and down, took in my entire outfit, sucked her teeth, rolled her eyes, and mumbled something under her breath about niggas that I couldn't quite make out. I was hot. Now, keep in mind I was newly rededicated to the Lord. This meant that I wasn't exactly filled with the Holy Spirit. So please don't think that I didn't entertain the thought of cursing her out, because honestly, that wouldn't have been beyond me back in the day. Instead, I nodded at her and kept pushin'.

I can't tell you what the pastor preached that day. I didn't hear the sermon. I didn't join. And if you want to know the truth, I almost didn't come back. That old heifer had really pissed me off. And I can now see how it was an attack of the enemy (Satan), designed to discourage me.

So I don't sound crazy, let me take a minute here to explain the very real concept of spiritual warfare. The apostle Paul reminds us that "our struggle is not against flesh and blood, but against the rulers, against the authorities, against the powers of this dark world and against the spiritual forces of evil in heavenly realms" (Ephesians 6:12). He encourages us therefore to "put on the full armor of God, so that when the day of evil comes, [we] may be able to stand [our] ground . . ." (Ephesians 6:13). I know that sounds real ominous, but it's really very simple. To the best of my knowledge it means that your beef ain't with me (or any other human being). Your real beef is with whoever or whatever is controlling me. Hold tight while I try to make something that could be potentially very confusing as simple as I know how. As humans we're all controlled or motivated by something. Our motivators can fall into only one of two categories: good or not good. God wants to be our sole motivator. As our Creator, He wants us to be filled with (controlled by) His Spirit all the time. If we submit ourselves to God's Spirit, then we will evidence love, joy, peace, patience, kindness, goodness, faithfulness, gentleness, and self-control in our daily lives (Galatians 5:23). Nobody can fault you if you possess all those characteristics. On the other hand, if you are controlled by anything other than God's Spirit, then you will display "sexual immorality, impurity and debauchery; idolatry and witchcraft; hatred, discord, jealousy, fits of rage, selfish ambition, dissensions, factions and envy; drunkenness, orgies, *and the like*" (Galatians 5:19–21, emphasis mine). There is no middle ground. In any given circumstance, you are either motivated by God (good) or by "other" (not good). The choice is yours. God will never force Himself on you. He waits for an invitation. The enemy (not good), however, intrudes as often as possible. He continually attempts to attack you in your most vulnerable, yet most powerful area—your mind.

You may ask, "Why?" What's so special about you that the enemy of our souls wants to get in *your* head? That's pretty simple, too. The enemy hates God. Since he can't get to God, he tries day and night to frustrate God's plans. Anything God values, the enemy tries to destroy. God loves all of humanity, so the enemy hates us. Since he's already going to hell, his goal is to do as much damage as he can to us and to God's plans on his way there. Think about it. If he can get in your head and get you to think wrong, then you're screwed for as long as he runs you.

Let me give you an example. Have you ever known a woman who was on the outside very pretty, but was convinced in her mind

that she was ugly? Even though she should be and could be running things, she acted like the hired help? Never giving eye contact.
Walking around hunched over. Mumbling all the time. Do you
know anybody like that? Despite the truth that she is fine, this
woman acts like she's ugly and gets treated like she is. Somehow
the enemy has attacked her mind and won. Maybe other children
or a parent told her all the time when she was growing up that she
was ugly. Maybe she caught beat-downs on the regular, or maybe
she was a victim of sexual abuse. Whatever the point of origin, the
enemy used it to tell her lies. She believed them and lives as though
these lies are true.

Then there was Malcolm X, born Malcolm Little. In his autobi-
ography, he recalls an incident from his childhood that shaped his
entire life. He told a teacher that he wanted to become a lawyer. He
told Malcolm that his dream would never come true because he
was better suited to trade work. He believed that teacher. In one
instant the enemy used that teacher to crush the dream of a young,
impressionable child. And because the boy was convinced that he
would never become an attorney, the man became a criminal. As
anyone who has ever listened to a speech Malcolm X gave or read
anything he has written can attest, he would have made a formidable attorney. He wasted many years of his life laboring under the
lies of the enemy.

The enemy is a mighty opponent, and we, as mere human beings, cannot conquer him alone. The only person in history who has
ever confronted the devil and won is Jesus Christ (Matthew 4:1–11).
If His Spirit, God's Holy Spirit, is in you, then you've got all the
power you need to defeat the enemy's attacks on your mind. You
just need instruction, found in God's Word.

Anyway, back to my experience in the sanctuary. The woman
who dissed me was very likely being controlled by a spirit of anger,
annoyance, hatred, or something like that. It made her express her
disapproval inappropriately. In response I got mad. What the
enemy wanted was for me to retaliate. Then she probably would

have responded the same way. And there you have it. It could have gotten real ugly, real quick, and ended very poorly. She and I would have been attacking each other even though we were just puppets for the enemy. Do you see how conflicts between families, communities, ethnic groups, and even nations can escalate? And while we're all at one another's throats, the enemy sits there laughing at us all, because he's managed to win on at least two fronts. Not only does he succeed in getting us to hate each other; he prevents us from working together to accomplish God's will.

What God would have had me to do in the situation would have been to pray for that lady. He would have had me see the situation with spiritual eyes, recognize her humanity, and offer her a kind word. I wasn't that mature then. I don't think I'm that mature now. The best I could manage at that time was *not* to curse her out.

Well, that's a very condensed lesson on spiritual opposition. There are many more qualified people who have written volumes on the subject. I just wanted to touch on it because it's something everybody encounters on one level or another. And it plays a role in what keeps people who need Christ away from the Church. Now that you're hip to it, can you think of a time when you were goaded by the enemy into acting a fool? Can you recall the last time when you were ready to go toe-to-toe with a fellow human being? Chances are neither of you was motivated by anything holy.

You don't have to be left defenseless, though. The Bible gives ample instruction on how to defeat the enemy in this area. Since the battle begins in the mind with wrong thinking, Paul begs us not to conform to the world's way of thinking, but to be transformed by the renewing of our minds. If we learn to keep God's perspective at the forefront of our thoughts, then we will be better able to understand and be excited by what He wants for us (Romans 12:1, 2). In other words, if we can just take our thoughts to the next level and focus on God rather than on the many distractions that compete for our attention, we could learn to think more like Him and understand His plan for us. This renewed mind comes primarily from reading God's Word, the Holy Bible, with the purpose of understanding God's original intent and applying His intent to our lives.

The next weapon in the arsenal against the enemy is resistance. James 4:7 states simply, "Resist the devil, and he will flee from you." It ain't deep. When the enemy figures out that what used to yank your chain doesn't bug you anymore, then he'll back up off that particular thing. Of course, he'll return with something else until he finds another weak spot, but inasmuch as you can resist temptation, you're straight. This is why Jesus is so bomb. Matthew chapter 4 records how the enemy came at Him with everything. He tempted Him with the best he had to offer. And J.C. was like, "Naw, man. I'm cool." I'm paraphrasing—but you get the point. Throughout Jesus' entire ministry, up until His last breath on the cross, the enemy taunted Him. But Jesus was focused. Because He never sinned, the enemy had no way to get at Him. Jesus even told His disciples that the devil had no hold on Him (John 14:30), meaning that Jesus had no weak areas through which the devil could gain access to His mind or behavior.

The best part for the believer is that the same power that was at work in Christ while He was here on earth is available to us through the Holy Spirit. When you accept Jesus' death as replacement for the one you should have suffered, then the Holy Spirit comes to dwell in you, to help you to be more like Jesus in every way. Your only job is to submit to His leading. You have to step back and let the Holy Spirit be the boss. That's really all it means to be filled with or controlled by Him. You do only what He approves of. Yeah, I know: It sounds simple, but it ain't easy.

Paul addresses this problem in Romans 7:15-25. I affectionately refer to this passage as the schizophrenic piece. Paul basically admits that he doesn't get it. He wants to do right, but doesn't. Instead he does the very thing he hates. He wills himself to do good, but is incapable of carrying out his own will, because his very nature fights him tooth and nail. He concludes by admitting how pathetic he is in his own strength.

Anybody who has ever battled an addiction of any kind knows exactly what Paul means. You hate that thing, but you do it. You hate yourself while you're doing it, but even your self-hatred isn't enough to stop you. So you just hate yourself that much more while you keep doing that thing. In the face of your addiction you have no choice but to admit how powerless you are and that you need help. If you're smart, you conclude that your help will have to come from an extremely powerful outside source. Paul is saying that our compulsion to sin is the same. And he reaches the same conclusion. In our own strength we're incapable of doing good. Any good that we manage to accomplish even accidentally comes only through God. "Thanks be to God—through Jesus Christ our Lord!" he exclaims (Romans 7:25). If we want to do this walk right and not just fake it, like so many do, then we've got to depend on the Holy Spirit every minute. We've got to be vulnerable to God and brutally honest with ourselves. It's not the most attractive proposition, but it's real, and, as my changed life testifies, it works.

The next way to overcome in spiritual warfare is by prayer. It sounds corny, but prayer works. Think about it. When you pray to God the Father, you are coming to the Creator of the universe to ask for help with your issue. Hmmm. Think He might have a li'l pull?

My boy Paul reminds us that the weapons of our warfare are not carnal (earthly) but mighty for the pulling down of strongholds (2 Corinthians 10:4). Simply put, pray your butt off. Bring every issue to God. Ask for His help. Pour out your heart. Praise Him for how good He is. And while you're at it, thank Him for sending Jesus to die for your sorry butt.

Prayer is not real complicated. It's just talking to God, telling Him about what's going on with you. It opens the door to communicate with Him. After you finish your part, be sure to shut up and listen for a bit. You don't want to miss His speaking to your heart. As you talk to Him more and read His Word more, you'll be able to recognize which thoughts in your head come from Him and which don't. When you're able to do this, then you can rebuke those thoughts that aren't like His. *Rebuke* is a ten-dollar word that just means to kick out. Whether the thoughts originate inside your head, like your last good idea, or whether they come from television, a conversation with a friend, or something you read in a book, if they don't sound like something God would say, scratch 'em. You don't have to go around talking to yourself, looking crazy. But you do need to reject suggestions that don't line up with His Word. For example, I know that God would never tell me to cheat on my wife. "You shall not commit adultery" is one of the Ten Commandments (Exodus 20:14)! So should that thought occur to me, I know that God did not send it and it has to go! I have severed relationships with colleagues who have made sexual overtures toward me. Once a woman lets me know that it's on, she's got to go. And I always make sure to tell my wife about it, too. I don't care what that sounds like. I'm serious up in this piece. That area is too tricky to mess with. Bump friends. I don't need any female friends. As a matter of fact, I don't have any who aren't already good friends of my wife's first and aren't like sisters to me. I have to be just that vigilant, and so do you. The enemy is always looking for a way in. That don't mean you have to be paranoid. You just have to be careful so you don't get caught sleepin'.

I was asleep on the job that Sunday way back when that older woman got me with that look at church. I thank God that He kept me from doing anything stupid (that day). I continued to go to that church for a while, despite the crazy stares from lots of older members. Some of them even felt the need to talk to me about my gear, about which the Holy Spirit has yet to convict me. I just learned to smile and move on. But I often think about what could have happened to me if I had been any less determined to follow

Christ that day. And I wonder how many new or not-yet believers have been turned off by that same spirit that manifested itself in that older woman that day.

You see, an attitude like hers isn't just about the clothes I had on. Her beef was with me and what she assumed I was about. She surveyed me and, for whatever reason, found me lacking. She decided, based solely on my outward appearance, that I was of no value to the kingdom—and possibly society at large. You may wonder how I know all that was going on in her head. She could simply have been suffering from indigestion. That is possible, but not likely; there was far too much venom in her words.

I don't know what exactly was happening with her that day, but I have encountered Christians who harbor the attitude I was certain that I saw in ol' girl. Any young person who has ever suffered at the hands of an older, disapproving person, or any person of color who has ever met the glare of a racist, knows exactly what I'm talking about. An attitude of superiority is ugly when it occurs in the world. But in the Church, in the Body of Christ, it's horrific. As a matter of fact, God hates it. The book of Proverbs lists several warnings against haughtiness, citing it as a characteristic that God detests (Proverbs 6:17). I'm sure this is true because of the level of rejection experienced by the person on the receiving end. That woman rejected me without even knowing me. And I won't lie: It pissed me off, and on some level it hurt. I could understand that kind of reception at a country club or even at a regular nightclub. But at church? Church is supposed to be the one place where everyone, anyone, can come without fear of being rejected, judged, or mistreated.

Eventually I did find a church home where that proved true for me. Because of my personal experiences at Faithful Central Bible Church in Inglewood, California, my time in the Word, and my sitting under the teaching of Bishop Kenneth Ulmer, I have come to understand that the Church is a hospital of sorts. It is a place where the sick, the lame, the deformed, the disabled can run as a refuge from the outside world. It should be a place where you can come and expect to get help, to be healed, to be treated, to be cared for. Bishop Ulmer would often announce to potential members that Faithful Central was far from perfect. He'd say that in the congregation we had "ex-everything": ex-pimps, ex-prostitutes, ex-gays, ex–crack addicts, ex-embezzlers, ex-fornicators. He'd always be sure to add "some of us ain't 'ex' yet." That always made me feel better. I was an "ex" in more ways than I care to count, and in some ways I'm still trying to become an "ex." I always like the fact that he included himself among the "us" who weren't quite "ex" yet. It makes him more human to me. That and the fact that he is always real with his. To say that Bishop is larger than life is somewhat of an understatement. Yet he remains one of the most humble men I've ever met. He is up-front about his past, having admitted to his congregation to having struggled through divorce, suicidal thoughts, and managing his own anger. It's hard not to love and appreciate a gifted leader like Bishop who embodies so many of the characteristics of Christ. Overall he is an extraordinary example of Christian manhood. In his humility, he has greatly influenced Faithful Central to attempt to live up to Christ's standard for the Body. He is an authentic Christian.

Admittedly, there are some churches that resemble hospitals where people are turned away because they're sick. They are places where the hospital staff ridicules the ailments of its patients, where patients laugh at other patients' weaknesses and deformities, a place where under the guise of concern they gossip about one another's disabilities. In all fairness, not all churches are this way. Many strive to become the kinds of places that desire to embrace and understand everyone, including the gay man, the lesbian, the prostitute, the pimp, the homeless, the drug addicted, the drug dealer, the child molester, the murderer, the pornographer, the adult-film star, the liar, the embezzler, the greedy business owner, the corrupt policeman, the shady politician, the fallen star, the adulterer, the fornicator, the spouse abuser, the animal torturer, the unwed parents, the difficult and rebellious teenager, the transgendered, the sexually confused, the gangbanger, the thug, and whoever else rolls up. The charge given to the Church is to see past the outside, past the sin, to the heart of the man/woman/child and to embrace them in the same manner Jesus Christ did when He walked this earth and as He continues to do in heaven.

After I became active at Faithful Central, I encountered something else I had forgotten that I feared about Christians. I have always hated regular folks being all up in my business. I especially didn't welcome Christians, mainly because I didn't want anybody judging me or thinking they could tell me what I could or couldn't do. When I was at Faithful Central, Bible-study leaders, discipleship leaders, and, in my case, even the teacher for the new-members class, Willie McBride, didn't think nothing about asking me questions about my sex life. When Sheeri and I first got engaged, it seemed like everybody and they mama was up in our BI. "So how y'all doin' in *that* area?" "Hey, brah, you hittin' it?" "So what's up, y'all?" were just some of the questions we fielded. Initially my response was "Damn! Can y'all give a nigga some privacy?" I'm certain I voiced that on more than one occasion, to which I was met with a straightforward no. It seemed that the more authentic the Christian, the nosier they were. Over time I came to understand that my boys were just keeping me on track. They all knew, especially the married ones, that the closer a couple gets to the wedding date, the harder it is to stay celibate. And you know what? They were right. Had it not been for their calling me out all the time, Sheeri and I would never have been able to keep our commitment to the Lord. The "interference" didn't end after we got married either. That was when Sheeri's girls really kicked in. They wanted to know if we were having enough sex. They wanted to make sure she was cooking for me, submitting to me, if we were praying together. Oh, Lord, the list is endless. Even though many of them have moved to different parts of the country, they still have permission to dig. Marriage and this walk require you to surround yourself with folks who will keep your confidences, hold you accountable to do what's right, encourage you when times get rough, and celebrate with you when things go well. I thank God for those nosy Christians who first butted into my life with probing questions. They have become my best friends and my biggest cheerleaders. I have made sure to return the favor.

What my experience with those guys taught me was that the Body must strike a balance between love and permissiveness. Continuing with the metaphor of the Church being a hospital, it must do its part to assist the sick with their healing. Of course, the only physician capable of healing the sin-sick soul is God Himself, in the person of the Trinity—the Father, the Son, and the Holy Spirit. But the role of the Body is to lead the sin-sick to the Master Physician and to hold them accountable for following the prescribed "medicine" as revealed in God's Word, the Holy Bible. Oh, yes, they got to make you take your medicine. Imagine a hospital where every patient was welcomed, but no one was treated and where there was no sterilization. A hospital like that would be a pit of disease, a starting point for plague and death. In his first letter to the Church at Corinth, Paul rebukes its congregants for allowing one believer, a man, sleeping with his stepmother, to persist in this behavior while remaining in the Church. "Don't you know that a little yeast (sin) works through the whole batch of dough?" he asks (1 Corinthians 5:6). Just as a person battling cancer seeks to remove the disease in his own body, through surgery and chemotherapy, so the Church must go after persistent, willful sin in its ranks.

Understanding that as humans we will never be sinless, once the Holy Spirit has seized our hearts and we have fully committed our wills to God, then we should sin less, or at least differently. As a believer, I should not struggle with the same things I did five to ten years ago. I should have all new struggles! That is to say that, as the Holy Spirit deals with me on one sin issue in my life and empowers me to conquer it, then I move on to the next. It's a lifelong process that is never finished until I meet God face-to-face in heaven, where

I will sin no more. But in the meantime, here on earth, I keep tryin' to get better and better. I am continually growing and becoming more like the Christ I serve. At any rate, it's the Body's obligation to hold me accountable, to encourage me when I fail, and to pray for me in my struggles.

As a believer, if I am sinning but refuse to turn away from it and continue to persist in it, then I gotta go. Because any church that puts up with me and my behavior runs the risk of my behavior spreading. Notice that I didn't say "if I'm struggling with known sin." Nor did I say "not struggling with something *I don't know* to be a sin." Struggling is very different from unrepentant persistence. And both are different from ignorance. Ignorance is easily solved. Once I realize what I'm doing is sinful, then I quit and repent. For example, I met a brand-new believer who had never been to any church before and who had never read the Bible. In her new-members class, she learned that sex apart from marriage was a sin. When she found out she told her boyfriend that she had to become celibate. He laughed at her, so she broke up with him. She was ignorant, but when she "knew better," she "did better," as the old folks say.

Struggling, on the other hand, indicates that I agree with God that my behavior is sinful, that I desire to change, that I am making the effort to do so, but with some difficulty. The Body's obligation to me in this area is to support me, to encourage me, and to hold me accountable for doing my best to fight this thing. My boys did this for me by being real with theirs. They shared with me not only past struggles from "back in the day," but current ones, too. We all prayed for each other. And we are all of us victorious day by day.

If you have come across Christians who seem to give off a holier-than-thou vibe, or who seem nosy, be patient with them. If you give them a chance, you may discover someone authentic who will love you enough to accept you with all your mess, but who will love you too much to leave you in it.

At the risk of running this hospital thing into the ground, let me just say this one last thing: The sick have an obligation, too. In the same way patients must follow the doctor's orders so that they can get healthy, so, too, should a person seek to follow God's way in order to be made whole. No person should come into the very presence of God Himself and expect to remain in his sin. Sin is a disease of the soul. God desires to heal us, to renew us so that we can function and thrive at our highest level—meaning in the manner and for the purpose He created us. Just as disease hampers the body from functioning at its best, so does sin prevent the person from performing as his best self, from living his best life. Just as a patient with a disease must make changes in diet and regimen in order to improve his condition, so must the new jack make changes to his lifestyle in order to have victory over the sin in his life.

The first step is salvation. As I mentioned in the first chapter, not one of us is perfect. The penalty for any wrong deed, the smallest lie, the tiniest indiscretion, is death. God would not be just if He allowed the sinner to go unpunished. But out of His love for us, He provided the only One who could bear full punishment on our behalf. A perfect man died for all the sins of severely flawed humanity. His sacrifice was acceptable. So all it takes to come close to God is to accept by faith that the sacrifice of Jesus Christ covered the sin that should have condemned you to death. Salvation gets us into heaven and spares us from the eternal torment of hell. But a victorious life on this side of death requires some work on our part. The Master Physician prescribes daily reading of and meditation on the Word (for right thinking about Him, ourselves, and the world around us); daily prayer (for open communication with Himself, the lifeline to an intimate, real, personal relationship with Himself and the peace and the immeasurable joy that results); and, last but not least, a bomb church home full of folks who are doing this thing for real.

12

This Game Ain't for Punks

Watch hip-hop videos and you'll see that in a lot of them it's all about the stuff. The cars, only the top of the line: Bentleys, Hummers, 7-series BMWs, and just about anything Mercedes-Benz makes. The locales: sprawling mansions surrounded by the white-sand beaches of the Caribbean, catered parties on the French Riviera, penthouse-apartment dinners backlit by the Manhattan skyline. The clothes? Only designer will do. The accessories: bling by Jakob the Jeweler, Harry Winston, and Rolex; shoes by Jimmy Choo, Manolo Blahnik, or S. Carter. Hip-hop's motto is "less is less and more is not enough." In videos and in real life, hip-hop's elite deliver the American dream by the truckloads. If you got it, flaunt it. Excess is never too much. Many having grown up with limited resources, hip-hop's biggest stars embrace their rich-and-famous lifestyles with a vengeance! No price tag soars too high and no indulgence hovers out of reach. Hip-hop sells the good life.

Apart from the obvious moral pitfalls inherent in indulging the desires of the flesh, many Christians buy it . . . the good life, that is. Many of us seek, if not idolize, the good life. Almost all the saved folks I know personally could just as easily push a Benz as they could a Honda. They desire to live in excellent neighborhoods, take family vacations to warm, sunny places, and to buy some toys here and there. In short, they want to get paid. In addition to their monetary goals, many people come to Christ seeking a better life in all areas. To us the good life means prosperity on every level—not just where money is concerned. Jesus' promise of providing abundant life covers ministry, marriage, friendships, careers, child rearing, and emotional, physical, and psychological health, to name a few topics. This is possible because there is no area in life where the Gospel isn't applicable. That's so deep to me. That means there is no issue or problem that can't be answered by God's Word. I don't know about you, but that gives me a tremendous sense of security.

Because of all the promises God makes to His children in His Word, it's easy to think that becoming a Christian means that you won't have any problems or suffer any adversity. To be real about it, the reason so many people come to Christ is because their lives suck. They are unfulfilled, and often so desperate they'll even come to the cross. This is a good thing. But doing so with the assumption that suddenly all your problems will disappear and your world will just simply right itself is not only untrue, but dangerous. Life for the believer is no bed of roses. At times it can be more like a tub of thorns. Anyone who undertakes this journey should know from jump that it ain't no joke.

It isn't very good marketing on my part to tell you that after salvation your life will probably get worse before it gets better. But I'm not trying to sell you Christ. I'm trying to tell you the truth. I like to think of this Christian walk as similar to a deep-tissue massage. Back in high school I used to play football. I'm a pretty solid guy, so I usually held down the position of defensive lineman. To say that I suffered my share of injuries is just the beginning. Sometimes I'd get hit so hard that my body would go into shock. Not the fallout paralysis kind, but the kind that registers no pain and allows you to keep on playing. Days later, sometimes even weeks later, ugly, painful bruises would appear out of nowhere and last for days at a time. Later in life I learned that if I had gone for deep-tissue massage, I could have coaxed those bruises to the top sooner and healed faster, albeit more painfully at first. That's what coming to the Lord is like.

All your life you've been getting banged up and beat down—emotionally, spiritually, psychologically, and for some, even physically. That's just life. Bad, horrible things happen to everyone—yes, even to "good people." The price of living in a fallen world is that perfectly innocent people become victims of the worst tragedies. My wife's oldest brother, who was really more like a father to her than even her own pops, was by everyone's account a great man. He loved his wife, cherished his children, and brought a smile to the face of almost everyone he met. He was a successful business-man with a bright future in corporate America. He possessed a gregarious personality that set even the stuffiest person at ease. He was a loyal friend and a fine son.

One day he got on a local commuter flight that crashed to the ground and burst into flames on impact. His entire family was devastated by the loss. To add insult to injury, it turns out that the crash of PSA flight 1771 was the result of a disgruntled employee's melodramatic attempt at revenge. Later reports would confirm that the employee had been fired days earlier for stealing seventy dollars (or some ridiculous amount like that) from the beverage cart. He returned, boarded the same plane that his supervisor was on, executed the pilots midflight, and crashed the plane into a hillside in Paso Robles, California. Everyone on board was killed, including Sheeri's brother Earl.

The family was devastated, especially Sheeri's sister-in-law, who had been married to Earl for seven years at that time. They had had two children, a two-year-old son and a nine-month-old daughter. Of all the surviving family, I think the children suffered the greatest, because they never got a chance to really know their dad, a loss that still plagues them both nearly twenty years later. People the world over were directly and indirectly affected as well. There had been close to two hundred passengers on that plane, some of them from other countries. All those lives devastated because of one man's selfishness.

Where was God when this happened? Why didn't He prevent that plane from going down? Why didn't He allow the perpetrator to get caught first? And why didn't He at least spare my wife's brother so that he could watch his children grow up? These are all questions that my wife had to wrestle with before she could move on in her relationship with the Lord. She had to learn, like so many Christians, that following Jesus does not insulate you from suffering. Salvation is no guarantee that you will live a life free from pain and drama. In John 16:30 Jesus promises, "In this world you will have trouble. But take heart! I have overcome the world." Holding on to the second half of that promise can be very difficult when the first half proves true.

In fact, following Christ can often lead to more drama in life. Being set apart is not easy and can often create a hostile response from the world around you. Before you come to Christ you've already been bruised by life's tragedies, yet somehow you manage to hold on. Sometimes the way you cope allows you to heal, but sometimes it just allows you to cope . . . to keep functioning in spite of what's going on. For example, when I was a kid growing up in Oakland, one of the things I had to learn to prevent being bullied was to hold my ground whenever possible. Bullies often tested younger kids by staring us down to see if we'd look away. If a kid looked away, they pegged him as weak and would harass him, steal from him, or beat him down. If you didn't look away, they'd taunt you by demanding, "What you lookin' at?" You had better come with some strong verbiage and be ready to square off quick if you didn't want your butt kicked. After I did this enough times in my neighborhood, dudes would leave me alone, for the most part. When I got older, initiating violent confrontation in order to literally beat bullies to the punch was an effective coping mechanism for me. You can probably guess that after I got saved I had to learn new ways to deal with threatening situations so as not to defame the name of Christ. Drawing blood first no longer fits my MO. After my first serious girlfriend cheated on me with her ex, I coped with my anger and pain by becoming a user of women. It worked for me for a good while. But when I came to Christ, I had to learn a new way to deal with that betrayal—His way. I had to forgive her and move on.

When you come to Jesus, the Holy Spirit begins to work. He starts massaging you so that those deep bruises will work their way to the surface and eventually heal. It's tempting to develop all new and unhealthy coping skills, the way a person trying to quit smoking will get addicted to chocolate, but pretty much the only coping mechanisms God permits are prayer, praise, and worship. God promises that if you bring all your pain to Him, He will heal you. He will help you to bear the pain, but you'll still feel it. The healing process is a lifelong one, which is at times unwelcome, painful, and potentially very embarassing. Even though God is ultimately working you out to get you to become the man or woman He's always wanted you to become, and using every experience that He's hand-picked since before you were born to accomplish His goal, it ain't a lot of fun. The cool part is that within the working out, God gives you joy, peace, and comfort. But in order to experience these you have to stay the course and not punk out. The result is a healthier, stronger, more mature version of you.

Pain, suffering, and disappointment present a problem for many Christians. It's a commonly held belief that since we're God's own, we shouldn't suffer. For the proof that this is not true we need look no further than the experiences of the Israelites, God's chosen people. Their relationship to God did not exempt them from suffering. True, the Israelites' suffering resulted from their disobedience to and rejection of God and His principles. But the same is true of us much of the time. Most suffering in our lives can be traced back to our personal rebellion against God. Some effects are immediate. Some take time to manifest.

Most Christians I know, however, can bear self-inflicted suffering more patiently than suffering caused by others. A woman who used to smoke a pack of cigarettes a day for forty years can reason out her throat cancer better than one whose nine-year-old develops the same disease. So what do you do when the suffering in your life results from some source other than yourself? What do you do when you pray prayers in those hard times that seem to go unanswered?

Some of us think that since we have a direct line to God's ear that He should always answer our prayers. All we need is to pray in faith without doubt. We name it and claim it. We blab it and grab it, claiming that unwavering faith is the key to getting our way. But any believer who has ever experienced unanswered prayer or a delayed answer to prayer figures out quick that there has got to be more to it than meets the eye. It can be confusing because Jesus said that all we have to do is to ask the Father anything in His (Jesus') name and God would do it (John 14:13, 14). Jesus also said that if we believe and not doubt that we can move mountains (Mark 11:23). So what happens when God doesn't do "it"? What's the next step when the "mountains" hold their ground?

My pastor, Reverend Jody Moore, calls this the "but if not" factor. The phrase comes from the biblical account of the Hebrew boys found in the book of Daniel, chapter 3. A quick synopsis goes something like this: The Jews had been carried off into captivity by the Babylonians. Hananiah, Mishael, and Azariah (who are better known by their slave names, Shadrach, Meshach, and Abednego, respectively) are drafted to serve in the palace for the Babylonian king, Nebuchadnezzar, an egomaniacal pagan with some serious control issues. Anyway, Nebby builds this giant gold image about ninety feet high and holds a dedication ceremony, at which he commands everybody to bow down and worship the idol. The Hebrew boys ain't feelin' him, so they don't do it. Some of Nebby's yesmen dime them out, and a furious Nebuchadnezzar propositions them. Basically he tells them they can worship the idol or they can face immediate execution by being tossed into a blazing furnace.

Smellin' himself, Nebby then says in verse 15, " 'Then what god will be able to rescue you from my hand?' " The boys reply that they don't need to defend themselves because God's got their backs. They tell Nebby that the God they serve is able to save them from the fiery furnace and that God will rescue them from the king's clutches. Them boys had guts. Facing execution, they tell the pagan king to do his worst because they know that God's got it. The part to pay attention to, though, is what they say next. In verse 18 they declare, "But even if he does not, we want you to know, O king, that we will not serve your gods or worship the image of gold you have set up." You may already know how the story ends. An indignant Nebuchadnezzar tosses our boys into the fire, but they survive. And not only that, but the preincarnate Christ shows up and walks them through the fire! They come out not even smelling of smoke, and Nebby is so blown away that he gives God Almighty his props. It's a bomb account.

The part that Pastor Moore focused on was verse 18, the boys' acknowledgment that God may decide not to save them. Facing death, they were like, "God's got us either way." They knew that either God would save them or He wouldn't. And they were okay with either choice. That impresses me a lot. The Hebrew boys knew their God. They knew that God wasn't with the split-loyalty thing, so they were down 100 percent. They knew He was able because He is all-powerful. No doubt they knew all about Moses and the Red Sea, Joshua and Jericho, and David and Goliath—to say the least. They knew of His goodness and trusted in Him so completely that they were willing to do right by Him, even if they didn't get the results they wanted.

I can tell you from personal experience, that's a hard place to get to, and it is the mark of a mature believer. I maintain that most of us believers are schizophrenic at our core. We know in our heads that God is good and that we want to follow Him. We may even earnestly be convinced that His way is always best. Yet we still have our wants and desires, which often conflict with His.

My wife and I recently miscarried. Actually she delivered a still-born, premature baby. We had gone to the emergency room of our local hospital because at her prenatal exam earlier that day the doctor had not been able to find a heartbeat. My wife called me in tears to explain. Sheeri is not prone to hysteria, so when I picked up the phone to her sobs, I knew something had to be really, really wrong. Immediately I started praying. I did my best to exercise active faith. I asked God to keep the baby alive, to heal him, to perform some kind of miracle for my unborn child! I knew He could and I believed that He would. I knew there was the possibility that He would not, but I didn't allow myself to go there.

The ultrasound proved our worst fears correct: The baby's heart had stopped beating and he was gone. My wife and I cried as the doctor explained that she would need to induce labor, so my wife would have to give birth to a dead child. I would like to tell you that in the moments before the news I had told God, like Jesus did in the garden, "not what I will, but what you will," and meant it (Mark 14:36). I had prayed that. I had prayed that God would have His way. I just couldn't believe that His will included taking my unborn baby from me. I didn't know how much I didn't mean "your will not mine be done" until the doctor showed us the baby's still heart. I didn't want God's will then. I wanted mine. I wanted my baby alive and literally kicking.

Eventually I was able to get to a place where I could worship God and even thank Him for our experience. I was able to get past my grief and recall God's faithfulness to me my entire life: His sparing me from an early death myself, calling me back to Him, giving me a beautiful and amazing wife and three other healthy children to love, and paving the way for my successful career. I couldn't be mad at Him because I really do believe that He allows everything to happen for my good and for His glory, even if it doesn't feel very good to me at the time.

As I look back over my life, some of my biggest disappointments and toughest trials have produced the character I have today.

And out of those same hard times have come incredible blessings and a deeper closeness to God that I would have never gotten otherwise. I know that God never wastes pain. And most important, I know that He grieves with me over the loss of my baby. I love Him. I worship Him. I submit to Him. I may never know why He didn't allow my child to survive, but I know enough about who He is to be satisfied with the fact that He does.

That's why this walk ain't for punks. If you're going to commit at any point, you should know this fact. It's hard, but then again, so is life. Unsaved people experience tragedy as much as the saved do. The difference is that saved people never have to experience the pain alone. God is a God who cares and who loves us tenderly. He is awesome and worthy of much props—all the time. And the fact that I can say that and mean it, along with everything else I've shared in this book, should be proof of His ability to completely transform a life.

How have you managed the tragedies in your own life? Have they wearied you? Have they made you bitter or fearful? Have they rendered you hopeless? I only ask because how you respond to the terrible things in life depends on who God is to you. Your ability to overcome them has everything to do with what you believe about Him. In hard times, if you look hard and ask Him to show you, you will see His hand of direction on your life. If you ask Him, He will share with you His perspective on things—not just in your life, but in the lives of others as well.

God is not some sadistic tyrant who takes pleasure in your suffering. Jeremiah 31:3 says that he draws us to Himself with loving kindness. He suffers when we suffer. He cares about our pain. He wants to see us live an excellent and fulfilling life. He ordered the universe and everything in it from day one. You are no accident. Your life has purpose. Every experience in your life is designed to escort you to your hand-selected, one-of-a-kind destiny. He is a kind and loving Father. God is never indifferent toward you. He has loved you with an everlasting love (Jeremiah 31:3). He is perfectly wise. He knows the exact combination of good and bad experiences required to mold you into the person He decided you should become, long before you were even a gleam in your mom's eyes. God is not powerless to help you. All power is His. Nothing is impossible for Him (Luke 1:37). He is perfectly sovereign, which means He needs no permission to carry out His plans. He is holy and good. There is no contamination in Him. He will never harm you—not even unintentionally. His love is perfect.

God does not change. This alone makes the Bible relevant. His promises and warnings still stand; you can claim both for yourself even today. His history with His chosen people helps you to understand your future with Him. He is dependable and faithful. He will never leave you nor forsake you (Hebrews 13:5). He is patient. He will wait for you to love Him in return. He is holy, which means His standards are high and right. You may not like them. They will cramp your style some—okay, a lot. But you'll be better off for it.

To be able to get to the place where you can embrace God's will for your life even when it conflicts with your own is gon' take some doin' on your part. This is where the real work comes in—the day-to-day grind that can take all the joy out of following Jesus if you don't get your attitude right from jump.

Have you ever seen a joyless Christian? This is somebody who is just broke down, going through the motions, just waiting to die so they can go to heaven. They scare me and I run from them. Don't become one of them. That abundant life I keep talking about is real—even in the really bad times. Even as my wife and I prepared for her to deliver our little one who had passed on, we had joy. I know that sounds crazy, y'all. But it's true. We weren't delusional. We weren't in shock. We were extremely disappointed and grief-stricken. Yet we were filled with hope. We entertained each other with stories about our other children that week. We talked on the phone to friends who prayed, cried, and laughed with us. We reflected on our life together so far. We reminisced about God's faithfulness to us in the past. We thanked Him for being with us right then and there. We praised God even through our tears, thanking Him for the incredible journey He has led us on and for giving us to each other. With the exception of a few saved nurses, the hospital staff didn't know what to do with us.

So now you know that if we're joyful even in the bad times, stuff must be jumpin' off in the Mitchell household every other day of the week. Our motto is, "Celebrate everything until God tells you otherwise." Our home is always filled with laughter and peace. If you're interested in knowing how to get that for yourself, I'll tell you.

The first thing you have to do is to accept Jesus. I know I keep bringing up that point, but what do you expect? I'm a Christian! I've already gone into detail in previous chapters about why you need to be saved; I won't run it into the ground. I will say again that whatever your plan is for your life, God's is way better. I am living proof of that.

The next thing you have to do is to know the Word for yourself! I can't stress how important this is. There is so much misinformation and just straight lies out there about God and His principles. You cannot afford to rely on the opinions of others. In the book of Hosea, chapter 4, God declares, "My people perish from lack of knowledge." That's true. Don't end up on the wrong path or in some cult because you got it twisted. And don't let just anybody tell you stuff about God or His Word. A good rule of thumb: If somebody teaches something you don't understand or agree with, challenge them to show you where it says that in the Word. Don't let fools get over on you. And more important, don't be a fool either. If you don't know something, then just say so. Don't risk leading somebody astray because your info is faulty. By all means, listen to your pastor and other folks who know the Bible, but make sure that you check their facts and interpretation, too. Bishop Ulmer taught me that. And if you don't get or agree with something they teach, ask questions! Bishop taught me that, too.

This brings me to my next point: Don't get caught up in the

man of God. Get caught up in the God-Man Himself, Jesus Christ. If you are a new believer or not very well versed in the Bible, read the gospel of John without commentary, praying to the Holy Spirit to teach you. Even if you aren't a believer and are just curious, I suspect that's a prayer that God will answer. Find someone knowledgeable, who is not a nutjob, to discuss it with, or attend a Bible study. You'll be surprised at what you learn.

Apart from John's gospel, there are sixty-five other books, all of which point to Jesus. Read them too. A good Bible that one of Sheeri's and my friends, Mrs. Sharnelle Blevins, a marriage mentor at FCBC, recommends is *The Daily Walk Bible* in the New Living Translation from Tyndale House Publishers. This Bible breaks the Word down into manageable daily chunks, which will allow you to study God's Word for comprehension and application. It works well for group or individual study. For those of you who prefer a more hip-hop-styled Bible, I recommend *The Message Bible*, a contemporary translation of the Bible with a lot of flava. It's also good for group or individual study.

Speaking of group study, a good interdenominational (they welcome all faiths and denominations) organization is Bible Study Fellowship International. They got a tight method. I haven't been able to attend a men's class near me, but my wife goes weekly nine months out of the year. Check their Web site, www.bsfinternational.org, for a class near you and try it out. In the United States their classes are mostly white, but don't trip. The fellowship is real and so is the knowledge. I have also heard of, but never attended, Walk Thru the Bible classes. Attendees that I know say this is a great way to understand the Word in a weekend! I think they usually set up classes through local churches around the country. Check the Web site, www.walkthru.org, and see for yourself.

The point is that you must study God's word for yourself every day. Once you develop the habit, it's not hard. Actually it's kinda exciting. Since the Holy Spirit authored it, the Bible is God speaking directly to you. That would make me at least a little curious.

Whatever you decide—BSF, local church, Walk Thru the Bible, personal study—just make sure that you focus on understanding the Word in light of Jesus Christ. He's the key to understanding both the Old Testament and the New Testament. If you focus on Him, you'll be able to tell a jackleg preacher from a true one. Also, when your pastor and other Christians fail you—and they will—your faith won't suffer like my grandmother's did, because it will be grounded in Jesus Christ, who never fails.

I know this setup seems endless, but it really isn't. My last two recommendations go hand in hand. First, make a real effort to leave behind bad habits and bad people. That's not to say that you should never associate with non-Christians. That would be stupid, not to mention impossible. But you should avoid being "unequally yoked" to folks who aren't walking in the same direction. You need to surround yourself with like-minded people for whom Christ is the standard and the Bible is the final authority. You need folks who will be serious about staying on the path and dedicated to helping you do the same. Bishop Ulmer calls this committing to folks who are "committed to your commitments." It's true in every other walk of life, so it shouldn't be any different when it comes to Jesus. People to whom success is important hang with successful people. It's that simple. If it becomes important to you to do this walk right, then find some folks who agree with you. I can tell you, it's hard to live right when all your homies are living foul. It's next to impossible to get up early for Sunday church services because you're hungover from partying with your boys the night before. If you are trying to quit sexin', don't go date a stripper! You feelin' me? At least try to find a Christian who's tryin' to be where you are. That don't mean you got to settle for a duck. There's some fly Christians out there. But guess what? They ain't at the club droppin' it like it's hot! (Well . . . not usually.) Get your behind to church.

Now for the second point. For every bad thing you try to change, replace it with something good. When it becomes clear that you have to ditch your dope-smoking boys, who watch pornos all the time, ask God to give you some other road dogs to kick it with, who are gon' support your efforts. When you realize your girls are interested only in hooking up and diggin' for gold, it's time to seek out women who can relate to the new you. The key is to get a support staff behind you. Find a church you can vibe with and go—regularly. Tell an aunt or a grandmother or your moms or somebody who's saved about your decision. Ask them to pray. Old people love to pray for you. The Christians in your life who are worth their salt been praying for your sorry butt all along. If you tell 'em about your decision, they'll probably bust a gut. So be careful in your delivery.

Okay. That's it. There's more, but this is a good start. If you aren't on board but know someone who is, tell 'em about what you just read. If you're saved and you got a knucklehead in your life, do likewise. Better yet, buy them a copy of this book. I can't guarantee that they'll read it, but you never know. At least this way they get a chance to experience the good life for themselves instead of looking at a faint reflection of it in music videos.

13

Last but Not Least . . . Do You!

It goes without saying that most gangsta rap artists have reputations for being less-than-law-abiding citizens. The fact that it's called gangsta rap means that if you perform it, then at some point in your life you should have at least known some gangstas, if you weren't one yourself. What an interesting transition it must be for the dude who grew up in the 'hood or on the streets to become a rap star. Having learned the ways of hustlers, pimps, and playas, once he makes it, he must function in a world of attorneys, record executives, and accountants. But if you want to know the truth from someone who has been in both worlds, they really aren't much different from each other. The fundamentals and the goals of each are the same: Get in. Get all the cash you can. Get out before your time expires. The only difference is the presentation. And even those lines are blurring. The more hip-hop gets absorbed into the mainstream, the fewer distinctions can be made between how the two aforementioned groups dress, speak, and entertain themselves.

Still, the artist who makes the journey from ghetto to boardroom faces some real challenges at the end of the day. Changing environments forces anyone to grow. But for the gangsta who prides himself on his rank, it must be difficult to maintain his authenticity while getting along successfully in what has traditionally been a white-dominated arena. He has to acquaint himself with the nuances and customs of a foreign culture, all the while taking pains to make sure that he is fully understood and not screwed over.

What I appreciate most about rap artists is that as they grow, become more business savvy, and generate more revenue streams, they manage to remain true to their roots. If you didn't grow up in a rough part of town, it may be difficult for you to appreciate the few benefits of growing up poor and/or "underprivileged." Many people who start out in the ghetto never make it out. But those who do bring with them character that can be obtained few other places. They fear few things and even fewer people. They have no need to impress those who don't understand. They don't apologize for their viewpoints. They know what they know and you'll be hard-pressed to change their minds about their fundamentals. They often exude a confidence that's easily mistaken for arrogance.

One of the things I like about most rap artists is that they don't come off as fake. They don't change who they are just because cameras are rolling or because an audience is present. Although this can work to their disadvantage when their behavior lands them in legal trouble, it usually is positive. Many of them, particularly Jay-Z and Mason Betha (formerly Ma$e) have confessed to "dumbin' down" their personas to boost record sales, but for the most part cats just are who they are. Snoop Dogg doesn't change his diction simply because Diane Sawyer is interviewing him. Busta doesn't change his gear because he attends an award ceremony. Even Reverend Run of Run DMC, who is now a pastor, keeps it real for the Lord. And ODB—man, that nigga looks the same in a mug shot as he do in a photo shoot. These dudes and many like them are authentic. I really, really dig that. Don't get me wrong; I don't agree with all the values they embrace. But I appreciate the fact that they don't switch up just because of who may be watching.

I mentioned earlier that one of my biggest obstacles to becoming a Christian was other Christians. I knew a few converts back in my day. And to be honest, they scared me. I did not understand how a dude could go from gangsta to choirboy overnight! Even on this side of the cross I still don't get that . . . not really. I see how, as you get to know Christ, He changes your heart. You are not the same person you were before encountering Him. That makes sense. But that change is usually a gradual one, which happens from the inside out by the renewing of our minds. I have observed that the more gradual the change is, the more likely it is to be permanent. The overnight transformation seems more cosmetic. A dude who used to smoke, sex, do drugs, run drugs, gamble, curse, and hang out in the club all the time gets saved, and suddenly he's spending every night in church, speaking in Christian-ese and quoting Bible verses all day long. Used to be if you asked him how he was doing, he'd answer, "I'm straight, man." Now he's talking about "Oh— I'm just blessed in the Lord, brother!" I don't trust that at all. It's not that the Holy Spirit can't spur radical change in any person— that's not what I'm saying. All things are possible with God. Radical overnight change just isn't likely to stay radical for long and isn't likely to touch the heart.

I've been studying the history of Israel and the minor prophets for the last year, and one thing that jumps out at me is that the Israelites were constantly backsliding. From the time God led them out of Egypt straight through to their life after captivity, they repeated the same cycle over and over again. They'd start faithful to God; then they would slip into the disgusting, repulsive practices of the surrounding pagan nations. God would discipline them, usually by allowing their enemies to overtake them and oppress them. They would whine, weep, and repent, and then God would deliver them. Then the whole cycle would start all over again. They continued this pattern for over four hundred years! All I can say is, God is patient, 'cause had it been me, I would have just left them fools alone and moved on to some other nation. And if that nation started trippin'—on to the next. But God never lies. He made a covenant with Abraham and his descendants and He's gon' see it through. He never breaks His promises. And He always makes good on His warnings!

Anyway, I point this out because as God's chosen people, even Israel struggled to remain faithful to God—over generations! What makes somebody think that they gon' flip the script overnight and never screw up again? True, Christians have God's Holy Spirit dwelling inside of them (1 Corinthians 3:16), and the Old Testament Jews didn't. Even still, the Holy Spirit doesn't make you instantly perfect. He empowers you to live out this faith with joy and victory. But you still sin. You still blow it. You still stumble. That's just the human condition. So when I see folks who undergo an instant total personality transplant I get suspicious and a little nervous. It has been my experience that either they have lost their minds or they're faking the funk while gettin' their freak on some other way. I'm not saying that's the case with everyone. I'm just sharing my personal observations.

I think the urge to fake total conversion is often founded in sincere motives. Experiencing coming to Christ can be so overwhelming, so eye-opening, so earth-shattering, that it can push you overboard. It's tempting to go from one extreme to the other, because you just want so much to leave your old dead life behind and embrace the new one that you can lose all sense of balance. You've probably seen this before in other areas. I saw a lot of it in college. Coming where I come from, I had nothing to prove about my identity as a black man when I got to college. Some of my suburban brethren weren't so secure. Here you have Spencer Hollingsworth III, a brother from Grosse Pointe, Michigan, who probably attended an all-white boarding school on the East Coast and who has dated white girls since kindergarten. Both parents are high-ranking professionals, making beaucoup dollars. After one semester at CAL, however, Spencer has changed his name to Muhammed Hussein Elijuwan X, and is sportin' dookey locks, sideburns, and dashikis, schooling you on the dangers of consuming too much pork, tolerating the white man's refuse (including his women) and capitalism's undermining of black America. And he's serious, too! You blow him off because you know that ten years after graduation he's gon' be Mr. Hollingsworth to you, pushin' a 600, vying for a partnership at Donaldson, Crane, Martin, and Goldenblatt, engaged to his once upwardly mobile black female counterpart, who has shelved her MHA to raise their three kids, Brad, Dane, and Baily, in Weston, Connecticut.

It's a question of balance. Spencer started out really far right. Part of his journey to discovering the self to whom he could be reconciled involved his going way, way, way left before he came back just a bit past the center.

It's the same with Christians. We start off on fire, 'cause this is good stuff. Unfortunately we usually have more zeal than knowledge—a dangerous imbalance. We're constantly talking about Jesus, the Bible, our church home, our pastor, this conference and that retreat. In the meantime, we alienate all our friends in the world (not always a bad thing), judge every person who comes across our path, and overspiritualize the meaning of a dirty sock in a laundry hamper, until we burn ourselves out or suffer through one too many disappointments or unanswered prayers. But this crossroad is crucial. What we conclude about God in our difficulty determines where we go next. Sometimes we return to our old lifestyle, declaring we "tried the Jesus thing" and it didn't work. Sometimes we hold on, but linger in bitter resignation that life may suck, but at least we ain't goin' to hell when we die. Sometimes we press in, wrestle with God, and stay in His face and in His Word till He gives us some answers we can live with and a lifestyle we can embrace with dignity and peace. Whatever we choose, eventually we'll be forced to live out all those Bible verses we've memorized. Know anybody like that? Be patient with them—especially if "them" is you. In the meantime, the persona we've adopted may fall apart while we discover our true identity in Christ. It can be embarrassing, but survivable.

I am sure that God never expects us to totally abandon our temperament. Let me explain. When you come to Christ, you could have a really foul personality. He doesn't strip you of it, but He does cultivate it. He does the same with your experiences. If we accept God's revelation of Himself in Scripture, then at the very least we must assume Him to be all-powerful, sovereign (meaning He does what He wants, when He wants, as it pleases Him), eternal (has always existed), infinite (without end), immutable (unchanging), and all-knowing. Operating from that guideline, He knows everything you have ever done and will ever do, and He always has. So if He has chosen you to become one of His own, His is a fully informed decision. God will never say about you, "Oh, I didn't know you were like that. That changes things." His being sovereign means that He let you do your dirt. That doesn't mean He was happy with it, but He allowed you to carry out your plans anyway because they fit into His plan. Given this fact, it is not necessary for you to switch over from Joe Cool to instant holy man in a single bound.

In Ephesians 4:22, 24, the apostle Paul exhorts us to "put off your old self, which is being corrupted by its deceitful desires" and to "put on the new self, created to be like God in true righteousness and holiness." This sounds like a command to instantly transform ourselves, but it isn't. According to G. Michael Cocoris in his *Formula for Family Living* publication, the "put on" and "put off" Paul uses refer to taking off and putting on clothing. Let's think about that for a minute. When you get dressed for work or school in the morning, you probably have a ritual. You take off your pajama top or T-shirt, then pajama bottoms, then draws. Hopefully you put on a new pair of draws, and then some socks, a shirt, jeans, some sneaks, and maybe a jacket. You don't suddenly pop out of all of your clothes, only to have them magically attach to your body all at the same time. You take off one piece, then replace it with another.

This is what you should do with habitual sin. As the Holy Spirit calls something to your attention, you take it off, then put on a godly replacement. You can't just abandon the bad behavior only to leave the space open. As a human being with a fallen nature, if you don't conscientiously fill that hole with something godly, something worse will take its place. For example, it does no good to stop drinking if you replace it with smoking crack. If, however, you replace drinking with working out, then you're at least headed in the right direction, as long as you don't get addicted to working out. If all goes well, then move on to the next vice—say, smoking— and try again. I can tell you from experience, this is a long, long process. I've got enough stuff to work on till Jesus comes back, so I can't trip on you with yours.

The key to success is to resist bending to discouragement along the way. Again my boy Paul comes through. "Let us not become weary in doing good," he reminds us. "For at the proper time we will reap a harvest if we do not give up" (Galatians 6:9). In other words, don't give up, homie; you will come up if you don't give up. That's a reassuring promise, 'cause trust me, as soon as you start dealing successfully with one thing, the Holy Spirit will show you more. But thankfully, mercifully, only as you are able to handle it. But keep your chin up. You ain't no more to'-back than the rest of us. The only difference is, now you know. And in the end, it's all good.

Equally as bad as putting off the bad behavior without putting on good behavior is putting on the good on top of the bad. This is what I think happens to the instant holy man mentioned above. In an effort to behave like he knows he should, this guy simply adopts all his virtues at once. To use our clothing analogy, he just puts on his work clothes on top of his pajamas. Yeah, it looks as stupid and uncomfortable as it feels. Eventually it's all gon' come off. Then he'll either go back to his old ways or adopt some new worse ways along with the guilt and hopelessness of having failed at being a

Christian. Don't let this be you. If you know you dirty and you want lasting change, your only hope is in Christ. Let Him do for you what He did for Lazarus; He resurrected him and ordered his grave clothes removed. Handle your business under His direction one article at a time and you will succeed.

In the meantime, if it ain't broke, don't fix it. Meaning, if it's not sin, leave it be. I remember I had this conversation with one of my wife's single female friends. Homegirl was fly, but real frustrated. While she, my wife, and I were chillin' at the house one day, she demanded to know, "Mykel, what's wrong with your boys?" She went on to say that it seemed like men got saved and got stupid. She wanted to know how it was that they could know how to approach a sister when they used be in the club, but were afraid to speak to her once they started going to church. Another one of our friends even went as far as to say that she had left the world behind and come to the Lord, she was ready to find a good saved black man to cook for, make babies with, and get started on the journey toward old age, but nobody was steppin' to her. She confessed that when she was in the world she got much attention. As a matter of fact, she still gets much attention, but not from Christian men. I understood what both women meant, because I had seen close friends of mine get saved and just turn into squares.

Dudes that used to spit serious game suddenly clammed up. Men who were hip-hop suddenly went corporate. Most of them were laboring under the assumption that their styles were sinful or displeasing to God. (Exactly how they came across this info I'm not sure. My guess is that it came from bad info they had had presalvation.) Many of the men I knew confided that they liked a lot of the women at church, but they didn't think it was appropriate to date them. Not appropriate? Where should you look for a girlfriend once you're saved? A club? They had it way twisted. But I'm afraid that their ignorance of God's Word repressed rather than freed them.

If you dated in the world, date in the church; just do it holy. If you were a drug dealer in the world, obviously you can't sell drugs once you get saved, but you can bring that knowledge and those same skills to the ministry. You know where the crack addicts hang out. Go there and hand out tracts or meals. You know how you used to make that money around the way. Do the same in your small business. Likewise, if you were a pimp back in the day, be a pimp for Jesus. You used to ferret out a woman's insecurities and use them to manipulate her for your gain. Now address those weaknesses with the Truth of the Gospels and build her up. Do you see? Use the skills He has given you to advance the Gospel in conjunction with the personality He gave you. You may not get it perfect from jump, but at least you can keep tryin' till you get better at it.

Become the person God called you to be, but do you! If you like hip-hop now, keep on liking it after you become a Christian— just know where it falls short of God's standard. If you work in entertainment now, don't let anybody force you to quit because you are now in a relationship with Jesus. If the Holy Spirit pulls your shirttails, that's different. But Sheeri and I have a friend whose father used to be a record executive at MCA back in the seventies and eighties. God spoke to his heart and he accepted Christ. Do you know his pastor pressured him to quit, telling him that he could not serve God and be a record executive at the same time because the music industry was too sinful? Kudos to him; he quit. That's commitment. But I maintain that he didn't have to. Nobody insists that doctors can treat only saved patients or that engineers can work only on church projects. So don't let anybody punk you. Be who you are and bring everything you got to the Body. The worst the Holy Spirit will do is refine you.

You don't have to look like me to love Jesus. And thank God I don't have to look like you. If you rock baggy jeans and a button-up, you don't have to buy a suit to serve God (unless you become a deacon at Faithful Central). But even in your deacon suit, you can put your earrings in (albeit after service) and sport your cornrows or locks. Do you get me? There is nowhere in the Bible that states there's only one personality for all, or that saved gear consists solely of a suit and tie or an ankle-length dress. God bless you if you roll like that. But if you don't, God bless you, too. Second Corinthians 3:17 states that where the Holy Spirit is, there is liberty. That means you are free to be who you really are. Just use common sense; exhibit dignity and virtue. Don't show up half-naked with all your goodies on display, but by all means rock yo' gear. Trust me, if anybody's got a problem with you, especially at a black church, they will tell you. Just make sure they got some Scripture to back up their complaints.

That reminds me of something I saw on the second season of MTV's *Making the Band*. Members of Da Band were praying before a performance. And Babs, the female rapper in the group, asked God to let them be "the sh———." One of the other members chastised her, saying that she couldn't say the S-word to God. But in this case I disagree. Obviously only God knows the condition of her heart. But I suspect that He would not refuse her prayer based on questionable wording alone. The apostle Paul asserts that none of us knows what we should pray, which is why the Holy Spirit stands ready to interpret (Romans 8:26). Moreover, Jesus Himself intercedes with God the Father on our behalf (Hebrew 7:25). It's pretty stupid-proof! Even if we don't get the words quite right or if we pray totally opposite God's will, we're covered. Babs became Sheeri's favorite member of Da Band at that moment. Am I advocating use of cursing in your prayers to God? No. Am I telling you to disrespect Him? No. What I am telling you is to be real with yours. The Psalmist states that he pours out his heart and soul to God (Psalms 42:4; 62:8). You can too in whatever words you have available. God can handle anything that you send His way. So tell Him everything. And don't be intimidated if you can't pray a sermon. He don't care about your oratory skills. Just about your respect.

A good gauge for how you should approach God is to think of how you would speak to a powerful, well-respected person. Once you figure that out, give God at least that much respect. After all I've seen of Babs on the show, I believe she would say the S-word to the President or the Pope without giving it a second thought. So for her that'll work till she has a reason to learn different. I come to God in formal, reverential prayer and worship about as often as I just holla at Him. He's my Lord and Savior as well as my Pops and confidant with whom I don't have to stand on ceremony. Either way, I prostrate myself before Him, because He's just that majestic. Maybe you ain't there yet. That's okay, too. With God, whole-hearted devotion beats performance any day. So come as you are with whatever is in your heart. As you grow, you'll find your footing.

I am so grateful to men like Bishop Ulmer; FCBC's associate pastor, Charles Brooks; FCBC's former youth pastors, Travon Potts and Troyvoi Hicks; and FCBC's former singles pastor, Donald Bell, who is currently the executive pastor at Covenant Blessings in Torrance, California. Had it not been for men like them, I would probably never have become a Christian. And I would never have learned just to be Mykel. All of them are men in whom I see elements of myself.

My wife's preface mentioned our membership at a predominantly white church with an older congregation. They are our family at Grace Bible Church. They are an incredible bunch of people whom my wife and I love dearly, even though we are no longer members there. From the very beginning, we felt at home and extremely welcome at Grace. And that's a big deal to us, given that we were the only black family there. A lot of times when you are the only chocolate folks in a group of whites, people don't know how to receive you. Some people totally avoid you. Some folks try to talk "jive" to you. They say things like, "Give me five," instead of just offering you a handshake. Or they say stuff like, "Holler!" when they should just say, "Good-bye." Y'know what I mean? Sometimes in their effort to make sure that you know you're welcome, they smother you. Or worse, if they've never been around any black people before, they treat you like a curious novelty, like you're the bearded lady at the circus. They ask questions of you as though you speak for all black folks, or as though you have a special understanding of all things urban—even if you were raised in the suburbs. My wife and I never experienced any of this at Grace. From the beginning we Mitchells were family, pure and simple. No one ignored the fact that we are black, but nobody tripped off it either. I love my family at GBC. Just as much or more than at any church I have ever attended, I found Christ's love most evident in the intimacy of their fellowship. Pastor Rob Warmouth often joked that "where two or three are gathered in Jesus' name [at Grace], there shall be potluck." And much to my delight, that proved to be very true.

Having said that, I know that if the folks at Grace had been my first contact with the Christian faith, I probably would not have embraced it so readily. Allow me to explain. I have not always been where I am today—mentally, spiritually, or emotionally. There was a time in my life that if something wasn't predominantly black, I didn't want to be bothered. As a Christian, I have grown to appreciate that Jesus' universality transcends that of my beloved hip-hop. He is completely relevant in every culture in the world and deserving of His rightful place as Lord. Whereas I used to go places playing "I spy the other black guy," now I'm hyped to roll up on another brother in Christ—regardless of race or color. Sometimes this world is so upside down to me that it feels like I'm finding my way through a lunatic asylum. When I spot another believer, it feels like I've connected with at least one other sane person. I can't explain the substantive bond that exists between believers. It's stronger than that of any frat, gang, race, or even blood relation. I have Christian brothers and sisters in whom I place more faith than members of the family I was born into. That's just real.

But like I said, I haven't always been there. And you know what? That was cool with God. That's why He sent me black men like me, whom I could relate to. And every last one of them is mad cool. They each have their own style. Bishop is smooth and polished.

Charles is bohemian and contemporary. Travon is the consumate musician—creative, deep, and just moody enough to be interesting without seeming strange. Troyvoi is the earthy intellectual. He's the only high school principal I have ever seen rock cornrows and pierced ears in class. Donald just straight rolls gangsta. Experiencing one of his sermons is like surviving a beat-down that you knew you had coming. He polishes nothing and employs no euphemisms. It hurts so good to listen to him, but make no mistake—it hurts. God knew that I needed to see men like these so that I could piece it together. If He could relate to them (and vice versa), He could relate to me (and vice versa)!

As a result of their examples, I have done my best to live my life with as much authenticity and transparency as possible, hoping that through my personality and experience someone may come to a better understanding of Jesus Christ. You've read some salty language in this book. Honestly I really struggled with whether or not to include it. I wrestled not only with my editor, but with the Holy Spirit, too. I don't seek to dishonor God with my words. But the truth is that I'm blunt like that. I've toned it down where He pricked my conscience, but left alone what I thought effectively made my point without offending Him. I take my cues from Jesus Himself, as well as from the rest of the New Testament. Jesus spoke to the common man. He used parables and references that his audience could relate to. He wasn't highbrow or any more intellectual than was necessary. All of the New Testament is written in common Greek, the language of the masses at the time. And each age has translated the Bible into its own version of contemporary speech. I've tried to share my experience in the same manner.

I alternate between slang, proper English, and relaxed grammar, because that's how I really talk every day. I don't always sound like I rolled right off of High Street—but I don't always sound like I attended a top-ten undergrad uni either. And I wanted this book to sound like me. I've been candid with my past and my struggles because I want you to see that I'm far from perfect. I'm no preacher, but I am a follower of Jesus Christ and just as valuable to the Body. I tell my story because I want you to understand and believe that if He accepted me with all my dirt, He'll accept you, too. If He cleaned me up and set me on the right path, He will do it for you. I was a dead man walking. He brought me to life. He didn't do it because I'm all that. For all intents and purposes, I'm just another nigga tryin' to make his way in the universe. I ain't no better than anyone else. That's what I want you to see. If He could love me, He can love you, too. He does love you—enough to die in your place. And therein lies your hope. Like I've said over and over again, it ain't nothing deep. God is simply good—all the time. And ain't we glad!

So should anything you've read make sense or make you curious, don't resist it thinking that you'll have to trade in your Ones for a pair of sensible loafers or your Manolos for a pair of Mary Janes. God made you exactly the way you are on purpose—with a purpose. So if you decide to come to Him, just do you, y'all. Just do you.

Epilogue

I've written this book with the hope that somebody, male or female, would read it and be spared some of the useless, painful experiences that I had apart from Christ. I've heard the saying, "If you can't be a good example, then be a horrible warning." I'd like to think that my new life in Christ represents the first half of that statement, while my BC days fit the latter.

Throughout this entire book two lives have been on my mind. One is already over and one is just beginning.

My son, Chase, who is six years old at the time of this writing, is still innocent. Having accepted Christ when he was five years old, he seeks after Him with the wide-eyed wonder and sincerity befitting a child. When he wants to be, he's really adept at applying the biblical truths he's learned in school, Sunday school, and at home to his own behavior and to life in general. I thank God for his eagerness to learn more about Jesus and his interest in Old Testament patriarchs. "Mommy, tell me a story from the Bible," is a regular request.

In so many ways he's years ahead of me. I smile when I think of the man he has the potential to become if he stays as close to the

Lord as he is now. I encourage him daily in his walk. In many ways he reminds me of myself before I allowed myself to be hardened by heartbreak, greed, and persistent sin. My prayer for everyone who reads this book is that you will become like my kid in regard to Christ. I pray that the Holy Spirit will make you curious, that He will draw you to His Word and prompt you to pray and worship. I pray that you will approach the Lord with the wide-eyed eagerness my son now exhibits, and that you will be satisfied by and made to hunger for the things of God both at the same time. I hope that you will turn to God and say, "Lord, tell me another story from the Bible," and that your heart will grow tender to the things of God.

I mentioned two lives. The other is that of my cousin Ray. His real name was Ramone, but no one but his mom ever called him that. I remember the day his life ended, the day he gave up. I was surprised to see him walking down the street alone. He had just left hours ago with my stepdad, Stan, my stepdad's girlfriend, and my two brothers. Ray was Stan's nephew and had come to live with my family for a couple of years. His mother sent him to us from southern California because he hadn't been doing well there. He was failing in school, hangin' with the wrong crowd, and behaving dangerously. She had hoped that taking him out of his element would give him a chance to start fresh and find motivation to do better on all fronts. Her hopes were realized. Living with us, Ray had begun to prosper academically, socially, and emotionally. He had found motivation to study and to behave better. He discovered new interests and new friends. His life was looking up. And we were glad to have him around.

After he came to live with us, my stepdad and mom ended up getting a divorce. As often as the mood struck, my stepdad would come get my brothers and my cousin so they could all hang out together. This was one of those days, except something really wrong happened. I would learn later from my brother that Stan and Ray had gotten into a really bad fight over Ray's not wanting to hang out with the group. Ray had challenged Stan—something that just wasn't done, especially by a child—and paid for it. Twenty miles from home, Stan cursed Ray out and yelled at him to get out of the car. Ray did and Stan drove off, leaving him with, like, fifty cents to get home, or something crazy like that. The young man I saw that day, who had covered twenty-something miles on foot, was a stranger to me. I don't know what happened to Ray in that instant that Stan flipped out on him. And I certainly don't know what happened to him on his way back to the house. He never talked about it. But he was never the same. The progress he had made while living with us had been hard-won. He was a bright kid, but he had some really bad habits that he basically had to unlearn to get along. He struggled in many areas, but he pushed through in many. That day I suspect he just quit. Somehow he must have figured that the struggle to do the right thing wasn't worth it anymore. He started slackin' off and eventually returned home to southern California, where he resumed his old life in every area.

Years later, after I, too, had moved there, I would learn of his murder. Years after that I would learn that it was a suspected suicide. Depending upon whom you ask in my family, it could be either. Either way it was a tragedy, but hardly a surprise. The day Ray's life ended was that day he quit. After that it was just a matter of his body catching up to his spirit.

Maybe you're like Ray. Maybe you've been trying to do the right thing, but you've grown tired. You may be living out the consequences of your bad choices as you read these words from your own prison, self-made or man-made. I was unable to offer Ray any hope, because I was lost myself. But that's not the case with you. If you've given up or are in danger of doing so, I especially invite you to try Christ. If anything else worked, then you'd be doing that and you'd be straight. The dissatisfaction you feel is not yours alone. All of humanity experiences it. Most people just do a better job at covering it up or distracting themselves from it than others.

God created us for Himself. Apart from Him we are doomed to be unfulfilled, lonely, and ultimately dissatisfied with everything we try to substitute for Him. You will never make enough money, achieve enough success, or impress enough people to conquer your own nature. Allow God to fill that gaping hole in your life, the one you've been pouring sex, alcohol, education, career pursuits, ambition, money, toys, drugs, relationships, shopping, and whatever into. He loves you and wants to satisfy you with things that will give you life, not take it from you. If you've become desperate enough to try Him, then read the prayer in the last page of this book and shake hands with hope. Given the choice, I hope you'll follow the example of my son and not that of my cousin. If you're not ready right now, that's okay. The invitation stands and cannot be revoked.

God bless.
Mykel Mitchell

Lord Jesus, I need You. I believe You paid the price for all of my dirt.

Please come into my heart right now.

Forgive me for all of the bad things I've ever done. Lord, I give You control. Help me to live right and to be the person You want me to be. I want every good thing You have ready for me. Bless me, and help me to stay focused on You. Amen.